THE TAROT
OF PRAGUE

A Xymbio publication
First published 2003
Xymbio
6-9 Bridgewater Square
BARBICAN
London EC2Y 8AH

Karen Mahony reserves the moral right
to be identified as the author of this work

Cards and book design by Alexandr Ukolov
and Karen Mahony, baba studio, Prague

baba studio
Bretislavova 12
Mala Strana
Prague 118 00
Czech Rebublic

www.baba-prague.com
www.tarotofprague.com

Printed and bound in Prague, Czech Republic by TRICO

All rights are reserved. No part of this book may be
reprinted or reproduced or used in any way, including by
any digital, electronic, mechanical or other means,
including photocopying or any other form of recording
or reproduction, or in any database, information storage
or retrieval system, without prior permission in writing
from the publishers.

British Library Cataloguing in Publication Data
A catalogue record for this publication is available form
the British Library.

© copyright Karen Mahony
ISBN 0-9545007-0-9

Karen Mahony

THE TAROT OF PRAGUE

A TAROT BASED ON THE ART
AND ARCHITECTURE OF THE
"MAGIC CITY"

XYMBIO

Contents

About the authors 5
The Tarot of Prague 7
What is Tarot? 8
The images and symbols used 12
The Magic City of Prague 15
The Major Arcana 26
Minor Arcana - Wands 100
Minor Arcana - Cups 145
Minor Arcana - Swords 191
Minor Arcana - Pentacles 233
Tarot Readings 274
Traditional Spreads - The Celtic Cross 283
The Prague "threshold" spread 288
Bibliography 292
Terms used 293
Index 396

About the Authors

Karen Mahony and Alex Ukolov run baba studio in the centre of Prague. Both are designers with many years of experience in both commercial and not-for-profit social design. Alex is a graduate of the Kharkov Fine Art University in the Ukraine and Karen did her post-graduate degree at the Royal College of Art in London.

Baba aims to produce design that is thought-provoking and socially useful but at the same time sensuous and enjoyable. There is a particular focus on collaborative and inclusive projects and on exploring Magic Realist and Symbolist design in different media.

The studio name comes from a global word that can mean "old woman" in Slavic languages, but also "baby" in English, "father" in Turkish and Bengali, and a very good cake in many languages...

www.baba-studio.com

Acknowledgements

We'd like to thank all the friends and colleagues who've generously given their help and encouragement, in particular we owe thanks to:

Ken Ganfield, Claire-Louise Hatton, Olga Kuzmina, Richard Oliver, Karen Wheller, and many the kind people from the Aeclectic and TarotL forums who have offered support and commentary.

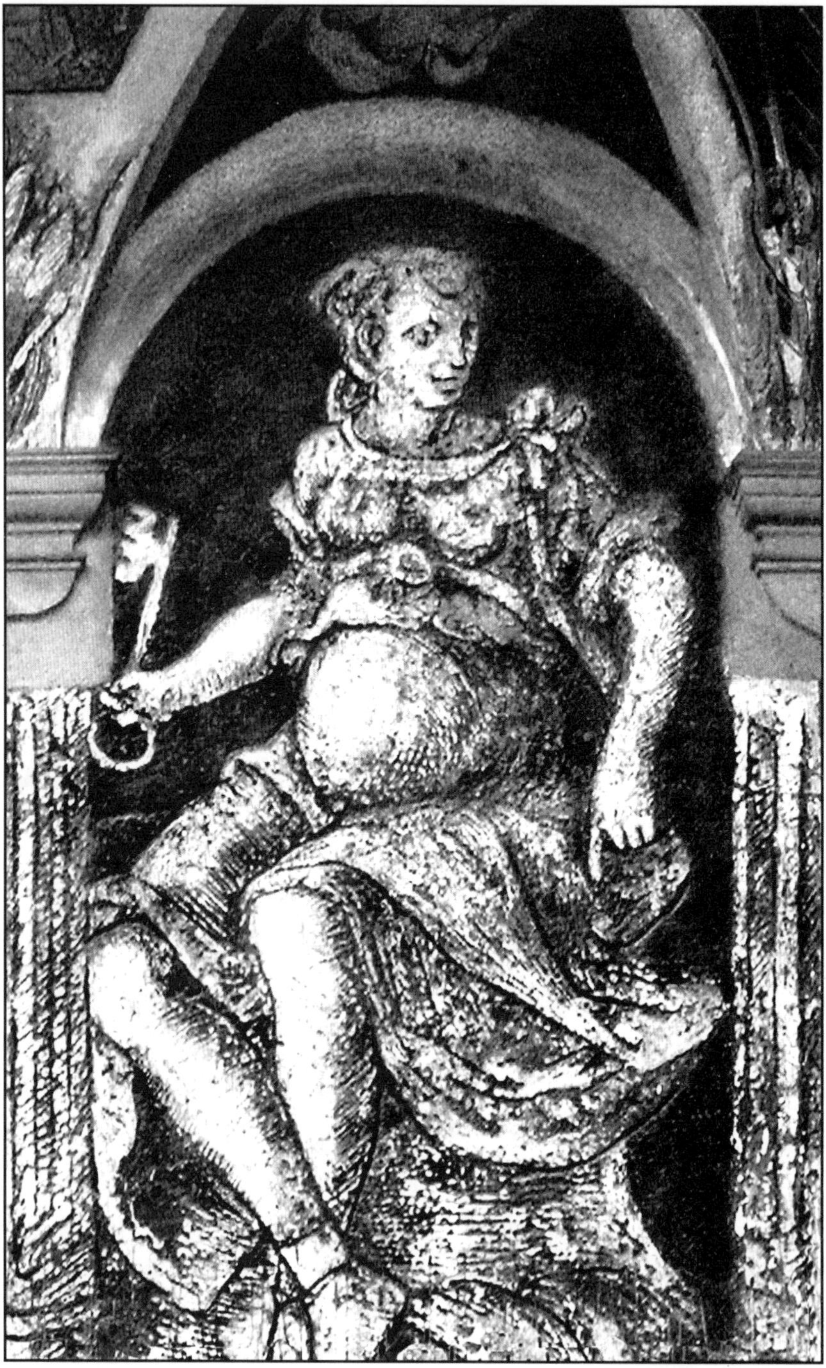

The Tarot of Prague

"Prague is a dear mother with sharp claws:
she never lets go of you"

Franz Kafka

Magic Prague, city of Art Nouveau and Deco, the Baroque and the Enlightenment. Yet also a place of gothic enchantment, alchemists and phantoms, the fantastic and fantastical. Ever since the reign of Emperor Rudolph II, who filled Prague Castle with curiosities and wonders as well as a succession of practitioners of astrology, astronomy, and alchemy, Prague has been known as a city steeped in art, esoterica and the occult. The surrealist André Breton called it "The Magic City", and this name feels as true today as ever.

We designed the *Tarot of Prague* to be a vibrant expression of the city. The images are collaged from thousands of original photographs of the streets and houses, the murals and statues, manuscripts and drawings, and even from the games that make up Prague's rich visual treasury. Each card is a picture in its own right, and many are so strongly narrative they seem like illustrations from fairy-tales that might have been, or traces of stories half-remembered. Together they form a deck that has a liveliness and *joie de vivre* that we hope represents some of the many facets of this fantastic Bohemian city.

This book is intended to be a guide to using the *Tarot of Prague*, and includes interpretations and explanations of the symbolism of each card and background information about the imagery. It also explains how to use the deck for readings, and, in addition to more in-depth information, has concise "short interpretations" and keywords to help you get started right away.

Whether you are a Tarot novice or an expert, we hope you will enjoy the far-reaching and stimulating interpretations that the deck affords, and that it will provide a new vantage point from which to look at the history and stories of Prague. We also hope it will help uncover some aspects of the Tarot that are new to you and at the same time enrich your experience of the Magic City.

What is Tarot?

Madame Sosostris, famous clairvoyante,
Had a bad cold, nevertheless
Is known to be the wisest woman in Europe,
With a wicked pack of cards.

T.S. Eliot, *The Wasteland*.

In popular myth the Tarot has become inextricably associated with disreputable fortune-tellers, gypsies, magic rites, and medieval witches, and in some cases even with ancient Egyptian rites and mysteries or with Voodoo. However, the factual history of the Tarot has very little to do with such ideas and is altogether more down to earth. All the evidence now points to Tarot originating in Italy in the 15th century, where it was a rather complicated card game similar to Bridge. The tarot (or "tarrochi" in Italian) decks of the time had four suits, each with ten cards (the "pips") and four Court Cards. In addition to the suits there were also usually twenty-two "trump" cards.

The trumps consisted of a series of named qualities, vices, virtues and religious figures, and generally included cards such as The Fool, The Devil, The Lovers, The Chariot, and Strength. These were fully illustrated, often with evocative scenes full of symbolism. The suits that made up the rest of the pack were most commonly called batons, coins, swords and cups. With the exception of the "Court Cards" (Page, Knight, Queen, King), these were usually not illustrated with scenes (the early "Sola Busca" tarot is one exception to this), but instead simply showed a pattern of the appropriate number of symbols, rather like those on ordinary 52-card decks of playing cards.

The imaginative images on the trumps may have encouraged people to use them for activities other than playing the game of Tarot. It does seem that from very early on playing cards, including tarot packs, were sometimes used for games of moral education or simple story-telling. There is a reference to a sermon in Switzerland that probably dates from the late 14th century in which there is mention of the pictures on playing cards being used to describe the state of the world and being valuable for demonstrating education and morals. However, it seems that actual fortune-telling or divination using the cards was not very widespread until a

The Tarot of Prague

professional psychic/fortune-teller called Etteilla popularised this in the late 18th century. Etteilla designed his own pack of cards, which is actually quite different from what we now think of as the classic deck of 78 cards. There has been much disagreement about just how significant Etteila was. He's been described as everything from the "father of modern cartomancers" (Levi writing in the 19th century), to an "illiterate but zealous adventurer" (Waite, *Pictorial Key*, 1910). However, he does seem to have been immensely popular in his time, and his deck of cards was a great success and versions of it are still available today.

In the 19th century there was definite interest in developing systematic ways of using cards for cartomancy, and in the early 20th century this interest exploded with the publication in 1909 of a set of cards now known as the Rider Waite Smith (RWS), developed by Pamela Colman Smith and Arthur Waite. Both were members of the famous esoteric society called The Golden Dawn (the poet W. B. Yeats was another well-known member who probably advised on the design of this tarot). The RWS cards differed fundamentally from most of the earlier tarot in that each card, including the "pips", was fully illustrated. This was the first 78-card occult tarot deck to depict meanings in this way, and it made the cards relatively easy for a beginner to understand. Waite and Smith also changed the names of some of the "trumps" and re-ordered them slightly. Because this was a deck designed for cartomancy, not for game playing, the ordinary suit cards were termed the "Minor Arcana", and the "trumps" the "Major Arcana" (*Arcanum* means "secret" in Latin).

This deck was an enormously influential innovation, and since its publication it has become the most popular model for modern tarot decks. The majority of decks these days are based more or less on Waite and Smith's cards. The *Tarot of Prague* also follows this system and this means that it can be used with most popular books about tarot interpretation and reading. It should be mentioned, however, that there are two other major systems used in modern decks: those based on the older playing cards which have no illustrated pips, known as the "Marseille" type, and those based on the deck that Aleister Crowley designed with Freda Harris in the late 1930s, called the "Thoth" type.

Most tarot decks based on the RWS system consist of twenty-two Major Arcana cards and fifty-six Minor Arcana cards divided into four suits: Wands, Swords, Cups and Pentacles (or Coins), each with four Court

Cards (Page, Knight, Queen and King). A few decks differ in small ways, and our own *Tarot of Prague*, for example, has two "Death" cards so that the preferred version of this sensitive card can be chosen for readings.

The cards in the Major Arcana, with names such as The Fool, The Magician and The Lovers, are considered the most important in the deck as they represent the more archetypal and profound aspects of life. When they come up in a reading they tend to be given more weight than Minor Arcana cards, which deal with more ordinary day-to-day affairs. There have been many theories about why these particular twenty-two archetypes were chosen. Some historians see this as mere accident and argue that the cards simply evolved from the pack of playing cards that happened to include this choice of trumps. Others believe that the Major Arcana is based on the ancient Jewish Cabbala, or see it as a careful and complete philosophical description of a journey ("The Fool's Journey") through life towards enlightenment. One recent theory is that the concepts on which the Major Arcana are based originally came from an Arabic culture, and that the twenty-two cards illustrate a mystical text or story (that unfortunately has not yet been identified). However, fascinating as theories such as this are, a detailed discussion of the original significance of the Major Arcana cards is outside the scope of this book. Many authors have debated the issue at length and it is a perennially popular topic in online discussion forums so there is ample opportunity to study this question further.

There has been much scholarship on the history of the Tarot, and serious academic research is still ongoing. So if the summary given here whets your appetite, please do refer to the Bibliography for ideas for further reading.

A note on the numbering of the cards.

The Major Arcana cards are now usually numbered, but there is considerable argument about what the "correct" system of numbering should be. When Arthur Waite and Pamela Smith produced their influential 1909 deck they decided to change the ordering commonly found in older packs. The reason for this was not stated clearly, but was related to the need for the deck to correspond more closely to some of the esoteric thinking of The Golden Dawn society.

The Tarot of Prague

Because of the continuing controversy about the best ordering system, the Major Arcana cards of the *Tarot of Prague* are not numbered. However, in this book we have used the ordering suggested by Arthur Waite. If you use numerology when you are doing your own readings, please decide for yourself which system of ordering works best for you.

The Images and Symbols Used

Prague is a city of innumerable faces...
Milan Špůrek, *Praga Mysteriosa*

The imagery of Prague extends from the medieval Gothic, through Baroque and Rococo to Czech Secessionism (Art Nouveau), Art Deco and some very distinctive examples of Modernism and Cubism. Although these styles are very different, and sometimes embrace a diverse array of symbols, they blend together surprisingly well on the streets of the city. The *Tarot of Prague* is designed to incorporate these different styles, so while our "Sun" is very Baroque, you'll see that "Temperance" is pure Art Deco, the Page of Swords is quite Pre-Raphaelite in feel, and the "Wheel of Fortune" combines some very old Gothic carvings with a 19th-century calendar wheel (which itself is an addition to a much older piece, the 15th-century Astronomical Clock). This means that you will find many different styles of signs and symbols in the cards, some of them very old in origin, others more recent.

In addition to these historical elements from art and architecture, we have also used elements from the traditional graphics of Bohemian playing cards. The deck we have used is a traditional one (ours is from WWII) with 32 cards divided into four suits, and it is commonly used throughout Bohemia to play a variety of card games. It's interesting that Czech (and German) fortune-telling cards also tend to use a 32-card pack, so it's probable that just as the old 78-card Tarocchi games deck evolved into the modern 78-card occult Tarot, the Czech Bohemian deck may also, in a simpler way, have evolved into a divination tool. Whether or not this is the case have used some of the graphics from these old cards in order to add another dimension to our images, and maybe to serve as a gentle reminder that tarot packs were originally used simply for card games.

The cards in the *Tarot of Prague* have all been created by photo-collage, but to use or enjoy them you don't need to know where all the elements of each image come from, or fully understand their historical or symbolic significance. Each card has been designed so that it is a complete picture in its own right, and anyone familiar with the traditional Rider Waite Smith pack will be able to use the deck quickly and easily. However, the Tarot is always a great deal more interesting when you can go beyond what you literally see on the cards and understand something of the underlying symbolism, so knowing something about the background of the card imagery will add much to your appreciation of the range of possible interpretations. We spent many months taking the thousands of photographs of Prague that were used in these cards and they come from a wide range of sources. These sources, their original significance and our reasons for choosing and combining them as we did, are outlined in this book. Like all symbolic images, they are very open to personal interpretation and we would encourage you to bring your own meanings to the pictures, as well as understanding ours.

A figure of Nox (Night) found on a building in Nerudova Street

STORY-TELLING WITH THE *TAROT OF PRAGUE*

What is true, is usually in the form of a myth
Nicholas Moseley, *Hopeful Monsters*

Unlike most decks, which tend to follow one style throughout, the look of each individual card in the *Tarot of Prague* is very distinctive. We felt this helped to capture the diversity of Prague, a city in which Cubist modernism rubs shoulders with medieval Gothic, and in which "high" art and "low" folk decoration can be found in the same street. Another reason for taking this distinctive design approach was so that every card can be treated as though it were an illustration from a individual folk or fairy tale, and this makes the deck particularly appropriate for story-telling and a narrative approach to readings. Many of the most sensitive and intuitive tarot readers are fascinated by the links between the Tarot and the archetypal motifs of traditional tales. When they interpret a tarot spread they will begin by constructing some sort of story or narrative around it. This does not mean that their interpretation is invented, far from it. The reason is simply that it's often easier to recognise and communicate fundamental truths in the form of stories.

When you lay out a spread with the *Tarot of Prague* you will see a pattern of cards in which some images may seem like fragments of stories, and we would encourage you to take some time to think about what the stories may be. Why is Puss in Boots lounging with the dreamy young man in the beer-hall in the Nine of Cups? How did a dove come to be nesting in the hat of the Page of Wands, and why does the lion in the Two of Swords look so anxious? As you imagine these stories, the pictures in your mind's eye will begin to take on a life of their own — as stories have always done — and you'll find that as you use the deck for readings your intuition is very much sharpened. The streets and buildings of Prague are full of stories, we hope that some of them are expressed in these cards and will take root and develop in your own imagination.

For more on reading and interpreting spreads, please see the section at the end of this book.

The Magic City of Prague

Prague is the capital of the Czech Republic, but is it the capital, in addition, of something purely abstract, a quality of mind perhaps, something that might fascinate a puzzled world? Every great city is constructed around a principle all its own... In Prague, the principle appears to be metaphysical... Are we to conclude that it is a city of mysteries that will never be fathomed, a city of mysticism and the occult?
Paul Berman *Slate*. June 1997 http://slate.msn.com/

Prague has long had the reputation of being not only one of the most beautiful cities in the world, but also one of the most mystical and atmospheric. There is no place quite like this capital of Bohemia, with its chaotic and rich mix of symbolism and imagery. Since its mythical foundation by Libuse, a Celtic queen who was also a magician and psychic, it has always been associated with enchantment.

Of course, it's true that to see Prague only as a mystic city is to caricature it. But while it is now a modern, growing hub of Central Europe, and Mercedes are considerably more common on the streets than magicians, it is still undeniably saturated with a distinctly odd atmosphere, and a vague and attractive sense of otherworldliness.

Where else, after all, can you sit in a café courtyard enjoying a cappuccino and look up and see looming over you the tower where the 16th-century alchemist Edward Kelley reputedly lived and practiced? Where else would your local greengrocer explain that the quaint old Baroque house on the corner used to be inhabited (and only 50 years ago) by a wizard? Where but in Prague can you meet a hip, young fashion designer who will confidently and matter-of-factly show you the exact location of the local Gate to Hell? (Apparently gates to hell are becoming a rarity in Europe, which perhaps is a good thing.)

Although Prague's links with enchantment do go right back to its foundation, the city's renown as a centre for the esoteric and the occult really became established during the reign of Rudolph II. It was this extraordinary period that really sealed its reputation as "The Magic City".

The reign of Rudolph II, patron of esoteric knowledge

When Rudolf II moved his court to Prague in 1583, the city became an academy of the occult. An accomplished amateur in alchemy, the natural sciences, physics, astrology and magic, he spent his time among paintings, objets d'art, cupels, luted crucibles...in the company of alchemists, painters and fortune-tellers.

Angelo Ripellino, *Magic Prague*

Rudolph was only twenty-four years old when he was crowned King of Bohemia in 1575. Raised at the court in Madrid, he was expected to follow the strict religious doctrines practised in Spain at the time. However, his early experiences of religious intolerance had quite the opposite effect on the young ruler. In fact he became remarkably, perhaps even rebelliously, open-minded about questions of religious and esoteric belief. Soon after he moved his court to Prague he began to invite to the city many outstanding figures in the arts, crafts, sciences and various mystical and philosophical doctrines.

Rudolph was a withdrawn and at times melancholic ruler, but he possessed an enquiring and intelligent mind and a fascination with arcane and hidden knowledge. As the writer Angela Carter says of the Rudolphine period "It was an age in love with wonders" (Angela Carter, *Alice in Prague, or the Curious Room*). As well as filling the Castle with alchemists, astronomers, makers of automata, artists, botanists, and other producers of marvels and mysteries, he also built up an astonishing collection of the rare and strange. This ranged from art, artefacts and occult objects, to exotic animals and plants. Most of this collection was lost, stolen or sold over the years, especially during the general destruction of the Thirty Years' War, but pieces continue to surface in Prague from time to time.

In those days the Danish-born Tycho Brahe was one of the most famous of the astronomer/astrologers working for Rudolph (there was of course much less distinction between the two disciplines at the time). He was known for his prosthetic nose, made of gold and silver and stuck on with special glue, which he wore in place of his own after losing it in a duel. It was Brahe who told Rudolph that his fate was tied to that of the African lion Oskar kept at Prague Castle. Rudolph did indeed die only a few days after the lion, so Brahe's warning seems to have been true. Images of lions can be found all over Prague, in all styles and all colours. Some are depictions of the two-tailed Lion of Bohemia, the regional symbol, but many of them are much more explicitly mystical beasts, often symbolically connected with alchemy, and hence, to some extent, with Rudolph himself.

The alchemists

I was in the Street of the Goldsmiths where, in the Middle Ages, those who were skilled in alchemy burnt the philosopher's stone and poisoned the moonbeams
Ewald Murrer, *The Diary of Mr. Pinke*

Prague has been inextricably associated with alchemy ever since the time of Rudolph. Rudolph seems to have been fascinated by the idea of the alchemical "Great Work", the aim of which was to create the mysterious deep red "Philosopher's Stone". This stone was incredibly desirable as it had the power not only to transform base metal into gold, but also to confer immortality on its owner.

Of the many alchemists who came to Prague during Rudolph's reign, the two most famous were undoubtedly Doctor John Dee from England and his assistant Edward Kelley (also spelt Kelly in some accounts). Dee is widely regarded as a serious and learned man. He spent a portion of his life as an advisor to Queen Elizabeth I of England, as well as to Rudolph in Prague, and was often referred to as "Elizabeth's Merlin". There are, however, varying views of Kelley. Most regard him as a Renaissance "con man" who tricked people into believing that he could turn base metals into gold. However, some believe that he really was able to see the future using a sphere of smoky quartz given to him and Dee by the angel Uriel. It's claimed that he predicted both Mary Queen of Scots' execution and the attack on the English fleet by the Spanish Armada. Kelley is rumoured to have lived for a time at a house called The Donkey at the Cradle, at 8 Janský Vršek in Malá Strana. The house is still there, complete with a very weird staircase, though, like so much about this man, it is debatable whether he lived there or not.

The period of Dee and Kelley is of particular interest to students of the Tarot. Dee claimed that it was in Prague and greater Bohemia that he spoke with the "Enochian Angels". These were higher spirits who by all accounts imparted a very ancient and secret wisdom to the two eager questioners:

Together they were fervently pursuing their alchemical experiments and their attempts at angel-summoning and practical Cabbala. To this period belong the séances described in Dee's spiritual diary, with their supposed contacts with the angels Uriel and Gabriel and other spirits.

Francis Yates, *The Occult Philosophy in the Elizabethan Age*

Enoch is considered to be the Egyptian name for Thoth, and the diaries of the conversations with the Enochian angels that Dee and Kelley recorded are believed to be part of the basis of the esoteric "Enochian" philosophy which Aleister Crowley drew on heavily for his *Book of Thoth* and the Thoth tarot. Crowley actually considered himself to be a reincarnation of Edward Kelley.

Rabbi Loew and the Golem

The activities of the alchemists were not by any means the strangest events believed to have taken place during Rudolph's reign. Far more fantastic was the creation of the Golem, a creature that the famous Rabbi Loew magically brought to life from the mud of the city to protect and defend the population of the Jewish ghetto of the time. It is rumoured that the Golem still lies hidden in the rafters of the Old New Synagogue and may revive once more if circumstances are right.

Rabbi Loew himself was extremely long-lived — if not quite as immortal as his Golem. It was believed that the rabbi could cheat death by recognising it in whichever guise it came. The story goes that one night during an epidemic of the plague he was walking through the cemetery and happened upon an emaciated woman wearing a veil and clutching a slip of paper. He tore the paper from her hand and ripped it to shreds. A fortunate act for him, as the paper turned out to be a list of those doomed to die and contained his name written in red ink.

Death finally came to Rabbi Loew, however, in a disguise he did not recognise: hidden deep in a red rose presented to him by a child on his birthday. He smelt the rose and fell down lifeless. As Ripellino [2] wrote:

"Death in a rose. Alas, Death in a rose."

Ghosts and hauntings

Now, long after Rudolph's reign, Prague's reputation for magic and peculiarity is still strong. Even today, surrounded by electric lights and friendly bars (or perhaps even because of the latter), people often claim to see weird figures and phantoms in the maze of small, winding streets of Old Town and Malá Strana. Most of the castles in the Czech Republic seem to have a "White Lady", and in old Prague nearly every locale seems to have its ghosts, sometimes threatening, but more often simply bizarre. One of the oddest is the huge dog with glowing black eyes that apparently emerges from the Martinic Palace in the little area of Novy Svět every night on the stroke of eleven. He accompanies any passing walkers as far as the nearby Loreto Chapel, which sounds like a truly terrifying experience. However, on reaching the Loreto the dog simply turns around and goes back the way he came, presumably leaving his erstwhile companions very relieved. An equally disturbing figure is the ghost of a Turk said to roam the courtyard behind the Týn Church. He carries a jewel box, and if you give him permission, will open it and display the contents: the head of his mudered mistress (for more on this story, see the Ten of Swords).

In addition to the hauntings by people, a terrifying goblin reportedly roams the Portheim Palace in Old Town, and spectral dwarves have been seen at the former home of one Josef Pisinger. A variety of animals are also said to haunt the city, from cats and dogs to horses and, oddly enough, polecats. As a recent article says of modern-day Prague:

Don't be fooled by first impressions. The ordinary does not exist here. Take the colourful house signs you see on the hillside street of Nerudova, used to mark a home before the more practical numbers. At No. 12 there are three criss-crossed violins. The home of an elderly violin maker? Too banal. Prague legend says it is the calling card of three crazed fiddlers who play a Czech mazurka before descending to the bowels of the city before sunrise.
"Poltergeists of Prague" *The Age* November 2 2002

One can only assume that they use the infamous "Gate of Hell" to do this; it's actually located not all that far from this particular house-sign. These crazed fiddlers are not, moreover, the only characters in the mythological history of Prague that are believed to have close contacts with the devil. Of these, Doctor Faust is probably the most notorious.

Doctor Faust and other devilish pacts

The story of Doctor Faust, who sold his soul to the devil for material gain, became well-known throughout Europe in the early Renaissance. There is absolutely no evidence that Faust existed, or, if he did exist, that he ever came to Prague. However, in Prague it is often claimed that he used to be a resident in the house now called the "Faust House". This large building stands in Karlovo náměstí (Charles Square), an area that has a formidable reputation for being frequented by phantoms and spectres. The house doesn't look particularly atmospheric or gothic now, as it was refurbished in 1769, but it is actually very much older than it appears. It dates from the 13th century and originally had a tower for fortification. In the late 16th century the alchemist Kelley owned the house. Kelley, and later another alchemist Mladota of Solopysky, carried out their chemical and alchemical experiments there. This seems to be one of the reasons the house became connected in the popular imagination with the tale of Doctor Faust Faust was also believed to have been very involved in mysterious experiments, obtaining assistance with these from the devil himself. However, while Kelley survived living in this house, people believe that Faust did not. It's said that one night his satanic master dragged him to Hell through a black hole in the ceiling. This hole is believed to still be there. No matter how often it is bricked up, it is found open again the following morning, with the odour of brimstone and sulphur hanging in the air.

The violinist Niccola Paganini, (1782-1840) was another visitor to Prague who left the rather awed inhabitants with the impression that they were seeing someone who had made a pact with the devil. Paganini did have an uncanny and death-like appearance. Some of the most atmospheric paintings of him were by the Czech painter František Tichý (1896-1961), and from what we can gather from Tichý's canvases, Paganini arrived in Prague "in a rickety pitch-black coach" as a "heap of black locks, stick legs and overly long tapered hands ending in fingers as twisted as convolvulus" (Angelo Ripellino, *Magic Prague*). It's no wonder that many people thought that this frightening figure's seemingly impossible skills with the violin must have had a diabolic source.

The Tarot of Prague

Vampires in Bohemia

In addition to pacts with the devil, there also seems to be a strong link between Prague and devilish vampires. This association also has a long history. In 1927, H.P. Lovecraft wrote *The Case of Charles Dexter Ward*, in which the young protagonist travels to Prague, where he unfortunately meets "an evil old man called Josef Nadek" who teaches him the secret knowledge for bringing a vampire back to life from its ashes. Being a Lovecraft story, horror follows horror in a complex plot that features several warning letters mysteriously received from Prague, all written in medieval language and referring to magical formulae and incantations.

In several modern horror films, Prague is mentioned as the birthplace of vampires (*John Carpenter's Vampires*, in which the vampire leader is a charismatic figure born in Prague in 1311, is one notable example). The recent film *Blade 2* played with this idea, setting the base of a powerful cartel of vampires in the centre of Prague. Prague was even featured in *Buffy, the Vampire Slayer*, with the city named as the place where the vampire couple, Spike and Drusilla, were attacked by an angry mob.

There is some historical basis for Prague being associated with vampirism. A recent article in *The Prague Post* described how archaeologists working in Bohemia often find what appear to be the graves of people thought to have been vampires. When the bodies were exhumed it was found that their limbs had been severed and their bones broken, in addition to having had stakes driven through them. It does seem as though the general Bohemian medieval attitude was "better safe than sorry":

> The most famous of all such graves was discovered in 1966 in Celakovice, 10 kilometers (six miles) northeast of Prague. There, archeologists uncovered 14 skeletons dating from the 10th century. The mouths were filled with stones and sand; the heads were removed from the bodies. Stories began circulating that the skeletons had fangs.
> "The land of the living dead…" a feature story in The Prague Post www.praguepost.cz

It's interesting to see the parallels between some of the ideas of alchemy and vampirism. Both involve the idea of achieving a kind of everlasting life, though in the case of alchemy this was sought in the form of the Philosopher's Stone, while in the vampire myth the path to immortality is altogether bloodier.

Fairies, sprites and thwarted demons

Moving away from the darker side of Prague mythology, there are cheerier beliefs. For example, it is thought that benign little people who smoke pipes, wear green and dispense good advice inhabit the Vltava, the river that flows through Prague. They are in many ways rather like Irish leprechauns, which is interesting, as many Czechs will tell you that the Bohemians have close historical links with the Celts. One of these sprites appears on the "Seven of Acorns" card in the traditional 32-card Bohemian pack.

Another more positive use of magic is the mysterious but lovely inscription on the first floor of the Old Town Bridge Tower. It is written with no spaces and is a palindrome (i.e. it can be read left to right or right to left):

SIGNATESIGNATEMEREMETENGISETANGIS
ROMATIBISUBITOMOTIBUSIBITAMOR

The translation of this would be "Revel yourself in the form of a sign (in the sky) in vain you reach for me, I am your desire. Rome, through movement (stars) suddenly love comes to you". It's purpose? Well, apparently it was put there to fool any demons that might want to harm the tower. It was believed that these demons, faced with a word puzzle, would read it again and again, unable to figure it out, until they became exhausted and went away. Who knows, perhaps it worked? Certainly the tower has survived the centuries undamaged, unlike many of the other medieval towers in Prague, a number of which have been struck by lightning over the years. We have used this inscription on The Star card, for which it seems most appropriate. It also appears on the back of each card, so the entire deck may come in useful for warding off demons, should the need ever arise.

Of course, whenever spirits in Prague are mentioned the "Green Fairy" comes to mind. This is the name given to absinthe, the bright-green liqueur (banned in many countries) that's known to induce strange illusions, visions and even dementia. This fairy needs to be treated with respect.

If you do visit Prague and go in search of esoterica, be careful where you go because people claim that Prague's streets move around. Gates will suddenly appear in a wall, leading to a never-before-seen garden, or a vista will suddenly open up: Was that tower spire really there yesterday? Surely that strange iron balcony wasn't in this road before? Supposedly there is even an entire house, At the Last Lantern, at the end of Golden Lane, that only appears on certain nights, and appropriately enough marks the bridge between the seen and the unseen.

So do the streets really move? Or is it just that their odd layout, twisting and turning and full of alley-ways, cut-throughs and crazy steps and statues, simply leaves people disoriented? Like so many things in Prague, it's hard to know the truth exactly.

Prague and the Tarot

The unmistakeably grotesque, feverish atmosphere of Prague literature, always a refuge for agitated, visionary characters, little men with whims as eccentric as a tarot pack gone wild.

Angelo Ripellino, *Magic Prague*

A journalist recently described the weird 16th-century court of Emperor Rudolph II as being full of people telling fortunes with tarot cards, but in fact this is highly unlikely as tarot-type cards were not widely used for telling fortunes until well into the 18th century. One can see an evocative reproduction of an early pack of cards in the alchemy display at the Prague Castle museum, but this pack would almost certainly have been used for playing games, not for divination. Nevertheless, there are some interesting links between the city and the use of the occult tarot, though they are quite recent.

In the mid-20th century, Madame de Thebes (actually Matylda Průšová) lived and worked at 14 Golden Lane. The house still has an old sign, now sadly extremely faded, that shows playing cards, a crystal ball and an owl. She is reputed to have had a live black tomcat, a very dead stuffed owl, and a slightly dusty ostrich feather hat. However, she was by no means out of touch with the world and the poor woman was actually put to death by the Gestapo during the occupation of Czechoslovakia in WWII because she refused to stop predicting the end of the war and a German defeat.

Pierre de Lasenic (1900-944, originally Petr Kohout) was another well-known Prague practitioner of the occult and magic. In 1927, with Jan Kefer and others, he founded the Bohemian alchemical and esoteric society, Universalia. Lasenic produced what is probably the first deck of Czech occult tarot cards (the originals are now rare, but a reprint is available from the Czech publisher Trigon). They are very similar to the pattern used in the earlier deck by Oswald Wirth (i.e. they are based on the Marseille system, not on Rider Waite Smith) but have some added symbolism that probably refers to Universalia rites and ceremonies. Lasenic eventually died a rather strange death from the lung damage he suffered in a sandstorm in the Valley of the Kings in Egypt. Sadly, his tarot pack is now largely forgotten and has not achieved anything like the same attention as some of those designed by his Western contemporaries.

Now that we've reached the twenty-first century, a city as steeped in art and occult history as Prague surely deserves a deck of its own that can speak to us now, as well as connecting us to the very long tradition of Bohemian esoterica. We hope that the *Tarot of Prague* will add a little to the appreciation and understanding of this tradition, as well as offering images rich in the symbolism of the "Magic City".

Number 14 Golden Lane, the house in which the famous Madame de Thebes read cards

The Major Arcana

0 THE FOOL

A boy stands on top of a stone platform that is borne by the figure of a young man flying high over the Prague rooftops. The boy is about to step off the platform but he smiles into the sun without a care about the danger. At his feet a little dog is jumping up and barking, maybe to warn him of the step he is about to take, or perhaps simply out of excitement.

Short Interpretation

There are times when simply trusting in fate and being willing to take a step into the unknown can actually be the wisest move. We can all be too careful and restrained at times, and sometimes we need to be brave enough to act with the innocence of fools and children. A naive faith that life is sunny and full of good things is now and again the right approach, even if it may look foolish to others. So let your thoughts roam free and take a chance. The next step into the unknown may result in something quite wonderful.

[Major Arcana]

Fuller Interpretation

Being wise by being foolish • Taking a risk
Stepping into the unknown • Light-heartedness • Trusting in fate

The Fool is the heart of the Tarot. It is about trusting, letting go and taking what may appear to be foolish chances. It is perhaps the most "Zen" card of the Tarot because, like many of the stories told by Zen masters it is about wisdom attained through apparent folly. It's about realising what you really desire in life (rather than passing fancies) and about having the faith, even the blind faith, to attain this.

The card has evolved visually over the years. In pre-Rider Waite Smith versions it was usually a simple picture of a beggar or a social outcast In the Visconti Sforza cards (circa 1450) the Fool is shown as a man dressed in tattered white and cream clothes with feathers in his hair. In the slightly later Tarocchi del Mantegna deck (circa 1465) he is also dressed in rags, but this time leaning on his stick and being harried by dogs. In Southern Italy the Fool evolved into a figure much more like a travelling entertainer, either playing an instrument or prancing about, as much madman as idiot.

In the modern "occult" tarot The Fool has become a much more powerful symbol. His position as a figure of folly outside the normal course of things is interpreted as a sign of his deeper mystery. To signify this, when the Major Arcana is numbered The Fool is usually left outside this numbering system, typically marked as "0".

So how does all this relate to the interpretation of this card? Well, it shows a figure who is certainly open, spontaneous, and able to act outside the rules. He is a kind of "idiot savant", and what looks like a reckless attitude in fact lets him do things that others would think impossible, or at least impossibly unlikely. Though similar to the Knight of Wands (another reckless character of the Tarot), it's important to understand the difference between the two. Whereas the Knight of Wands is seen as having a wilful and sometimes selfish "devil may care" attitude, the Fool is not at all self-seeking or egotistical. He is reckless with his own safety but not with that of others, and in every sense he is of a higher order than the Knight.

The Fool in Tarot is, interestingly, very similar to the fool or "youngest son" found in a whole genre of fairy tales. He is the innocent who is sent out into the world to do an impossible task and, simply because he does not realise it's impossible and because he trusts the various odd figures who offer to advise and help him, he actually manages to achieve his task, and is frequently also rewarded in some unforeseen magical way.

The *Tarot of Prague* Fool is depicted as being outside the usual order of things. Rather than flesh and blood, he is made up of stars; he is actually Aquarius, an astronomical/astrological metaphor, rather than a real person. He is not tied by physical boundaries or by the normal rules of the earthly world.

He and his dog trust themselves to a flying pillar, something that is clearly ridiculous but does give the sense that they can interact easily with another plane of reality. As the Fool steps off into thin air his dog seems to be trying to pull him back, but it's clear enough that he wouldn't come to any harm if he fell into the void.

Sources

The Fool is taken from Al Sufi's (also known as Ali Sufi) Astronomical Atlas from the 15th century, a copy of which is part of the collection of the Strahov Library. Traditionally, the Fool is associated with Aquarius, so we used the image of this figure contained in the atlas.

The bright little dog is from the "Eight of Bells" card in our old 32-card Bohemian deck.

The platform carrying them over Prague is held by one of the carvings in the corner of an archway under the Old Town Bridge Tower. In the original it depicts a young man in the company of an older woman, and in the opposite corner are the figures of a young woman with a much older man. In spite of various names given to these carvings such as "student with a lady" or "man with courtesan", there isn't really much explanation of what they represent.

[Major Arcana]

THE MAGICIAN

I THE MAGICIAN

A powerful-looking young man stands in front of a small gaming table. On the table are symbols of three of the Tarot suits: Cups, Pentacles and Swords. He holds two magic wands, both alive with leaves. His table has checkerboards on it, implying that he may be seen as a figure of power or as a simple trickster or player of games. Maybe he is both? This Magician may sometimes play pranks, but he is also able to channel his power towards higher achievements; he is focused, active and consciously in control of the elements. Behind him is the figure of Mercury, a symbolic link to transformation and alchemy.

Short Interpretation

Often called the card of artists, The Magician is about great creative potential. You can work brilliantly in many areas if you focus and really use your knowledge and your abilities. If you believe in your own creativity you can achieve almost anything and it can be magical.

Fuller Interpretation

Creative force • The power to transform • Applied energy
Thrilling concepts brought to life • A flash of inspiration

The Magician is a powerful card with an interesting history. It was originally called the Battalier, Juggler or Pagat, and depicted a simple street performer, much like the hucksters that deceive people with the "shell game" trick in the streets today. However, over time the meaning of the card has changed from this trivial entertainer or trickster to something much more like our current idea of a wizard. The Magician now stands for focused energy and creative ability. It is a card of clear action and a sharp awareness, though there remains an implication, in some readings, of something rather tricky, a little like the Norse god Loki who had tremendous power but was not above playing tricks and practical jokes. Like Loki, this Magician is able to harness some of the power of the heavens and bring them down to earth, but the way in which he does this may not be predictable or easy to deal with. However, the consequences will be exciting and often incredibly productive.

The figure in the background of this card is Hermes, also known as Mercury. In alchemy, Hermes/Mercury was the God of Transformation (and the metal "mercury" named in his honour has the strange quality of being a liquid metal which has no definite shape). The Magician has many mercurial qualities. He is a quicksilver figure who transforms, transmutes and, on occasion, manipulates. He is in some ways like an alchemist, someone who can turn the ordinary into something precious and rare, just as the alchemists sought the ability to turn base metal into gold. However, it's important to realise that while the alchemists laboured for years to reach this goal, there is nothing painstaking or labour-intensive about the Magician; everything is done effortlessly in a moment of energy and inspiration.

The Magician is often called "the card of artists", but it can in fact mean a powerful burst of creative activity in any field. This action is effective because it is focused on changing real things. He (or she) is someone who can channel power in a practical way, with the ability to take raw energy and transform it into something usable. This power might seem overwhelming in some situations, but it's not wise to try to restrain such a powerful burst of inspiration. In a reading, whether this card indicates

[Major Arcana]

that it is you or someone else in your life who is able to harness this power, it signifies that it's best to stand back and let it electrify and energise the task at hand. The results may be startling and beyond anything you could have imagined.

Sources

The Magician is taken from a sculpted bronze relief of Jan Neruda, the Czech poet and writer. Appropriately, the sculpture is on the street named after him, Nerudova Street, above the door of the House of the Two Suns where Neruda lived. However, in our card we have laid a mask from an Art Nouveau house in Old Town over the original face. While this is not obvious when you look at the card, it is in many ways significant that the Magician wears a mask – he can manifest himself in many guises.

The odd little games table is adapted from a very old table in the Strahov Library. Much of the furniture on display there seems to incorporate odd faces hidden in the carvings.

On a more general level, an association with magicians, street performers, tricksters, quacks and alchemists features strongly in Prague's history. This may be partly because many of the numerous alchemists who passed through the city during the reign of Rudolph II were probably practising deception and sleight-of-hand rather than real magic.

The background of this card shows Mercury (Hermes) with his winged helmet. He is holding the distinctive "Caduceus" wand, made up of two intertwining serpents or, as in this example, circles. Mercury has always been considered the patron of alchemy, and different versions of his wand can be seen in many alchemical images. This particular chiaroscuro painting of Mercury is from the remarkable and rather mysterious set of paintings on a building in Ungelt (behind the Týn church). Other cards that use these paintings include the Three of Cups and The Star.

The Tarot of Prague

II THE HIGH PRIESTESS

A beautiful but stern woman is seated between two pillars that have carvings of masks and shells. She holds two precious books. On the cover of one is the *Monas*, the mysterious symbol of Rosicrucian alchemy. The other book is open, and she is pointing to a line written there. At her feet, a defeated serpent is coiled around a globe, a golden ball in its beak, a crescent moon behind its head. Behind the veil stretched between the pillars, the towers of a fabulously gilded church can just be glimpsed.

Short Interpretation

The High Priestess is about the inner mysteries of life. She may indicate clairvoyance and other "occult" powers, or she may simply be about the power of intuition. But whenever she appears it will be a time of insight and inspiration. Even if this feels profound and visionary, don't look too hard or too long. Life is also about action and about everyday events. Search within, but stay in touch with the world, too.

Fuller Interpretation

Spirituality • Inspiration • Inner vision • Self-knowledge
Seeking deeper truths • Soul searching

This is another card of great power, but it's an inward looking, reflective and spiritual power, rather than an active one. While the Magician works with raw external energy, and channels it into earthly matters, the High Priestess finds the power and energy within, and helps to bring it to conscious awareness. She is the card of visionaries and of inspiration.

The history of The High Priestess card is particularly prone to cause huge arguments (could this be because the whole notion of a powerful female figure in an intellectual/spiritual realm arouses strong emotions?) In earlier cards she was always shown as a female pope and known as The Papessa. Much later, this was changed to the High Priestess and she began to be shown with some of the attributes of Isis, the Egyptian goddess, rather than with the typical papal triple tiara that was originally on this figure. The argument rages on as to whether the early tarot Papessa was a figure of reference or heresy. In other words, was this image of a powerful woman to be regarded with respect or shock? Was she very conventional in meaning or openly anti-establishment?

These are really questions for the historian, but they do have some bearing on how we can interpret the meaning of this card now. It's important to realise that there is a nonconformity about the High Priestess that makes her quite different from the Hierophant. The spirituality that she signifies is not constrained within the structures of an established system of beliefs; it is much more likely to indicate a deep individual search for the underlying meanings of life, and a certain mystery. The High Priestess stands for knowledge that is hidden or held privately rather than communicated through laws or policies.

At times the lack of social involvement that is at the heart of this card can seem cold. The High Priestess is always impressive, but she can also be quite daunting. While her spirituality can simply take the form of "soul searching" and looking inwards, it can also manifest a powerful intuition, perhaps to the point of clairvoyance or other occult powers. This can be disturbing or even frightening. Less alarmingly, The High Priestess can also stand for patience and passivity and the faith to let events unfold without intervening, simply trusting in the unconscious, instinct and imagination.

The imagery used on this card is particularly laden with significance. The symbol on the front of the Priestess's book is the mysterious *Monas hieroglyphica*, which first appeared in the work published by the magus John Dee in 1564 (some years before he came to Prague) and which he regarded as being at the heart of his philosophy and knowledge:

> Dee's *Monas* is a combination of the signs of the seven planets, plus the symbol for the zodiacal sign, Aries, representing fire. It must have some astral significance; alchemical operations seem implied through the fire sign; it is also some kind of mathematics or geometry; but above all it is Cabala... It is a profound secret, which Dee wonders whether he has sinned in publishing.
> Frances Yates, *The Occult Philosophy in the Elizabethan Age*

This same symbol appeared much later on the opening page of *The Chemical Wedding*, one of the three major works of Rosicrucianism and alchemy which are believed to have been very influenced by Dee. The use of this symbol indicates that the knowledge of the Priestess is hidden and not to be shared.

The serpent below the feet of the Priestess shows that she can crush the Devil beneath her feet, that she is much more powerful than he is. The crescent moon is a traditional symbol on this card. It can be associated with both the Goddess Isis and the Virgin Mary.

Sources

The High Priestess herself is taken from one of the figures on the base of the statue of Charles IV at Křižovnické náměstí, the small square that stands at the Old Town end of the Charles Bridge. The crescent moon and the serpent coiled around the world are part of a carving found at the Strahov monastery. In the original, it lies at the feet of the Virgin Mary.

The pattern on the veil is part of the mid-16th-century sgraffito decoration on the Míčovna (Ball Games Court) at the Castle. Boniface Wolmut did the work between 1567 and 1569. For other cards that use figures from this sgraffito, see The Empress and the Seven of Pentacles.

The church glimpsed through this veil is the Loreto, an important

Baroque pilgrimage site dedicated to the Virgin Mary. The lavishly decorated church contains a 17th-century replica of the "Santa Casa", the house believed to be the site of the Incarnation (the moment at which Mary was told that she would conceive a child by the Holy Spirit). This house is supposed to have been transported by angels from the Holy Lands to Italy during the crusades. There is a charming local belief that the Loreto tower is one of the places on earth where good souls can rest for a moment when they choose to leave paradise to travel the world. These angelic visitors are believed to be present at the Loreto quite often.

The pillars can be found on a late 19th-century building on Karmelitská Street in Malá Strana. The house is very high, and the street not particularly wide, so most passers-by don't look up to see the other decorations on this house, which is too bad because there are some beautiful though slightly disturbing scenes of classical figures with fauns. Similarly, the relief masks on the pillars seem to show the tension between civilisation and untamed nature.

The Loreto church, a famous pilgrimage site for centuries

The Tarot of Prague

THE EMPRESS

III THE EMPRESS

This Empress is young, but calm and wise beyond her years. She is made up of mosaic pieces, representing all the facets of the earth, and is surrounded by an abundance of fruit and flowers. She is dressed in a silk and gold robe that is reminiscent of an Indian wedding sari, and her cloak is covered in hearts. Behind her is a picture of a woman embracing her children, while a tropical parrot looks on.

Short Interpretation

Mother Earth, Mother Nature — the Empress is all natural things in abundance. She is a powerful figure, though not a frightening one unless you cross her. Show respect for the natural world and embrace all it can offer, and the Empress will repay you with the fruits of the earth.

[Major Arcana]

Fuller Interpretation

Abundance • Fertility • Growth • Passion • The Life force

The Empress is the classic Earth Goddess. She is natural and in touch with the senses. She is also healthy and earthy, and very much attuned to plants and animals. In this way she is somewhat like the Queen of Pentacles, but whereas the Queen is a domestic Earth Mother, the Empress is much grander and more like Ceres, the goddess of harvest and fertility or, in modern terms, Gaia, who is the Earth herself. The Empress commands nature at its most profound and gorgeous. She represents motherhood, but also more generally the life force. She is deeply passionate, and has strong feelings that are sometimes unrestrained by any rational thought. She usually represents the positive side of strong passion, which can be enormously life enhancing and energetic. However, in certain readings her complete reliance on emotion can indicate a refusal to consider things in a more logical, empirical way, and an inability to look coolly and rationally at the simple facts.

This card hasn't changed much over the years. In some decks the Empress is shown with wings, but in others she is simply sitting on a throne that rises behind her like wings. Our card very much keeps to the traditional composition, but our Empress is more Asian than European in appearance. With her sari-like garment she suggests hot climates, bright sunlight and lush vegetation. She gazes serenely forward, crowned not with the golden crown that she holds in her hands, but with a tiara of stars.

Behind her is a picture that shows another side of the Empress: that of mother and loving nurturer. The birds and fruit on this picture are again signs of fertility and vitality.

Although she represents the Earth and the senses, it would be a mistake to see the Empress as being in any way domestic. She is motherly but she is not homely or tamed. Like nature itself, she is free from the control of mankind and this is one reason she is celebrated and revered.

Sources

This card is based on one section of the mosaic façade of the Municipal House (Obečni dům) in Prague. This was the work of Karel Spillar and is called "Homage to Prague". The whole building is a feast of Czech Secessionism (the Central European version of "Art Nouveau"), and this façade is a particularly fine example. We have added the starry crown and the lush foliage, in accordance with the Rider Waite Smith tradition, but even without these additions, the figure, surrounded by fruit and flowers and backed by a cloak of hearts, is the Empress incarnate. For another example of a card based on the Obečni dům mosaic, see the Knight of Pentacles.

The mother with two children in the background is based on a figure of "Charity" that is part of the mid-16th-century sgraffito decoration on the Míčovna (Ball Games Court) at the Castle. The artist was Boniface Wolmut.

One odd fact about the pictures on the Ball Games Court is that when they were restored in 1952, in the Communist era, the Communist szmbol of hammer and sickle was added between the figures of Faith and Justice. It is still there today, though no doubt not for long. The Seven of Pentacles also uses figures from the same sgraffito.

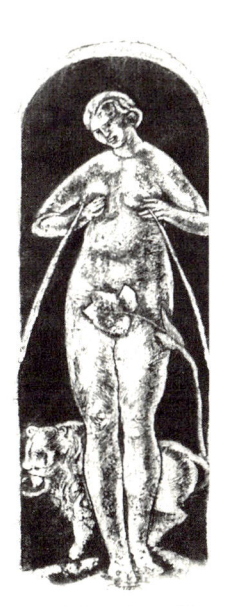

Depiction of a goddess
(probably Hera) from
the House of the Minute

[Major Arcana]

IV The Emperor

A stern and somewhat inflexible looking man sits enthroned and with crossed legs. He holds a sceptre and wand, symbols of authority. Behind him another figure, who looks more like a Roman emperor, plays with a crescent of red spheres.

Short Interpretation

The ultimate rationalist. Don't ask the Emperor if he is in touch with his emotions — the answer is definitely No! However, there are times when using the cold logic of the Emperor is the best approach. Some things just need to be thought through lucidly and without getting drawn into sentiment. However, once you know the rational choice, don't forget to ask yourself if it also feels right.

Fuller Interpretation

Rationality • Structure • Reason and Logic • System • Authority

This card is very much about the head rather than the heart. The Emperor is rationality personified, very much an archetypal father figure and an immensely strong source of influence on those around him (this does not mean that the Emperor is always a man, sometimes a woman will take this role). Rationality is rightly valued in our modern society. It is the root of enlightenment and self-control, and vital to good judgement and guidance. However, even while we value the logical and the empirical, we need to remember that emotion and intuition are also fundamental to a balanced approach to life. The importance of rationality should not go unappreciated, but in a reading this card may indicate the danger of letting it take over your life to the exclusion of feelings and intuition.

Appropriately, as The Emperor is very much about conservatism and keeping to the rules, this card has remained virtually unchanged over the centuries. He is always shown seated on his throne (though in some versions this is a simple block of stone or wood) and he always holds a sceptre. Earlier cards often showed a griffin or eagle. The eagle was probably a reference to the Imperial Eagle of the Roman emperors, and of course stood as a symbol of authority.

What is notable and interesting about older versions of this card is that the Emperor is almost always shown with his legs crossed. This is a very traditional pose that Crowley, in *The Book of Thoth*, states is a symbol of the Cross, but that other commentators have associated with the lame Fisher King, a very ancient mythical figure who is both ruler and victim.

The image in our card follows this "crossed leg" tradition but in a rather different way. The figure in the foreground is the rather rigid Emperor that we are used to seeing. His legs are crossed, in a formal and almost ritualistic way (in no way is this a casual pose) and his clothing is carefully arranged. His expression is controlled and neutral. He looks thoughtful and intelligent, but he shows no emotion.

In contrast, the figure behind him refers more directly to the Roman associations of this card. He is the more sensual Imperial Roman Emperor. He is lounging in a relaxed way, but if anything this gives the impression that his authority is even more absolute because it doesn't have to be conveyed by a formal pose. He gazes at a perfectly arranged semicircle of red spheres. The geometrical symmetry fascinates him, as does their colour, the bright red that stands for Imperial power and perhaps also indicates the energetic ability to bring about change through logic, self-discipline and good judgement.

The contrast between these two images should remind us that the Emperor can take different forms. He may seem like a fairly rigid character, full of self-restraint and control, but in his other aspect he may exert his authority in a way that seems on the surface to be more relaxed. Whichever form the Emperor takes, however, he is always fundamentally a symbol, for better or worse, of absolute rationality.

Sources

The Emperor is one of the statues depicting the Kings of Bohemia on the Powder Tower in Náměstí Republiky (Republic Square). The name of the tower comes from the fact that until the 17th century this tower was used to store gunpowder. The statues were done by three sculptors, Čapek, Seeling and Símek, and date from the mid-19th century.

The "Roman Emperor" in the background is one of the figures in a series of elaborate, gilded Art Deco decorations on a house in Václavské náměstí (Wenceslas Square), near the intersection with Vodičkova Street. Although these decorations are spectacular, they are placed so high up that pedestrians on the street below rarely notice them.

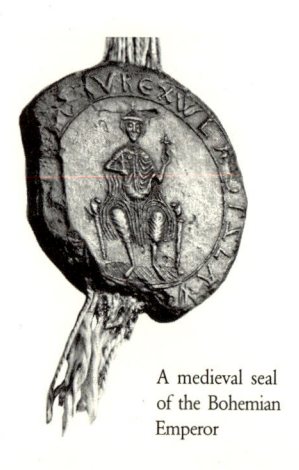

A medieval seal of the Bohemian Emperor

The Tarot of Prague

THE HIEROPHANT

V THE HIEROPHANT

An imposing elderly man stands in a library. A woman pleads for help — or is she an acolyte pleading for guidance? At first this Hierophant seems to be a fearsome figure, but if you look more closely his expression is stern but benevolent. However, even though the woman at his feet is both vulnerable and sensual, he completely ignores her, lost instead in more intellectual thoughts. The books behind him are symbols of authority and organisation, but his learning is not only from books. At his feet lies a globe that implies that his knowledge can also be far-reaching and even, within recognised and orthodox limits, quite exploratory.

Short Interpretation

The card of established authority and received knowledge. This can mean religious authority, or simply formal or structured education, systems of government, or the organisation of games or of business. When The Hierophant appears you may need to look at the role that orthodoxy and conformity play in your life. There are times when following the accepted rules are necessary and satisfying, but are you getting the balance right? Is there too much or too little conformity in your life? Are you looking for an authority figure, or simply trying to buck the rules? It's time to think carefully about these questions.

Fuller Interpretation

Establishment • Rules • Order • Education • Civilisation

The Hierophant is a card that tends to arouse strong feelings. To some people the established norms represented by the card seem stifling and restrictive. To others, it is these very structures that allow civilisation and learning to flourish. On a personal level also, someone who is a natural rebel may see nothing but a threat in the call to convention that The Hierophant stands for, whereas a person who has lived by the rules may tend to see the card as a very positive symbol of much that they value.

The Hierophant may appear in a reading to indicate that you feel the need for some order in your life. This may take the form of studying or learning in a structured way, probably for a qualification. It can also mean following a disciplined regime, or a system of rules or beliefs. There are certainly times when one needs to bow to a higher authority and be willing to control one's personal opinions in order to learn from someone (or some system) that has more established knowledge. While institutions can feel rather large and overwhelming to the individual, there are also times when being part of an established structure is empowering and rewarding and can actually allow you to accomplish remarkable things.

However, the downside of The Hierophant is a possible lack of intuition and emotion. While he symbolises the ability to explore the far reaches of any discipline (i.e., he is in no way limited in his intellectual thinking), he may be unable to step outside the agreed structures and think intuitively.

In early cards, The Hierophant was "The Pope", and of course carried specific associations with the established church. However, in the later "occult" tarot this card evolved into the less specifically Christian "Hierophant". In our card, the figure shown is very much a recognised figure of established religion, but of Judaism, rather than Christianity. The image is a statue of Rabbi Loew (Jehuda Low Bezalel, 1520-1609), the almost mythical spiritual leader of the Prague Jewish community at the time of Rudolph II, and a highly respected scholar and expert in the Cabbala.

There are many legends about Loew, perhaps the most famous of which is the story of the creation of the Golem (see the Five of Cups). Though to our modern eyes his use of Cabbalistic magic seems unconventional, in Loew's time he would have been seen as fairly orthodox — very appropriate to the figure of the Hierophant. We have shown him standing with the Theological Room in the Strahov Library in the background. This library is particularly appropriate as it not only represents the established theological knowledge of the time but also contains a remarkable collection of texts on the Cabbala.

Sources

This forbidding but impressive sculpture of Rabbi Loew is by Ladislav Šaloun, and is located at the entrance to the Prague Town Hall, which is just beside Josefov, the old Jewish quarter of the city.

Rabbi Loew (Yehuda Low Ben Bezalel) was the Chief Rabbi of Prague. He who lived a long life from 1525 to 1609 and is perhaps most famous as the creator of the Golem, the man made of mud to protect the Jews of Prague (for more on the Golem, see the Five of Cups).

The library in the background is at the Strahov monastery. It is one of the most famous old libraries in Central Europe, with a particularly fine collection of theological texts, including many volumes on the Cabbala. There is also a very famous collection of books on the properties of plants and herbs.

The room shown here is the Theological Room, which contains about 16,000 books, including the precious Kralice Bible. The globe is one of several 17th-century globes kept in this room.

[Major Arcana]

THE LOVERS

VI THE LOVERS

These Lovers are clearly Adam and Eve, but although they have eaten from the Tree of Knowledge they are not afraid. Instead, they seem very wrapped up in each other's tenderness. The stag beside them is a traditional symbol of faithfulness — perhaps here standing both for their steady devotion to each other and to a higher power. Above them is an angel depicted in Art Deco "Egyptian"-style and carrying a banner that reads "Nothing better here below".

Short Interpretation

The Lovers card represents not only passion, but also strong emotional relationships and values, or beliefs based on emotions rather than rationality. Desire can take many forms. It can be powerfully sexual but it can also refer to less sensual loves. Unlike The Devil card, The Lovers signifies that giving yourself up to passion, when it is truly based on love, can be an act of generosity that can lead to both happiness and spiritual calm.

Fuller Interpretation

Passion • Love • A powerful relationship • Desire • Faithfulness
Sexuality • Emotional values

This card is about love, but also often specifically about sexuality and desire. The type of love symbolised by The Lovers is essentially earthly, though this does not mean that it should be considered any less valuable than a more spiritual love. It signifies a love that is both powerful and faithful, a precious thing in its own right. It also stands for passion and desire within the framework of a deep emotional relationship.

The Lovers card has an interesting history. Early versions were usually simply called "Love" rather than The Lovers, and showed cupid shooting an arrow at a couple. Some early cards focused on the aspect of choice in love, showing a scene in which a man (or in one case a woman) stands between two potential lovers. In modern cards the scene tends to be simplified to show one couple only and has come to be focused (in what is perhaps a very modern tendency) to show an emotional and, by implication, sexual relationship. However, the early meanings are still possible, and in some readings this card can be interpreted as indicating that it's time to choose between types of love; maybe a more base attraction as against a "pure" and selfless love? It can also refer to the need to make choices between types of relationships, for example, perhaps between opposing loyalties to friends and family.

The image on this card is that of the first lovers, Adam and Eve. These lovers are totally wrapped up in each other, although they have lost the Garden of Eden. Above them an angel (perhaps one of the angels who chased them out of Paradise) carries a banner which says "Nothing better here below", a reminder perhaps that although they have lost one paradise they still have love, the best thing that earth can offer. The stag is an early symbol of fidelity and faithfulness and also, interestingly, of longevity. On some older tarot (notably the Florentine Minchiate) it was an attribute of Father Time (which is The Hermit in the modern deck). Here, on The Lovers card, it can be read as a sign that time cannot conquer true love.

[Major Arcana]

Sources

The figures of Adam and Eve, together with the stag, are from the sgraffito on the façade of the House of the Minute in Old Town Square, believed to date from 1600. The House of the Minute is situated prominently on the "Royal Route" traditionally taken by the Bohemian kings on the way to their coronation. The façade is covered with pictures of Biblical and mythical scenes, and also with representations of various virtues. At the very top of the house are portraits of historical rulers.

The angel is from the cloisters of the Vyšehrad cemetery. It is particularly striking because of its Art Deco Egyptian-style design; Egyptian motifs were very popular in the Art Deco/Secessionism period.

The quote on the banner is taken from *The Chemical Wedding* by Christian Rosencranz. This whole text focuses repeatedly on the meanings of love, both those that are apparent and the underlying "Rosicrucian" esoteric meanings. Part of one of the poems contained within the text reads:

> There's nothing better here below,
> Than beauteous, noble, Love;
> Whereby we like to God do grow,
> And none to grief do move.

The Tarot of Prague

THE CHARIOT

VII THE CHARIOT

A mature, intense-looking woman drives a chariot drawn by two eagles, one dark and one light. These eagles are not easy to control; one of the birds is squawking at her, as if to question her authority, but she remains calmly in charge. Although the chariot is flying high above the ordinary life of the city, there is a down-to-earth confidence about the charioteer. Perhaps this is because she knows she will succeed in driving this chariot to wherever she wills it.

Short Interpretation

You are absolutely determined to reach your goal and succeed, even if it means sacrificing everything else in life. It's a great thing to have such tremendous faith and confidence in yourself and in your abilities, but consider balancing this focus with some less forceful and driven behaviour. You know you'll get there. Push towards your goal by all means necessary, but not so ruthlessly that you hurt yourself or someone else.

[Major Arcana]

Fuller Interpretation

Iron control • Clear aims • Willpower • Confidence
Tenacity • Focus

The Chariot is about reaching goals through strength of will and concentration. This requires determination and an ability to focus on the goal to the exclusion of all else. It also implies having tremendous faith and confidence in yourself and in your ability to focus your energies. The charioteer is not a cold person, but someone who is able to master their emotions and demonstrate strong discipline and authority whenever it's needed. This card is about victory, but of a much more controlling and self-willed type than that of the "victory card", the Six of Wands. However, The Chariot is not a straightforward depiction of victory or war. Tarot historian Tom Tadfor Little has, for example, said that this symbol is also about general attributes such as mastery and control and can sometimes indicate brutality and megalomania or the use of excessive force. This kind of iron will can be appropriate and an asset in hard times, especially when it is needed to respond to an attack, but it can quickly turn negative when it is used to simply exert power for its own sake.

In the case of The Chariot, it is particularly obvious that the interpretation of the card depends entirely on context. In some circumstances the iron control of The Chariot shows itself as wilful dominance, whereas in others it is more about the ability to apply the appropriate level of forcefulness when it's needed.

The victory signified by The Chariot can be a victory of intellect as well as willpower. Arthur Waite, in his 1909 book *A Pictorial Key to the Tarot*, described this card as showing a person who had answered the notorious riddle of the sphinx, the ultimate intellectual challenge. However, Waite also points out that the rational and physical victories that are symbolised are only that, and higher spiritual success is not implied, so in some ways the will of the charioteer only effects the intellectual and material planes. The determined-looking woman driving the chariot is a little similar to the figure in "Strength", but she does not look as though she is physically exerting herself but rather shows her strength of character by controlling the difficult and wilful eagles that draw her vehicle.

She is flying above the Royal Route in Prague the route that the Bohemian kings travelled on their way to their coronation. This is a reminder of the power and control that, for better or worse, status and position can lend. By having a woman rather than a man behind the reins we are reminded that strength, drive and control can be attributes of either gender.

The charioteer controls the eagles with a wand tipped with a glowing eye. This is an old symbol of the eye of God; a similar symbol has been used in many cultures and religions. It is included here to show that the control represented here is not primarily physical. It comes from the spirit, and from having the knowledge that allows you to see where you are going, and to believe in your ability to get there.

Sources

The use of a woman rather than a man as charioteer is actually quite ancient. The early Minchiate and Visconti Sforza decks both show a woman on this card. Of course, anyone British will be familiar enough with depictions of Boudicca driving a chariot, and the woman charioteer is a common enough subject of monumental statuary in many other countries and cultures.

The woman charioteer used on this card is from the fantastically decorative, stuccoed and painted ceiling of the Theology Hall at the Strahov Library. The room dates from 1671, but a local monk, Siard Nosecky, decorated the ceiling later, in 1721. The ceiling shows seventeen scenes, depicting the thoughts of J. Hirnhaim, who was then the Abbot, and represents the theme of human knowledge.

The street shown in the background is Ke hradu, a sweeping road that turns from Nerudova Street up towards the Prague Castle. This steep slope is the very last leg of the Royal Route to the castle.

[Major Arcana]

More about the Royal Route

The Royal Route is the road traditionally taken by the Bohemian kings on the way to coronation. It begins at the 15th-century Powder Tower, runs the length of Celetná Street (past the House of the Black Madonna), across Old Town Square and Little Square, then down Karlova Street and across Charles Bridge. It crosses Malostranské Square and goes all the way up Nerudova Street before turning a steep corner and climbing up Ke hradu to Prague Castle. It is about three kilometres long.

The reason for this particular route is that for centuries the Bohemian kings had their residence in the town, close to the Powder Tower on the site of the present Obecni dům (Muncipal House). The Royal Route was therefore the way between the king's court and the St Vitus' Cathedral where the coronations took place.

There have been some recent theories that the Royal Route was in fact intended as a "ground map" of the process of the alchemical "Great Work" (e.g. see Milan Spůrek's *Praga Mysteriosa*). While there is little real evidence to support this, it's interesting to note that Tarot has also been regarded by some as a "royal road" to enlightenment. The Swiss Antoine Court de Gébelin (1719 1784) claimed that the word "Tarot" was derived from the Egyptian and meant "the royal road", from "tar" (road) and "ro" (royal). (Although in fact neither of those words is to be found in most Egyptian dictionaries.) Inspired by Gébelin, Etteilla wrote several books and pamphlets on this subject. In more recent times, this theory has been further developed, and the idea of the Tarot as a Royal Road has been connected to the Cabbalistic Tree of Life (e.g. see Stephan Hoeller's *The Royal Road*).

Many of the elements used on the *Tarot of Prague* cards were taken from buildings that can be found on the Royal Route. Here are some examples, given in the order in which the elements that they incorporate appear on the route:

The Empress Obečni dům
The Knight of Pentacles Obečni dům
The Emperor The Powder Tower

The King of Swords The Powder Tower
The Hanged Man (Black Sun) Celetná Street
The Knight of Swords Old Town Square (at the entrance to Celetná)
The Knight of Wands Old Town Square (the Astronomer's Clock)
The Wheel of Fortune Old Town Square (the Astronomer's Clock)
The Knight of Wands The House of the Minute, Old Town Square
The Lovers The House of the Minute, Old Town Square
The Six of Swords The House of the Minute, Old Town Square
The Ten of Swords The House of the Golden Well, Karlova
The Three of Cups Clam-Gallas Palace, Karlova
The Two of Cups Charles Bridge
The Queen of Cups Charles Bridge
The King of Pentacles Charles Bridge
The Moon Charles Bridge
The Star (palindrome inscription) Old Town Bridge Tower
The King of Pentacles Malá Strana Bridge Tower
Death St Mikulas (Nicholas) Church, Malostranské Square
The Moon (the face of the Moon) Nerudova Street
The Ace of Cups (the Lion) Nerudova Street
The Chariot Ke hradu
The Seven of Cups St Vitus' Cathedral
The Hanged Man (the Golden Door) St Vitus' Cathedral
The Ace of Wands St Vitus' Cathedral

[Major Arcana]

STRENGTH

VIII STRENGTH

A young woman is standing and calmly holding open the mouth of a lion. Her hair is red, like the lion, and she wears flowers in her hair and on her delicate dress. Behind her is a wall on which there is an sgraffito picture showing Hercules performing this same task with the Nemean lion (one of the beasts that Hercules had to defeat as part of the trials set for him). He is using sheer physical power to overwhelm his lion.

Short Interpretation

Confidence and serenity are at the core of real strength. Strength isn't about force, but comes from the knowledge that you really can achieve what needs to be done — calmly, quietly, but in a way that overcomes all resistance.

The Tarot of Prague

Fuller Interpretation

Strength of purpose • Patience • Determination • Fortitude
Quiet confidence

This card signifies the measured strength that comes from confidence rather than physical force. It reminds us that confidence and calm are at the core of real strength. Strength isn't about brute force; the source of true strength comes from the knowledge that you really can achieve what needs to be done — calmly, quietly, but in a way that overcomes all resistance.

In early versions this card was often called Fortitude, which perhaps better conveys its real meaning, which is less about physical strength and more about courage and standing firm against adversity. A variety of images were used for this card. Sometimes they showed a man rather than a woman. Often he was forcing open the mouth of a lion, but in some versions he was shown simply standing with a lion and brandishing a club. All these images are very similar to medieval and Renaissance representations of Hercules, an enormously popular symbol of strength. In most old European cities you can see numerous depictions of Hercules fighting with a lion. However, even in early Tarot, Strength was also often shown as a woman. She was usually depicted either as carrying a heavy marble pillar with ease or, in the version that is now the most common, effortlessly opening the mouth of a lion.

In this card we have shown both male and female depictions of the scene. This partly shows that Strength can be a quality of either gender, but also represents the different meanings of the concept. In the sgraffito image in the background, Hercules is showing his brute strength: he defeats the lion simply because he is physically stronger. In the foreground image, however, it is unthinkable that the slight woman would actually be physically stronger than the lion. She possesses different and more powerful kinds of strength: force of character, of purpose, and of will. With these, the image implies, we can achieve anything.

Sources

The woman is in the style of Alfons Mucha, the most famous artist of the Czech Art Nouveau. The lion is taken from a very old wooden sculpture currently in an alleyway in one of the streets near Týnská, in the area behind the Týn church. The original shows a male figure straddling the lion and exerting considerable physical force. This is a common subject in old sculptures and usually depicts Daniel, Hercules or Samson.

The sgraffito is from a wall in an inner courtyard of the Martinic Palace. The whole series shows scenes from the mythical life of Hercules and the biblical stories of Joseph. This is a Renaissance building, part of which dates from the mid-16th century. It was in ruins for much of the 20th century, but has now been beautifully and painstakingly restored. For more cards that use the sgraffito panels from the Martinic Palace, see The Fool and the King of Swords.

The sgraffito depiction of Hercules and the Lion at the Martinic Palace

The Tarot of Prague

THE HERMIT

IX THE HERMIT

It is twilight. A hooded and cloaked elderly man walks across a lane of tiny painted houses. He is holding a staff and a lantern shaped like an hourglass. Above him is a sign that shows all the equipment of the alchemist's laboratory.

Short Interpretation

There are periods when you need to withdraw a little from the everyday business of the world and look inside yourself. The Hermit reminds us that life is short, and we need to find time in our hectic lives to meditate on who we are and why we are here. It may sound introspective and even a little frightening, but in fact if you take some time out for contemplation you'll find it makes your life richer and your mind more active.

[Major Arcana]

Fuller Interpretation

Introspection • A quest • Meditation • Deliberate withdrawal

The Hermit signifies the need to be quiet, focused and meditative in order to see things with more depth and clarity. This may involve a period of withdrawing from the everyday concerns of the world in order to be alone to think. This card often symbolises some kind of quest, but it is not a quest for anything physical but rather one aimed at uncovering hidden truths and shedding light on them.

From the early Tarot of Marseille onwards, this card has usually shown an old man dressed like a monk, carrying a lantern and leaning on a large wand or walking staff. However, the name of the card has varied considerably over the years. Significantly, in 14th and 15th century Italy the card was called The Old Man, Time, or The Hunchback. In these cards he is more typically shown carrying an hourglass (this was a motif that was sometimes associated with Death as well as Time — for an example of this see our Death card). It seems, therefore, as if this card used to be not so much a depiction of a hermit but of Father Time himself. This implies that the position of the Hermit in the Major Arcana may be a reminder that time overcomes all, and that old age signals the nearness of Death. It's a rather grim interpretation for modern tastes, and the meaning has evolved into the more optimistic interpretation of the figure being associated with meditation, introspection and the quest for truth. However, these things very often come with maturity, so perhaps the two interpretations can be reconciled without too much difficulty. In a reading, the surrounding cards and the question being asked will help you arrive at the appropriate interpretation.

In the *Tarot of Prague* design we combined the traditional symbols so that the Hermit holds an hourglass that glows like a lantern. It is both a symbol of the passing of time and of enlightenment. He stands in Golden Lane, perhaps the most famous street in Prague, known as the "Street of the Alchemists". There are many myths surrounding the Lane. The Czech author Karásek wrote in his play *Král Rudolf* (*kral* is Czech for king):

The Golden Lane... is the city's soul. So much energy, so much magnetism of occult forces is concentrated there that experiments which fail elsewhere will succeed there.
(Karásek, *Král Rudolf*)

The Golden Lane has become a powerful symbol of alchemy, though in fact the houses here were probably never home to any alchemists. Regardless of its true history, the Golden Lane will always stand as a symbol of alchemical endeavour and of the long study and inner transformation that lay at the heart of the "Great Work". It's therefore very appropriate as the setting of this card.

Sources

The Hermit figure is adapted from one of the statues in a group of statues from the 19th century standing in a small park on Smetanovo nábřeží (Smetana Embankment). For other cards that use this group, see The World and the Knight of Wands.

The street of tiny, old, painted houses in the background is the Golden Lane, the so-called "Street of the Alchemists" which is within Hradčany (the Prague Castle complex).

The collection of alchemical instruments shown at the top of the card is taken from a house sign on a building in Konviktská Street.

A wall painting of a scholarly monk from the Storch House in Old Town Square

[Major Arcana]

More about Golden Lane

In the Golden Lane in the Hradčany
Time almost seems to stand still
If you wish to live five hundred years
Drop everything, take up alchemy

Vitězslav Nezval, *U alchymistů*

Golden Lane is a tiny and very pretty street inside the complex of buildings that make up Prague Castle. The whole lane, including the houses, is only eight metres wide at its wideSt Nowadays it is often crowded with visitors, who go to admire the atmospheric and picturesque little houses. Years ago, however, Golden Lane certainly wasn't a desirable location. Jan Neruda provides some insight into what it was like living there:

The lane is very narrow, scarcely a pace and a half wide... From the lane one goes into an entry hall, barely one yard by one yard in size, and from there to the main and only room, sometimes two yards by two yards, sometimes measuring even less. The ordinary tenant, a so-called "lodger", lives on the first floor, and cannot really use his flat for anything other than sleeping, because, owing to its low ceiling, he can hardly even sit upright in it".

(Jan Neruda, *Pictures of Life*)

The lane is centuries old, and by 1566 there were already records of eighteen "lodgings" there. The structures were indeed not much more than lodgings, very small in size and mostly without any water or even rudimentary sanitation. Things improved later when some windows were knocked into the back of the little houses. However, even today many of them have just one room and an attic that is only tall enough to crawl into. This has fired the imagination of many writers such as Angela Carter:

Prague, the capital of paranoia, where the fortunetellers live on Golden Alley in cottages so small, a good-sized doll would find itself cramped, and there is one certain house on Alchemist's Street that only becomes visible during a thick fog. (On sunny days, you can see a stone.) But, even in the fog, only those born on the Sabbath can see the house anyway.

(Angela Carter, *Alice in Prague or the Curious Room*)

Fortunately, like most of the other houses, number 14 is visible at all times. It was home in the 1930s and 40s to Madame de Thebes, arguably the most famous tarot reader Prague has ever had. There is still a (very faded) sign on the house showing her cards, an owl and a crystal ball:

With her black clothes and old-fashioned hat with ostrich feathers, this chemist's widow, whose real name was Matylda Průšová, aroused curiousity even from a distance. Into her living room, crammed full of bizarre objects, including stuffed owls and a wooden eagle hanging from the low ceiling, customers came daily, yearning to hear what the future had in store for them...Owing to her frequent predications about the imminent end of the war she was arrested by the Gestapo and, during the last interrogation, tortured to death.

Frantisek Kadlec, *Golden Lane*

Although Madame de Thebes has certainly gone down in history, by far the most famous resident of the street was Franz Kafka, who lived there from 1916 to 1917, at the tiny house at number 22. It is there that he wrote his story *The Country Doctor*.

Nowadays Golden Lane is most popularly associated with some of the wilder imaginings about alchemy and magic. This quote from a website is fairly typical of the kind of thing that gets said:

During the 16th Century black magic and the occult sciences were practiced in Prague - the famous center of alchemy - on Golden Lane or the "Street of the Alchemist" as it was known. The infamous Doctor Faust lived there, as did Paracelsus, Cornelius Agrippa and the monk Tritheim.

www.madametalbot.com

In fact, none of these people lived there and it is doubtful that any alchemists did. It was in the White Tower at one end of Golden Lane that some alchemy labs were set up (nowadays it houses an exhibition and re-creation of a lab that shows how it may have been), and this tower was also used as a prison. The alchemist and magician Edward Kelley was imprisoned there in May 1591 when Rudolph II finally decided that he was a charlatan and had him convicted as a fraudster.

[Major Arcana]

WHEEL OF FORTUNE

X Wheel of Fortune

A golden wheel shows the cycle of the year. Each day is recorded in writing, and each month is shown in a picture. Around the Wheel there are four figures holding scrolls — a winged lion, an eagle, a winged bull and a boy. Presiding over all is a small horned figure pointing with one hand at the book he holds in the other. The devil is there as a warning, reminding you that all the actions in your life will be noted.

Short Interpretation

A turning point in your life. Whatever your fortunes now, things may soon change. There are always going to be ups and downs, and things aren't entirely in our control, but this doesn't mean we are entirely at the mercy of fate. What matters is how we deal with our fortunes. When you are up, don't be complacent, enjoy your luck but remember that it won't last forever. If you are down, then think of this only as a phase. Don't give up, the Wheel may be about to turn again and things should get better.

Fuller Interpretation

Ups and downs • Luck — good and bad • A change of fortune • Fate
Passage of time

The Wheel of Fortune reminds us that nothing, whether good or bad, stays the same forever. There is always movement and change in life. It is important to acknowledge fate and to understand that in spite of all our efforts we are to some extent subject to our destiny. As Carl Orff put it:

The Wheel of Fortune turns
I go down, demeaned;
another is raised up;
far too proud
sits the king at the summit
let him fear ruin!
for under the axis we read
about Queen Hecuba

Carl Orff, *Carmina Burana*

The Wheel gives hope in adversity, but also cautions against falling into complacency or smugness when things are going well and we feel on top of the world.

It isn't by chance that this card is numbered "ten" and so is at the midpoint of the traditional numbering sequence of the Major Arcana. It is there as a kind of a centre point around which the varied cards of the Tarot turn. The Wheel of Fortune is, of course, absolutely neutral. When the figure of Fortune is depicted (as she sometimes is on this card) it is nearly always as a blindfolded woman, similar to the traditional depiction of Justice. It's a reminder that fortune is blind to position or status, so each of us is equally at the mercy of chance. When this card comes up in a reading it often implies a turning point and change, for better or for worse. However, whether it sometimes simply signifies a more generalised force of destiny or fate. It might even be a straightforward reminder that nothing stays the same.

As well as the Wheel, our image shows the four figures traditionally featured on this card: a winged lion, a bull, an eagle and a man. It also shows a little devil at the top of the card. This is not to imply that the

[Major Arcana]

Devil is in charge, but simply to warn that if you don't take responsibility for your own fate then you risk being controlled by it. In the Tarot, The Devil is always about the loss of control over your destiny. In the original carving from which these figures are taken the devil was there as a warning that your actions would be noted and recorded. The long index finger with which he points towards his book was originally known as "the Mother" finger, the one that pointed, controlled and cast spells.

The Wheel of Fortune is another card with an interesting and enlightening history. In early versions it sometimes showed four pictures of a man at various stages of his life. One figure was at the left of the wheel, and obviously on his way up, one was on top, and the third was on the right and falling down. The final figure lay under the Wheel. In each case there was some text explaining his position on the Wheel – "I will reign", "I reign", "I have reigned", and finally "I am without reign".

In later cards the figures were usually animals, and there is much debate about how this change happened. Some people argue that it may simply have been a misinterpretation of the imagery of poorly-printed, old woodcut cards. Whatever the reason, by the time the Rider Waite Smith deck appeared in the early 20th century the four figures had become the familiar winged eagle, lion, ox and man that represent the biblical Evangelists.

In our card, the Wheel is very richly illustrated; there is a picture for each month of the year as well as zodiac symbols and a piece of text for every day. It reminds us that in the course of a single year many events take place, some important, some trivial. Nothing is forever, because time always moves on and, as the cliché goes, the only constant is change. The four figures surrounding the Wheel are particularly delicate and attractive in their styling. These are not the forbidding figures of some biblical illustrations of the Evangelists. They are gentle and approachable, even smiling. However, they carry long, long scrolls on which the good and bad actions of mankind, or of any one individual, are recorded. So even though we seem to be subject to unpredictable fate, the scrolls that these figures hold remind us that every little thing we do is in some way accountable. The image on this card implies that it isn't just the tiny devil at the top that threatens to record our mistakes. The kindly figures that surround the Wheel will also take note of our good deeds and benevolent actions.

The Tarot of Prague

Sources

The Wheel is the "calendarium" that shows the signs of the zodiac and forms the lower part of the famous Astronomical Clock in Old Town Square. While the main mechanism and the face of the clock date from the early 15th century, this lower decoration is much later. Josef Manes painted it in the mid-19th century. It shows the signs of the zodiac, a picture for each month, and a text for each day of the year. The disc advances one day at midnight, so that in a year it completes an entire revolution.

The figures around the Wheel are medieval carvings. The originals can be found at the side entrance to the Týn Church. The carving shows all four figures with the little devil in the centre, so they have been used on this card very much as they are arranged in the original, although we have made the devil smaller because in the original he looked rather too much like the dominant figure, which would hardly be appropriate for the meaning of this card.

The Astronomical Clock in Old Town Square

[Major Arcana]

XI Justice

A woman balances lightly on the back of an elephant standing on a globe. She is holding a pair of scales and a glowing sword. Behind her there is a highly-decorated wall, drawn entirely in black and white, showing a phoenix rising from ashes.

Short Interpretation

Justice has been done. You have got what you deserve, whether this is good or bad, and there is real satisfaction in knowing this and in taking responsibility for this outcome. If times are not so good, then be honest with yourself and think about whether this is in any way because of your own past actions. However, if times are great, enjoy it even more because you know it's deserved and you worked hard to make it happen.

Fuller Interpretation

Cause and effect • Fair play • Reaping the rewards • Consequences
Responsibility for actions

Fairness, ethics and honesty are all part of the meaning of Justice. Depending on circumstances, true justice can be most welcome or very much resisted. When this card comes up in a reading it may mean that you are getting exactly what you deserve, and that can of course be satisfying or threatening according to what you have done. Justice demands that you look back at the actions that have lead to the current situation, and recognise realities. This doesn't just mean that we need to take responsibility for our negative actions — sometimes it's almost as hard to take credit for good deeds and see that a happy situation is often not just due to luck but is the result of hard work and the right decisions. In addition to justice or retribution, this card can less dramatically indicate waiting for a decision and/or accepting responsibility. Even in this interpretation, though, there is a demand that cause and effect be recognised and that we willingly face up to justice and fair play.

In the image on this card, Justice stands balanced on an elephant. This signifies the need to remember the actions and decisions leading up to the present. True justice needs to have a long memory. As the old saying goes, if you don't think about the events of the past you may be condemned to repeat them. The elephant is standing on a globe to signify that justice often needs to be seen in a broad context; sometimes it's important to think through the consequences of our actions from the perspective of its wider effects, as well as just the local ones. Remember the two aspects of Justice: it's not just about recognising and taking responsibility for any damage your actions might cause, it's also very much about realising how you have made a positive difference — and can continue to do so.

The phoenix is a symbol of justice in Japan. However, that isn't the primary reason we have included it in this card. What we had in mind is that the phoenix is also a symbol of death and rebirth, of reincarnation. When reincarnation is combined with the concept of justice, we arrive at the idea of karma. Even if justice does not seem to have been done in this world, the good or bad karma that you accumulate may be taken into account in another world or another life.

[Major Arcana]

Sources

The black and white sgraffito façade is taken from the front of the elaborate and beautiful mid-16th-century Míčovna (Ball Games Court) that is part of the Prague Castle complex.

The elephant is taken from the "Eight of Leaves" from our old pack of Bohemian cards. Engagingly, it isn't very anatomically correct (unlike the more domestic animals like the horse and dog also shown on the Bohemian pack). This is probably because the artist had never actually seen an elephant and had to use a little guesswork.

The figure of Justice herself is taken from a remarkable marquetry door in the Wallenstein Palace. This dates from 1623-29 and was designed by the Italian architect Andrea Spezza. The door was actually taken from an even earlier house that was one of several demolished (in spite of their owners' protests) to make way for the palace. Albrecht Wallenstein was a remarkable man who, through two advantageous marriages and skilful military exploits, grew to become immensely rich. His palace (in which he rarely lived) incorporates a fabulous collection of mythological, astronomical and astrological paintings and sculpture. This door is just beside the entrance to the famous painted corridor of mythical scenes, all based on Ovid's *Metamorphosis*. The even more remarkable astronomical/astrological corridor is on the floor above (but has been closed to the public for some time). Wallenstein's personal encounter with justice was the result of his plotting with the Saxons and Swedes against his patron Emperor Ferdinand. When this was discovered, the Emperor wasted no time in having Wallenstein assassinated.

The intricate marquetry door at the Wallenstein Place.

The Tarot of Prague

More about Wallenstein

In 1608, at the age of 25, Albrecht von Wallenstein had his horoscope cast by the famous astronomer Johannes Kepler. Wallenstein was born at 4:36 p.m. on September 24, 1583, under the sign of Libra. Kepler's horoscope said that the young man would be "alert, lively, eager and restless, curious of every kind of novelty, unsuited to the common manner and behaviour of mankind, but striving after new, untried or extraordinary ways." Also that he would have "a bent toward alchemy, magic, and enchantment, community with spirits, scorn and indifference toward human ordinances and conventions and to all religions, making everything proposed by God or man to be suspected and despised". Kepler also predicted that his character would be "unmerciful, without brotherly or matrimonial love, caring for no-one, devoted only to himself and his desires, severe upon those placed under him, parsimonious, covetous, deceitful, inequitable in his dealings, usually silent, often impetuous, also belligerent and fearless." These predictions turned out to be quite correct, as Wallenstein rose to prominence with a brilliant but ruthless military career and developed a keen interest in esoterica.

Sixteen years later, in 1624, Wallenstein insisted on Kepler casting another horoscope for him. Kepler was quite reluctant, but did so because by this time Wallenstein was very powerful. This second horoscope turned out to be remarkably accurate, so much so that it's become very famous among historians of astrology. In it, Kepler predicted that in March 1634 there would be some terrible confusion in the country that would affect Wallenstein. In fact, Wallenstein was assassinated on the Emperor's orders in February 1634. It has been said that he didn't defend himself partly because he felt that his death was fated.

There is one last curious fact about Wallenstein. It is claimed that one of the rooms that is closed to the public contains a graphic painting that shows a man being stabbed by assailants, and the painting looks very much like a depiction of Wallenstein's own manner of murder. In fact, this picture was commissioned by Wallenstein himself — a year before he was assassinated.

[Major Arcana]

XII The Hanged Man

A young man hangs upside down, caught in a large knot of rope. However, he seems entirely at peace, his expression almost beatific. His hands encircle a radiant black sun. Behind him is a golden door.

Short Interpretation

A strange moment of enlightenment. You may need to let go of your usual sense of your own identity and relinquish control in order to gain the insights that are now possible. Don't be afraid to allow your world view to be turned upside down. This state of trance-like clarity is a rare thing in life and can lead to great peace and understanding.

Fuller Interpretation

Transcendence • Meditation • Enlightenment • Letting go of the ego Detachment from material things

The Tarot of Prague

The Hanged Man is not about death but enlightenment. In one sense, this type of transcendence can be thought of as the death of egotism. The card usually draws on very old symbolism to show a man, perfectly calm, hanging in a state of trance. It is one of the most obviously "spiritual" cards in the Tarot and is quite closely related to The Fool. However this particular sense of "letting go" is about suspending action and giving up control, rather than (as in The Fool) taking a chance. The Hanged Man can also refer to enlightenment through sacrifice; particularly of the ego, and the ability to put a higher cause before personal interest In some readings, it can also be about turning things around and seeing them from another angle. However, this fresh view is not brought about by logic, but simply by "letting it be". While the card is entitled the Hanged Man, it does not stand for either a man or a woman. It's a state of mind attainable by anyone willing to give up ego and will and detach themselves from the material world.

The history of this card is a very strange one. In early cards it was sometimes labelled "The Traitor", and indeed being hung upside down, in the manner the card shows, was one of the traditional punishments for traitors. However, over the years this very negative aspect of this card has been completely replaced by a more transcendental and spiritual interpretation. The idea of blame or guilt is now completely forgotten.

In our card the image departs from the usual RWS picture to emphasise the transformational and mysterious aspects of the image. The young man with piercing blue eyes looks angelic. He already seems to be not quite of this world. His legs are entirely hidden beneath an enormous coil of rope. In one sense this rope has become exaggerated and monstrous, but in another way it is actually supporting the suspended man. He does not look trapped by the knots of rope so much as hanging in a strange ecstasy of transcendance and meditation.

The Hanged Man holds a Black Sun, the alchemical sign of transformation and "mirror images". It is a powerful symbol, representing the part of things that cannot be seen but that are nevertheless real. In alchemy, things have their apparent and visible nature and qualities, and also their 'mirror images', a concept which is actually surprisingly similar to the modern concept of anti-matter and black holes. The Black Sun in this card is also the face of a man, so it is a reflection, or the "part that can't be seen" of the Hanged Man himself. This 'mirror image' aspect is an important part of the meaning of this card, but can be hard to understand. It implies that the Hanged Man literally sees the world turned upside down and inside out. He is something like the character of Alice when she went through the looking glass and saw the world transformed into something odd, new and only half-recognisable. In this position the Hanged Man can see facets of the world that are usually hidden. This is one reason why he is essentially an isolated figure: to clarify his vision he has given up his ego completely and the reactions of others have become utterly unimportant. He wears a wreath of golden pomegranates because since ancient times this fruit has been a powerful symbol of the continuity of the cycle of death and rebirth:

All the trees lose their leaves, all
Trees but the pomegranate.
I alone in all the garden lose not my beauty,
I remain straight.
When my leaves fall,
New leaves are budding.

"Garden Song" translated by Ezra Pound and Noel Stock
from sources taken from Egyptian papyri (1567-1085 BC)

Sources

The Hanged Man is based on an angel on the ceiling of the main corridor of the Strahov Library. The thick rope around his waist and his beatific expression are both part of the original figure. The Black Sun is an important symbol in alchemy and can be found all over Prague. This remarkable example is from the façade of a house in Celetná Street.

The door that forms the background is one of the gothic Golden Gates at the St Vitus' Cathedral. For five hundred years, from 1406, these gates were the main entrance to the cathedral. They get their name both from their colour and the red and gold mosaics of the Last Judgement situated above them. A fragment of these mosaics is used on our Judgement card.

The wreath of pomegranates is from a ceiling in the Wallenstein Palace. The whole palace is full of symbols of birth, death and transformation, and so pomegranates, a symbol of rebirth, are perhaps a predictable element to find there.

The Tarot of Prague

| DEATH | DEATH |

XIII DEATH

The *Tarot of Prague* has two Death cards. One is in the rather shocking Baroque tradition of Memento Mori ("remember that you will die"). The painting that it is based on is genuinely frightening and disturbing, but also powerful and moving. The other card is much more jolly, styled in a slightly tongue-in-cheek gothic mode, with Death and his horse represented by wooden puppets lurching across a craggy landscape full of hidden figures.

As the tarot Death card is often particularly sensitive, we suggest you choose the one you or your querent feel most comfortable with.

Description – "Memento Mori" card

Death is seen walking among ordinary people. Everyone, whether man, woman or child, will meet Death in some form, and in this picture the grim reaper can be seen nine times, in many different guises: as a robed figure, as a death's head, as an archer and as a skeletal figure of Time. Some of the people see him, but others are unaware of his presence.

Description – Puppet card

An armoured knight sits awkwardly astride his puppet horse. The landscape behind them is a dark grotto of stalactites from which faces peer out. Above them is a sundial featuring a grinning skeleton holding a scythe and an hourglass.

Short Interpretation

The Death card isn't often about a physical death. It just means that one part of your life is about to finish, and though this may be traumatic, in the long run it can be a good thing. There may be something that you need to finally finish so that you can go on to new things. It's a time of renewal and change. Don't be afraid. Let your old self die away so that you can become a new, and stronger, person.

Fuller Interpretation

The end of a cycle • A difficult transformation • Death of identity

The Death card nearly always stands for the end of a cycle or phase in life. In many ways it can mean the death of one identity, and, by implication opening the way for the birth of a new one. Rarely does it stand for physical death. However, it can still be a disturbing card to see.

Often we find the idea of letting our familiar self "die" terrifying, even when the death isn't physical but rather the death of a kind of behaviour, personality trait, or identity. In modern society we tend to spend so much time building up a sense of our own individual selves (we're even sometimes told to regard ourselves as a "brand" that has to be consciously designed and maintained) that the idea of giving this up is really very difficult.

One example is that of a mother whose children leave home. Suddenly, instead of seeing herself primarily as a full-time mother caring for her children, she needs to find another identity. Equally common is the case of the dedicated professional or craftsperson who retires. Instead of being primarily defined by their job, he or she has to find another role. Changes like these can be terribly hard for the individual.

Some clinical therapists are actually of the opinion that such changes in identity are physically dangerous for certain kinds of people, who may simply get ill and die rather than undertake such personal transformation. The Death card speaks about this and helps us confront our fear and see that this "death of one of our selves" happens to everyone.

So is the Death card primarily about transformation? Not quite. Rachel Pollack explains it thus:

"Contrary to what many believe the card of Death does not actually refer to transformation. Rather, it shows us the precise moment at which we give up the old masks and allow the transformation to take place"

Rachel Pollack, *Seven Degrees of Wisdom*

In other words, what we see in this card is the need to give ourselves up to the possibility of the necessary transformation. It's the difficult moment of letting go that we must go through in order to be able to move on with a new self-identity. Whether this is physical death, or the transitional state arising from the death of one of our identities, the experience is one that we all have to pass through. By understanding this we can find not only courage but also wisdom.

At first glance, the picture shown in the "Memento Mori" card might seem very grim. It's a particularly vivid example of the Baroque fascination with death, and the widespread medieval tradition of pictures that graphically represent death. In fact, if you think about it, it's as much about affirming life as it is about remembering death. Yes, we will all die, so therefore we should make the most of our time and live well. The very blunt images characteristic of the Baroque were intended to shock people into valuing their lives, and making something good of them. Death is the great leveller, and pictures like that shown on this card tell us that death will touch all of us, regardless of our status or position in life.

The picture in the "Puppet" version of this card is a little more gothic and probably scary rather than truly frightening. It's a better card to use with querents who may not want to face an image as graphic as that shown on the other version. The horse and rider are both puppets, implying that Death is not in control but is merely in the service of higher powers, which you may regard as God or Nature. The grotesque little faces peering out from the rock remind us that death touches everyone.

Sources - Memento Mori

These pictures of Death are mainly taken from the Baroque murals in the church of St Mikuláš (Nicholas) in Malá Strana. The church dates from 1283, but was rebuilt during the 17th and 18th centuries. The murals form part of one section, the "Chapel of Death", that is entirely devoted to admonishments to remember death and judgement. The paintings are by Josef Kramolin and date from the mid-18th century.

One interesting fact about St Mikuláš Church is that Mozart is known to have played the organ there when he was staying in Prague, though what he thought of the Chapel of Death has not been recorded.

The sundial is from 1658 and is painted on one of the external walls of the Clementinum complex. Death was often shown in this way, holding an hourglass, an oil lamp, or a clock, all intended to show that our time passes swiftly.

Sources - Puppet

The puppet figures are modern; there are many puppet shops in Prague, some of which have works that display high-quality craftsmanship.

The faces in the rock are from the "grotesquery" in the garden of the Wallenstein Palace. This is a very weird structure (though one that would actually have been very fashionable when it was built in the mid-17th century). It is made to look like the walls of a limestone cave, covered in stalactites in which are hidden numerous faces of men, devils and animals, alongside a great many serpents. Like so much in the Wallenstein Palace, it seems to both question and mock the meaning of life and death.

Both this card and the "Momento Mori" card use the same sundial, though in this card it's used in a slightly more prominent way.

More about Memento Mori in Bohemia

Throughout Europe, from the Middle Ages to the Baroque, pictures, texts and symbols that encouraged the viewer to "remember that you will die" were commonplace. Even some gravestones from this period carry the disturbing, if slightly comic inscription "remember that as I am now, you shall be". Figures of Death were routinely inserted into all sorts of artwork and decoration. Even on something as flamboyant and joyful as the façade of the mid-16th-century Míčovna (Ball Games Court), a building used for physical recreation and enjoyment, there are two laughing skulls clutching hourglasses in their teeth. In the modern age, this seems shocking. We have grown very used to denying death. Of course, with better health we generally enjoy a longer lifespan, but, more than that, we simply don't see or experience death as often as our forebears.

The paintings in the St Mikulaš (Nicholas) "Chapel of Death" are quite mild compared with the famous Kostnice Ossuary at Kutna Hora, which is in fact quite recent, dating from the mid-19th century. The Ossuary holds the bones of about 40,000 people, and many of the bones have been assembled into decorative or allegorical objects. There is a large chandelier composed of bones, a bizarre tableau of a bird skeleton (actually made from human bones) pecking a skull, and various candelabra. Even an enormous coat of arms has been made from the bones of the people interred there. While this seems morbid and disturbing, there is actually a profound lesson, which is that your body does not matter, its parts can be used for mere decoration after your death. What matters is how you live your life.

The skeleton that stands by the Astronomical Clock

[Major Arcana]

XIV Temperance

An orderly but elegant Art Deco figure, dressed in white, is standing holding two cups above her head and pouring water from one to the other. Around her, shining fish hang in a pattern of perfect symmetry.

Short Interpretation

In spite of the name, this card is more about balance than temperance. It signifies a time when you should look at your life and make sure that all aspects are in equilibrium. This doesn't necessarily mean abstinence, but it does mean following the old adage of "all things in moderation".

Fuller Interpretation

Balance • Moderation in all things • Harmony • Compromise "The middle way" • Synthesis

This card is about moderation and achieving a balance in life. It can also signify harmony, co-operation and a willingness to reach compromises. It is the card of the middle ground, of tolerance and avoiding extremes, whether these are of thought, attitude or action. Because "moderation in all things" is often cited as the key to good health, this card can also stand for health, healing and general fitness and vigour. A less immediately obvious meaning is that of synthesis; the ability to find the right mix and join things or people together.

Temperance is one of the three classic Virtues shown in the Major Arcana (the others being Strength and Justice). In early Tarot this card was sometimes called Balance, and perhaps this name conveys a fuller and broader sense of its meaning. It doesn't just mean abstinence from anything obviously harmful (such as excessive alcohol, or any other potentially addictive substances or habits), but also more broadly signifies the necessity of moderation and 'common sense' so you can enjoy all the aspects of your life in a healthy and sustainable way. This restraint and self-control in all pleasures used to be seen as a profound virtue, indeed one that was in some cases essential for the redemption of the soul. This may be one reason Temperance has traditionally been shown as an angelic figure.

The figure of the woman shown on this card is placed in a perfectly symmetrical arrangement of stylised vines and fishes. While she looks sensual, her sexuality is veiled and restrained. She wears a white headdress that is part helmet and part halo. She is active, but also calm and controlled. She signifies the inner peace that can come from temperance and balance in all things. The fish that surround her represent not only fluidity but also aspects of creativity (in older tarot cards fish often carry this meaning). What's implied here is that creativity can be supported by moderation. The idea that you have to follow extremes to be creative does not always hold true – temperance may be a better path to follow.

Sources

This card is based on an Art Deco façade in Široka Street in Josefov (the Jewish quarter of Prague). The figure is a beautiful example of restrained but quite extreme Art Deco styling, and manages to convey a sense of strict control, further emphasised by the symmetry of the design. We added the cups she is holding, and her tiny pair of wings, but apart from that we made very few changes to this image.

XV THE DEVIL

A couple fight and tear at each other. Above them the Devil is laughing and it is he who is obviously in control of their situation and behaviour. The whole image is colourless, everything is in harsh black and white.

Short Interpretation

Don't let yourself be controlled by destructive behaviour or influences, whether these are unhealthy addictions or obsessions, or simply overly materialistic and greedy behaviour. You may find yourself surrendering to anger or ignorance, when deep down you know that this is only making you feel depressed and disgusted. You can overcome this by focusing more on what you know to be the better things in life. Faith, hope and charity are always there — you just need to rediscover them.

Fuller Interpretation

Lack of self-control • Unhealthy obsessions • Giving in to impulse
The glamour of sin • Greed • Addictions

This is both a violent and a disruptive card, though like all the "dark" cards of the Tarot it does conceal some positive messages as well. When The Devil appears in a reading it often indicates growing obsessions, sometimes combined with a sense of being tied down and controlled. It can mean giving in to unhealthy compulsions or simply believing too much in the physical and sensual sides of life and forgetting about spirituality. It can also apply to situations in which you, or someone near to you, is being wilfully ignorant and refusing to see the truth. The Devil certainly has "glamour", and it's worth remembering that the old sense of this word was a spell or enchantment. Old stories tell us that the Devil often has a deceptively attractive surface appearance. We may at first enjoy the feeling of giving up control to something that's dangerously glamorous, and for a time our friends may find us more fun if we do so. But ultimately this can lead to a terrible sense of being trapped in a downward spiral. In the end, we can only really be happy when we are prepared to take responsibility for our own actions and desires rather than allowing ourselves to be controlled by them.

Everything in this card is depicted in stark black and white. This symbolises that a tendency to see things in extreme black-and-white terms can often lead to anger and conflict. The inability to recognise compromise is frequently a sign of unhealthy fanaticism.

In readings, The Devil can sometimes be associated specifically with addiction (the fact that the devil in this card originally presided over a beer hall makes him particularly apt for this interpretation). This can be a physical addiction such as a dependency on alcohol or drugs, or it can signal a subtler psychological addiction, such as being locked into a familiar cycle of destructive behaviour. Lastly, The Devil can simply indicate a situation in which someone has lost their faith and hope and has succumbed to hopelessness and despair. This may sometimes manifest itself as depression or anger.

[Major Arcana]

Sources

The image of the Devil is taken from one of the façades in U Fleků, a very old beer hall in Prague (the wall paintings there have also been used on the Ten of Cups and the Five of Swords). If you believe that "demon" drink is an invention of the devil then you might like the U Fleků paintings (three of the four paintings have depictions of devils). The one we have used is possibly the most frightening. It has been combined here with a much older sgraffito image from a wall of the Martinic Palace. The original shows a biblical scene from the life of Joseph. It's the famous scene in which Joseph refuses to 'lie with' Potiphar's wife, which was a very popular subject in Renaissance art.

Another figure of the devil painted on the walls of U Fleků beer hall

The Tarot of Prague

XVI THE TOWER

Two figures are falling helplessly from a burning tower. Around them everything is in flame, and even the water reflects the livid flames. It's a violent scene, and it looks as though these people did not choose to jump but have been forcefully flung from the tower. The expression on their faces is of despair and resignation.

Short Interpretation

An earthquake in your life. You are going through a huge upheaval and change. It may feel cataclysmic, or even catastrophic, but it's important to realise that it isn't all negative. Sometimes dramatic disruptions have to happen and, difficult as they are, they can lead to a release, or eventually the opportunity to start anew. Even if it's an uncomfortable time, don't despair. When the dust settles there may be something positive that results, and useful lessons to learn.

Fuller Interpretation

Cataclysmic change • Explosive events • Dramatic disruption
An earthquake in your life

Change is often hard, and sudden change is even more difficult. The Tower is about change that is so unexpected and extreme that it can feel explosive. When this happens it can be cataclysmic. Sometimes The Tower can mean a release of anger or emotions that have been bottled up or denied. However, while The Tower is generally an unsettling card it is not necessarily completely negative. The sudden and dramatic disruption that it signifies can bring about a necessary transformation. While this can be an unpleasant or even distressing experience, it may be a good thing in the long run and can actually result in some startling insights.

This card hasn't always been called The Tower; in older decks it was sometimes titled Fire, Hell or The House of the Devil. In some ways it brings to mind the Tower of Babel, and has much the same sense of confusion, chaos and loss.

The image on this card shows a tower going up in flames. Around it other buildings seem to be on fire and the river in front of the tower reflects the conflagration. The figures falling from the tower seem to be flying through the air, almost as if an explosion had flung them out. This card does imply a very sudden change, violent in its power. Of the cards in the *Tarot of Prague* deck, it's one of the few set at night. The huge changes that The Tower signifies do tend to happen when you have been, in some sense, stumbling around in the dark. The sudden flames can seem horrifying, but in an odd way they can also be illuminating.

The falling figures look oddly fragile, as though they will shatter when they hit the ground. But the implication is that after the hard fall you will be ready to pick up the shards of your shattered life and get back on to your feet.

Sources

This image is taken from a small gouache painting in the collection of the Strahov Library. It shows a scene from the sacking of Prague by the Swedish army in 1648.

The Tarot of Prague

The figures falling from the Tower are both taken from the remarkable stucco façades over the doorways to St James' Church in the Old Town just off Ungelt. Ottavio Mosto did these carvings in 1695. They show St Francis, with St James and St Anthony of Padua.

For another card that uses a picture from this façade, see the Six of Wands.

The original painting on which we based The Tower.

XVII THE STAR

A woman sits calmly pouring water from two jugs. Behind her is the figure of another woman who kneels beside a fountain that has the head of a benevolent looking lion. On a pillar in the distance there is a strange inscription that is a palindrome and so can be read in either direction.

Short Interpretation

You are experiencing encouragement, faith, hope, good health and general well-being – and it's a wonderful feeling. The Star means all of these good things, together with the ability to remain tranquil and optimistic in both good times and bad. It's a card that signifies openness and an ability to see the truth behind the surface. So use this time to accomplish your dreams, because the hope and inspiration that you feel right now will make many things possible.

Fuller Interpretation

Hope • Recovery and healing • Generosity • Peace and calm

The Star is first and foremost about hope. It isn't surprising that this card comes directly after the upheaval and dangers of The Devil and The Tower. Hope is the first thing we need to find to pull ourselves out of bad times. There is both openness and tranquillity in the figure of the Star. She is naked (one of the few figures in the traditional Tarot who is shown unclothed) and she appears to perform her task of pouring water quietly and calmly. There is a sense of peace and tranquility about the whole scene.

The Star often appears in a reading as a sign of the recovery and healing that comes after a period of immense turbulence or trouble, especially when this trouble has been emotional or psychological. Sometimes this card shows the possibility of achieving peace and finding renewed hope and inner strength even when difficulties are ongoing.

In our card a myriad of little stars are flowing from one of the jars to signify that light and joy can come in many small ways as well as in larger, more dramtic forms. In the background a young woman draws water at a lion's head fountain. This image implies that the water The Star pours also flows like a fountain, continually and without end, and serves to remind us that the well of hope also never dries up. Hope is always there as an inner resource that we can draw from in times of need.

The inscription on the pillar in the distance is a symbol of the way in which the hope promised by The Star can act as an almost magical defence against evil. It is in fact the talismanic protective palindrome on the Old Town Charles Bridge Tower. It reads:

SIGNATESIGNATEMEREMETENGISETANGIS
ROMATIBISUBITOMOTIBUSIBITAMOR

This means "Revel yourself in the form of a sign (in the sky) in vain you reach for me, I am your desire. Rome, through movement (stars) suddenly love comes to you".

It is there to guard the tower from demons and to keep it safe from harm.

Sources

The statue of the woman pouring water is located in Mariánské náměstí, just beside the Clementinum in Old Town. In the background is a painting from the wall of the Granovsky House, built in 1560, in Ungelt (or 'Týn Courtyard') just behind the Týn church. It is part of a wonderful group of chiaroscuro paintings that show biblical and mythical scenes. Other images from this group have been used in the *Tarot of Prague*, for example, in The Magician and the Three of Cups.

The "magical" palindrome can be seen on the Old Town Charles Bridge Tower where it presumably still deters demons. A version of it can also be seen on the back of every card in our deck, where we hope it will serve as a small piece of good magic.

XVIII THE MOON

A darkly-hooded woman with stars on her gown stands quietly. She gazes at the pale flower that she holds, and seems to be lost in her inner thoughts. On her head is a crescent moon. At her feet a cherub crouches with a fishing net, displaying the crawfish he has caught. Beside him a little dog rests his head on his paws and seems to smile. The river and two towers behind them are drenched in moonlight.

Short Interpretation

The Moon is the card of the sub-conscious, and signfies the visitation of strange dreams and desires. This may all feel a little weird, but it can also be wonderful. At such times you will be fired by your imagination, you will be able to get in touch with the more mystical and magical side of life. Don't let it bewilder you, instead learn from your dreams and let yourself see and feel things more intuitively.

[Major Arcana]

Fuller Interpretation

Dreams and visions • The subconscious • Bewilderment
Magic and enchantment • Imagination • Psychic abilities

This card indicates dreams, visions and all the strange enchantment of the subconscious. While The Moon is often a positive, or even an exciting card for someone who is relaxed about such things and confident in their own psychological health, it is sometimes rather frightening to get this card in a reading if you are feeling mentally disoriented or in some way troubled by nightmares or a disturbed imagination.

It's worth remembering that the sense of fear that The Moon can provoke is fear of the unknown and the nameless, rather than of anything very concrete. It's much more about what you imagine could happen than about real events. It can therefore indicate phobias and general anxiety, and also about forming false and unrealistic notions or following strange fancies and half-truths. In many ways, The Moon is about the dangers of falling into neurosis. But in its positive aspect it can also be about a fantastic and fertile imagination and the joy of the bizarre. This can run wild, but can also be a source of visionary dreams and a window to the unconscious.

In the folk belief of many countries the Moon is often associated with bewilderment and disorientation. In Shakespeare's *A Midsummer Night's Dream* all the characters seem to behave quite madly in the moonlight, running after false loves and strange transformations. When morning comes, they wake up to reality again. The Moon card can connote a situation just like that — being "moon mad" (remember that the word "lunacy" comes from Luna - the moon) and chasing after all sorts of delusions that will look quite different when you wake up and see things in the rational light of day.

Historically, this card has had several incarnations. The basic elements of moon, water, dogs (or wolf and dog), and a lobster or crawfish have usually been present. However, there are also variations that show a woman with a spindle (the Moon's association with spinning and with spinsters is an old one) and also a simple version that shows a woman holding a crescent moon, or with a crescent moon on her head. It's this last depiction of the Moon that you can find in statues around Prague, often contrasted with a male figure of the Sun.

The Moon card has always been loosely associated with witchcraft. Witches are of course seen as creatures of the night, and of the new moon and full moon in particular. In our card the woman is heavily veiled, just as Hecate, the Queen of the Witches was often shown. She isn't a frightening figure, but she is withdrawn and inward looking. The flower in her hand is a reference to the use of herbs and flowers in spells and enchantments. In colour, it is like the "Moly" flower that Circe (who is also a type of Moon Goddess) used to enchant Ulysses' companions in the old Greek story of the Iliad.

Sources

The figure of the Moon is based on a statue of "Nox" (Night) at 5 Nerudova Street. It is high up on the house and is partnered with an equally striking figure of the Day.

The background is the Vltava by moonlight. One of the two towers is the legendary medieval Old Town Charles Bridge tower (for more on this tower and the spell it carries against demons, see The Star). The other is the tower that forms part of the complex of buildings that stands on Novotného lávka, which also features in the background of the Two of Pentacles.

The little dog is from the "Ten of Leaves" card on our old Bohemian deck. Though it's usual to show two dogs on this card we felt that one was quite enough to howl (or smile) at the moon.

The cherub and crawfish are from an imaginative and well-executed Art Deco façade in Spálená Street. It shows every sign of the zodiac, all done in a suitably heavenly blue and gold.

Sundial from a chimney of the Lobkowitz Palace

[Major Arcana]

XIX THE SUN

A man in lavish Baroque dress balances on the back of a circus horse. Behind them is a formal garden full of flowers and flooded with sunlight. Above them is an old painted sundial. Everything is bright and sunlit.

Short Interpretation

You can see things clearly, and the world looks wonderful. Everything seems much clearer than before and you can move ahead with confidence and energy. When you feel this much energy and well-placed confidence in yourself it lends brilliance to all you do. So let your talents and abilities shine forth, you are sure of success.

Fuller Interpretation

Blinding insights • Magnificence and richness • Confidence and success • Vitality and the life force

The Tarot of Prague

Everything about The Sun stands for straightforward, physical radiance. After the rather veiled, inward and disturbed vision of The Moon, The Sun refers to enlightenment and a childlike joy and pleasure in the world. If The Moon touches on "lunacy", then The Sun is about "lucidity", about being clear and seeing things with a brilliant sharpness and focus.

When this card comes up in a reading it can indicate a sudden ability to gain a clear view or insight about an issue. It can also represent deeper knowledge, but one based on an understanding of the world and its magnificence rather than extensive knowledge of details or facts. The Sun is a card of great optimism and confidence, as well as of a tremendous and life-giving energy. It's also about an almost childlike clarity of vision.

The card shows a man balancing lightly on a horse in what looks like a scene from a circus. This is a reminder that the sun is both spectacular and enjoyable, but also very much part of a cycle. Just as the circus horse and rider go round and round the same circuit, so must the sun. So while the card may be about expansiveness — the sun does shine over everything — in another sense it is also about keeping within the natural order. Unlike The Fool, The Sun is not outside the structured universe, but in fact is very much a signifier of such order. The success that this card indicates will come in a very worldly way and will be visible to all.

It's worth adding that many Astrologers categorise Prague under Leo, the sign of the sun.

Sources

The Sun is based on a statue on the House of the Sun and Moon on Úvoz Street in Malá Strana This is a very steep street and it runs alongside Petřín Park. The house stands at the top, overlooking the park.

The garden in the background is the Vrtbovská garden, a Baroque terraced garden, full of murals and statues and topiary, which offers a wonderful view of the city. The sundial in the background is hidden away on the back of a palace near the castle. It is one of the most elaborate and well-preserved painted sundials in Prague.

The horse, which pays homage to the original Rider Waite Smith illustration, is from the "Nine of Bells" card in our old Bohemian pack.

[Major Arcana]

XX Judgement

An angel lifts the lid of a coffin. She is not looking at what she is doing, however, but stares straight ahead, her eyes following whoever looks at this card. Her expression is clear but neutral — she seems, in some way, to look through you to see the truth. Behind her is a medieval scene of the Last Judgement. Angels are calling the dead to a new life, and they rise from their coffins to follow the call.

Short Interpretation

This is a time of rebirth and renewal. Look back on your past life without regret and try to put old grievances, faults or worries behind you. You now have the opportunity to take the first steps towards a way of living that is more fulfilling.

The Tarot of Prague

Fuller Interpretation

Rebirth and renewal • A more meaningful way of life • A new reality

This can initially seem a forbidding or even alarming card. Nowadays we often find the idea of judgement frighteningly absolute. However, the main thing to realise is that the Judgement card shows souls going to Heaven, not to Hell, and is essentially about the possibility of being reborn and having the opportunity to go on to better things. It's a card about judgement, not unkind blame, so it carries messages of fairness, responsibility and also of hope.

This card is different from the Death card because it isn't about the difficult moment of making a change but about what comes next. In the judgement indicated by this card you are not really asked to make any decisions — they have already been made. Instead you are being given the chance to accept these and move on to a new and more meaningful way of living and being.

The image shown, of angels pulling people from their graves on Judgement Day, is a very old one, and variations of it can be seen at many religious and secular sites all over Prague. Our card combines a very old scene of judgement (from a medieval mosaic) with a much more recent one in Art Nouveau style. By combining these the image implies that whatever age we live in, judgement about the basic morality of our actions remains constant.

Sources

The card is based on the mosaics from the "Golden Door" of St Vitus' Cathedral at the Prague Castle. (The door is so named because the mosaics have very rich red and gold backgrounds.) The original shows souls going to Heaven as well as those being driven to Hell by some alarming-looking demons.

The angel at the front is a much later Art Nouveau piece from one window on the inner cloisters of the graveyard at the Church of St Peter and St Paul in Vyšehrad.

XXI THE WORLD

A confident and laughing woman, surrounded by a laurel wreath, is dancing and holding two wands. At the four corners of the card are a man, a lion, a cow and an eagle. Everything glows with a golden light.

Short Interpretation

A strong sense of completion and fulfilment that makes you feel so exhilarated that your feet don't touch the ground. This card indicates a real sense of achievement and happiness that goes beyond words. You feel at one with the world, and at this moment your place in the Dance of Life is perfect.

Fuller interpretation

Rapture and joy • The love of life • Ultimate fulfilment
A state of spiritual and emotional ecstasy

The Tarot of Prague

The World is a card of completion, fulfilment and achievement. It has very much the same sense of lightness and unbounded joy or rapture that you can see in The Fool, but added to this is a sense of achievement and profound insight. If The Fool is at the beginning of the journey of life, then The World represents the joy of successful completion.

The World card in many ways represents finally arriving at enlightenment after a long journey of experience and self-discovery. This fulfilment is not simply material (as represented, for instance, in the Ten of Cups), but goes much deeper. It means enlightenment and self-knowledge, and the joy that comes from understanding the true meaning of life. This is why the figure of the "World Dancer" on this card carries two magic wands. While the Magician can channel the energy of the cosmos into earthly achievement, the Dancer is able to act as a conduit of energy between heaven and earth. She is a symbol of cycles, connections and the integration of many elements. The four figures surrounding her, representing Earth, Air, Fire and Water, reinforce this sense of balance, connectedness and joyful completeness.

If you look at this card in terms of Zen thought, it shows the moment of Nirvana and the realisation that 'everything is nothing, and nothing is everything'. Though this insight may seem nonsensical (like the mad risk-taking of the Fool at the beginning of the Tarot Majors cycle), it is actually the highest, and therefore the most sublime, kind of wisdom. It is for this reason that images of the Buddha so often show him laughing, and why the feeling of this card is, for similar reasons, so light and unserious. The World Dancer is simply sheer joy. In the end the meaning of life turns out to be both foolish and wonderful.

The evolution of this card is particularly interesting. It has always carried a rather optimistic and joyful picture, but early renditions of it often showed a haloed figure (seated or standing) that undoubtedly represented Christ, rather than a more ambiguous figure of joy. Surrounding him in these early images were a man (or angel), a lion, a bull and an eagle, symbols which traditionally represented the four Evangelists, as well as the four elements and four of the signs of the zodiac:

Man (angel)	Lion	Bull	Eagle
Matthew	Mark	Luke	John
Air	Fire	Earth	Water
Scorpio	Leo	Taurus	Aquarius

Other versions of this card depicted a woman holding a trumpet and crown and floating above scenes of everyday life, or a figure standing on top of a globe. These early cards were usually called "Fortune" rather than "The World".

Throughout much of its history the central figure has been somewhat androgynous, and though in later cards (roughly from the early 18th century onwards) the figure does appear to be a woman, she is sometimes quite boyish. It is hard to know if this was entirely deliberate or whether the crudeness of early woodcuts resulted in figures that were hard to interpret and sometimes looked androgynous.

However ambiguous the figure, it seems certain that at some point there was a purposeful shift from showing the figure of a young man (who could always potentially be interpreted as Christ) to that of a woman. Nowadays we always associate this card with a picture of a joyfully dancing young woman. This achieves an interesting balance in the Major Arcana: it starts with the Fool, a young man who represents an unconscious and naive "foolish wisdom", and finishes with the image of The World, a young woman who stands for the achievement of insight, enlightenment and a kind of "wise foolishness".

Sources

Our World Dancer is taken from a fresco on the roof of the Theological Room at the Strahov Library. The fresco is by Franz Anton Maulbertsch (1724-1796) and, appropriately, it is called 'Struggle of Mankind to Gain True Wisdom'.

Surrounding the central figure are a man (who may actually be more of a dwarf or gnome), a lion, a cow and an eagle. These figures were taken from photographs of small sculptural figures that make up part of a 19th-century group of statues in a park near the river on Smetanovo nábřeží. The whole group has a fairytale quality. For other cards taken from these statues, see the Page of Wands and the Six of Swords.

The Tarot of Prague

As the sculptor of these statues chose to use a fairytale figure rather than a man or an angel (which would have been more typical for this card), and a cow rather than a bull, we chose to follow this schema. This actually seems to expand the number of potential meanings because of the multitude of associations that can be made with fairytale literature (the cow appears in European fairytales a good deal more often than the bull, and it is always a benign, and often magical, figure) while still allowing interpretations based on the more traditional meanings given in the table above. The original composition is quite magical in its own right and also includes a female sphinx with wings and a wonderful mermaid with two tails that can be seen on the King of Cups.

Both the wreath and the wands that the Dancer is holding are taken directly from the title card of our old Bohemian card pack, although we changed the original colour scheme of red, yellow and green to a more suitably celebratory gold.

A section of the painting on which

MINOR ARCANA - WANDS

Wands

The Wands element is Fire, and this suit is about action, energy, and speed. Wands tend to indicate an adventurous spirit with plenty of courage and liveliness. On the negative side, this can at times take the form of an impulsiveness or hastiness that borders on the irresponsible. However, the ability to act is of course essential in achieving anything, and a reading that is lacking in Wands may indicate an inability to turn ideas or emotions into actual realities. On the other hand, the action and energy of Wands can only be put to really good use when it is balanced by the intellect of Swords, the feelings of Cups, and the practicality of Pentacles.

At their most positive, Wands show the ability both to begin new projects and actively develop them. The Ace of Wands is a great card to see in a reading if you are about to start a new business or enterprise, as it indicates the presence of the necessary forcefulness and energy. The Two and Three of Wands both point to some positive aspects as such a project develops and takes on its own momentum. In the case of the Two though, there may also be a sense of sadness about seeing a project grow beyond that initial "start-up" excitement. With the Four of Wands comes a sense of real freedom, the ability not only to begin something, but also to do it with the courage and self-confidence necessary to step away from the old routines and try something fresh.

As in all the suits of the Minor Arcana, when we come to the Five some of the more difficult aspects of the suit begin to appear. Instead of fruitful actions that bring success, the Five indicates silly activities that it would be better to avoid; actions that result in petty annoyances and quarrels. However, in the Six the more cheerful and successful side of Wands comes to the fore again. Often called the "victory card", the Six of Wands shows how inspiring it is to accomplish and be acknowledged for something you've worked hard at, though this card also warns that care should be taken not to be too self-assured about your abilities.

The Seven of Wands indicates that constant action can become a struggle. Some people will enjoy battling continuously through their life, for others this can be exhausting. In the Seven the fight is successful, but seems tiringly endless. Like most of the Wands, the Seven implies that the option of inactivity feels almost impossible. The Eight is in many ways

[Minor Arcana]

the essence of Wands: speed and action in a number of directions at once. There is usually no particularly negative or positive implication to this. How all this activity is interpreted very much depends on circumstances, and on whether the work is likely to be useful or not.

Having said this, at first glance the Nine does seem to show, uncharacteristically for this suit, a scene of inaction. However, this is a temporary and tense moment, a mere lull before a burst into further activity. Looking at this card you can see one of the central characteristics of Wands: the need to be "doing" all the time, even if this is simply the mental activity of staying alert and ready. This card is about something who is briefly resting, but who can never be truly at rest.

With the Ten this issue of constant action has become a real problem. Overburdened by the large number of projects that have been taken on, the "plate spinning" Wand, usually able to manage so much at once, suddenly feels trapped and weighed down. The Ten of Wands shows that exhaustion is the inevitable culmination of too much action for too long – it's sometimes essential to find time to rest, recuperate and do nothing.

Court Cards

In the Wands, the Court Card qualities are applied to action. The Page of Wands therefore indicates the start of some exciting activity. All the Pages can be about news, but in this particular case any such news is likely to be about things that demand real energy. Forceful and faithful, the Page will perform such tasks with enthusiasm, confidence and honesty.

The Knight of Wands has the enthusiasm of the Page, but to the extent of often being quite reckless and uncaring about other people's needs. Like all the Court Cards in this suit, the Knight of Wands is very charismatic and attractive, and can certainly get things done. However, he tends to take risks and get bored very easily, so though you can rely on him for adventure, you certainly can't look to him for commitment.

The Queen of Wands is altogether more reliable. Her well-balanced nature means that she can temper the Wands urge for immediate action with the proper consideration for other people's feelings. Mind you, this is a very attractive Queen indeed, and she may inadvertently leave some broken hearts in her wake. However, she is so cheerful and honest that any unrequited admirers will soon recover and simply enjoy being in her company. She radiates vitality and can quickly lift anyone's spirits.

The King also has a similar ability to inspire and cheer, but he is an altogether more forceful presence. He can, in fact, be rather dominating, but he also creates a lot of excitement around himself, and his bold flair and personal charisma usually means that he gets away with assuming leadership on almost every occasion. Often an eccentric, he gets away with any potentially shocking unconventionality by applying the sheer force of his personal charm.

The overall message of Wands is that the thrill of action can be wonderful, especially when accompanied by passion and charm. Action is necessary in order to achieve anything, and when energies are applied in the right way, what is achieved can be very great indeed. However, action for its own sake can quickly become a burden, and instead of leading to accomplishment can just leave you tired, hostile and weighed down. Find a balance, be prepared to act when needed, but also learn to recognise those moments when calm contemplation might actually be more effective.

More about the Court Cards

The Court Cards in Tarot have acquired a reputation for being difficult to interpret. Certainly, in early writings such as Waite's *Pictorial Key to the Tarot* there seems to be very little to distinguish them. But in fact, they are not so difficult if you understand the essential qualities of each suit and also the main traits of each Court. Regardless of the suit, they share some characteristics. The Pages tends to signify enthusiasm, energy, exploration and a certain naiveté. They also refer to messages and news. The Knights of the Tarot indicate action in some form, and a growing sense of responsibility not shared by the Page. All the dilemmas surrounding the Knight cards are basically about the need to strike a balance between action/impetuosity and responsibility/duty. The Queens are by far the most rounded cards, and show the best qualities of their suit in a balanced, creative and thoughtful way. They manage to combine emotional and social sensitivity with the ability to get things done. The Kings also show social responsibility, but they carry a greater sense of authority and a worldliness that outwardly may look like power and success, but inwardly can feel like a burden. The Kings all tend, to some extent, to repress their desires out of a sense of duty.

It's important to remember that all the Court Cards can be interpreted in alternative ways; either they can be understood as standing for an actual person, or they can more broadly be taken to indicate a particular kind of personality or a type of behaviour. In earlier Tarot, the Court Cards were usually thought to signify a person, and on seeing a Court, people made pronouncements such as "A young countryman with golden hair will become important to you". This is now generally considered much too crude an interpretion. When they appear in a reading these days the Courts will usually be taken to indicate broad character types rather than definite features such as gender, age, profession or appearance.

One last point about the Courts: remember that while these cards usually stand for some behaviour by another person who is an influence on the querent, they can also often point towards such traits in the querent's own behaviour. Bear this in mind when you are deciding how to interpret one of the Courts in a spread.

Page or Princess?

In the *Tarot of Prague* we decided to make all four of the Page cards rather androgynous visually, so that each can easily be read as either a young boy or a young girl, as you prefer (or perhaps according to whichever seems more appropriate in any particular reading). In fact, of course none of the Court Cards are gender-specific, but by approaching the Pages in this way it makes the visual representation of gender in the cards somewhat more balanced.

It may seem quite modern to have this figure open to interpretation as a girl, but in fact, the idea of women as knights (if not as pages) occurs in medieval literature. Contrary to the prejudices we may have about the medieval period, not all women were, in fact, presented in the literature of the time as hopeless victims or decorative objects. In Ariosto's *Orlando Furioso* (late 15th century) one of the central characters, Bradamante, is a very beautiful female knight who takes full part in combat. So in fact a female Page is not really such a new or radical idea.

The four *Tarot of Prague* Pages can be regarded as either boys or girls.

[Minor Arcana]

ACE OF WANDS

A hand holds a wand wreathed in lushly flowering vines. Behind it is a richly carved panorama of the city, in which a river and two towers stand out prominently.

Short Interpretation

Express yourself creatively and with enthusiasm. Be confident and courageous, and don't be afraid to trust your own abilities. If you put all the energy you now have into a new project, you can be sure you'll succeed.

Fuller interpretation

The beginning of a project • Enthusiasm and action
Opportunity and optimism

Wands are always about action, and the Ace is no exception. It's about opening up new possibilities and opportunities, and all the enthusiasm and energy that accompanies this. It's a time to believe in yourself and in your ability to be enterprising and inventive, and also a moment to feel sure of success. This is an opportunity not only to build up your self-esteem but also to inspire others with your bravery and optimism.

This card shows a hand holding a wand that is both strong and full of vitality. The wand, encircled by tendrils of vines, is bursting with life. It is held against a panorama carved in a warm natural wood, that shows the entire city. Take this as an indication that at this moment the world, or at least part of it, is your oyster, as long as you choose to seize the moment and act with energy and confidence.

Sources

The image of the Wand is based on one held by a statue in the Wallenstein Palace Gardens. These are reproductions of Baroque statues made by Matthias Braun in the early 17th century. The originals were looted from Prague as war booty by the Swedish forces after the war of 1648.

The relief of the City of Prague is taken from a large and detailed Baroque wood carving in the St Vitus' Cathedral at Prague Castle.

The carved wooden relief used in the Ace of Wands

[Minor Arcana]

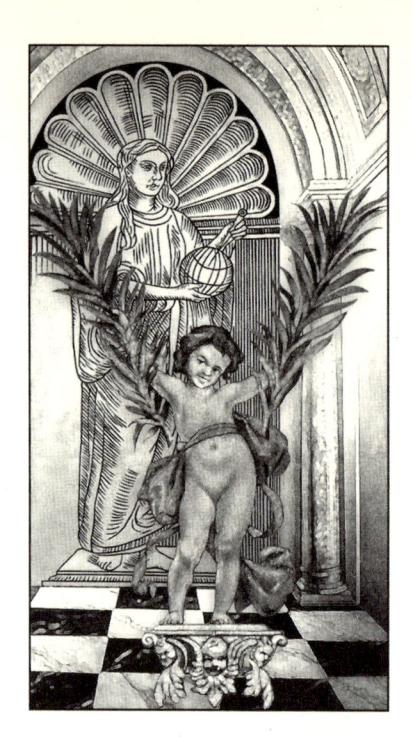

Two of Wands

A young child stands triumphantly on a pedestal, holding two lush green branches. He gives the impression that he is about to step off and walk away; his light garment billows with movement. Behind him is a rather two-dimensional wall painting of a woman gazing rather sadly at the globe she is holding. She looks as though she is confined within her niche.

Short Interpretation

This is a moment of success as you now have an opportunity to launch your projects on to the world. It ought to be a time of great happiness, and in a way it is. But somehow there is a lurking sense of restlessness, perhaps even some depression. You find yourself looking at what you've done and wondering if the achievement isn't rather small. Don't submit to this sense of "flatness". Look again, and see your work only as the start of something that will get bigger and better. This is just the beginning.

Fuller interpretation

Limited achievement • "Is that it?" • An enterprise grows up
Restless satisfaction

This card signifies achievement, but it's a success that is somewhat tempered by a feeling of dissatisfaction. The woman in the card is holding a globe and looking at it, but she seems bored or depressed. She literally looks "flat" compared to the energetic and fully three-dimensional child in the foreground who holds up his two wands enthusiastically.

The Two of Wands is about the contradictory emotions that come when a new enterprise grows up. It may appear in a reading when you have successfully launched a vibrant new project into the world, but instead of feeling totally satisfied you find yourself unsure of how much it really meant, and what your next move should be. The feeling then, could be summed up as one of achievement, but with the underlying question "Is that it, then?"

If this sense of flatness threatens to leave you feeling depressed, take another look at the project, represented in this card by the confident and happy child brandishing two lush and vibrant wands. Remember that getting your venture to the current point required all your enthusiasm, daring, originality and self-confidence. It's still somewhat new and, in reality, probably hasn't reached the point where it can really carry without you. So instead of succumbing to dissatisfaction with what you've achieved, look at your work again in terms of its potential growth and what still needs to be done. If you pull yourself out of this flat period and begin to put your energy back into the task at hand you can take it far beyond your current horizon. Try to go beyond this feeling of boredom and restlessness and instead refocus and re-energise your enthusiasm.

Sources

The woman with the globe is part of a very lavish, monochrome red-and-white sgraffito decoration from an early 19th-century building in Vodičkcova Street. The whole façade is completely covered in paintings of the classical skills and virtues, and makes a welcome contrast to the grey buildings surrounding it. The young cherub holding the two leafy branches is from a 19th-century wall painting at Senovážné náměstí in Prague 1.

[Minor Arcana]

Three of Wands

A man stands at the top of a flight of steps and confidently surveys the world in front of him. He is leaning on a virile-looking bull, and behind him are three tall wands. In the background a group of men planning an expedition cluster around a globe excitedly.

Short Interpretation

This is a time to be far-sighted and exploratory. The projects you have worked on are about to be launched on the world and now it's time to be a leader and look outwards. You are bursting with self-assurance and your "mission and vision" are very clear right now. Survey what's been achieved and be confident about making ambitious plans for the future.

Fuller Interpretation

Being visionary and exploratory • Looking for uncharted areas
Leadership and direction • Launching your projects on the world

In the Three of Wands the original ambition that motivated the beginning of a project has developed and become broader than in the more restricted Two. This card is about expansion and the willingness and self-confidence to explore new ground. This probably has to do with business or work, but can also refer to other, less material projects, perhaps about self-development. Whatever the mission, this card shows that it will be done with vision and leadership. It's very much about looking outward, and taking action rather than being introspective.

The picture on this card shows a strong figure leaning against an ox. But he is not resting, rather he is taking a moment to survey what he has done and to plan his next moves. The ox represents strength and endurance, but also signifies "ploughing your own furrow", i.e. putting in the hard work needed to achieve your personal goals. This image is not about teamwork but rather a picture of an opinionated and passionately committed leader, who will confidently take things in his (or her) chosen direction.

The ox and plough play an important role in the legend of Prague's foundation that makes them very appropriate to the meaning of this card. When Libuše, the celebrated "Magician Queen" of Bohemia, married, it was to a young man who was found ploughing in a field with a team of two oxen. In spite of his lowly position in life he became Libuše's husband and helped her establish the benevolent Přemysl dynasty, which grew and thrived from that point.

The background of the image shows a group of men planning an expedition. This communicates some of the excitement and drive that the Three of Wands stands for. When this card appears in a reading it is time to think in broad terms and let your enthusiasm and drive help you achieve your goals, however ambitious they may be.

Sources

The statue of the hero with a bull is from the Pražskátržnice market in Bubenské nábřeží, Prague 7. It is untitled, but probably represents the

[Minor Arcana]

Přemysl husband of Libuše, first queen of Prague. Because of the legend of Libuše and Přemysl (see more about this on the next page) their Celtic dynasty "The Přemsyls" has always been associated with oxen.

The painting of the planning of an exploratory expedition is from the ceiling of the Theological Room of the Strahov Library. It is one of a series of seventeen scenes painted in 1721 by a local monk, Siard Nosecký, depicting the thoughts of the Abbot of the time (who was called Hirnhaim). The subject is man's search for knowledge

For other cards that show paintings from the Strahov Library see The World and The Chariot. A picture of the entire Theological Room can be seen as the background of The Hierophant.

More about Libuse and the Foundation of Prague

According to Bohemian mythology Libuše (Libussa in German) was the Celtic founder of Prague. She was the daughter of King Krokus and his elfin wife. Being half elf, Libuše was blessed with great beauty and magical powers, one of which was the ability to foretell the future. Her character was highly regarded:

She was content with the wonderful gifts that she had inherited from her mother, without attempting to increase them or turn them into a source of gain. Her vanity did not extend beyond her awareness that she was beautiful. She did not crave riches, nor did she desire to be feared or honored.
Johan Karl August Musaus Libussa (this version from Zipes, *Spells of Enchantment*)

However, her Bohemian subjects became unhappy that they were ruled by a woman and demanded that she marry so that they would also have a king. Libuše reluctantly agreed to this and told her nobles the magical method by which they would find the man she would marry. She told them to follow her white horse, that should be allowed to go free, without saddle or bridle. It would lead them to a place where a man would be found eating his meal from an iron table under the open sky, in the shade of a solitary tree. In some versions of the story, she also said that the man would be ploughing with oxen.

Her nobles did as she told them, and after many hours were led to a field where a lowly young ploughman had stopped to eat – placing his meal on his plough (the iron table) and, as predicted, sitting in the shade of a large, isolated wild pear tree. His name was Přemysl, which means 'The Thinker'.

After they explained their mission he set his oxen free (which, according to different versions of the legend immediately sank beneath the earth or vanished up into the sky) and went with them back to the queen. Realising that he was not only intelligent, but also kind and attractive, the queen married him and together they founded the "Přemyslid" dynasty in Bohemia.

[Minor Arcana]

One day, Libuše had a vision that she should found a city "whose glory would reach to the sky". In her vision she saw a place in a forest thirty cubits from the castle. She told her nobles that when they arrived there they would find a man carving a wooden threshold in the middle of the forest. She said that the city should be founded on that spot and that the castle they would build there should be called 'Prague' (Praha), after the Czech word that means "threshold" (*prah*).

The man was found as her vision foretold, and the city of Prague was established on this site. It is believed that Queen Libuše still sleeps under the hill on which her first castle, Vyšehrad, was built and that if Bohemia is ever in great danger, she will awake and come riding to the rescue.

An early 20th century relief depicting the moment that Libuše's husband was found

Four of Wands

A group of women wrestle playfully in front of an archway. They are brandishing wands wreathed in flowers. They seem excited, almost skittish. One of them has broken away and strides forwards, glowing with happiness and holding a wreath triumphantly above her head. Flowers lie all around as though strewn on the ground.

Short Interpretation

You feel like breaking out of the old routine and doing something much more adventurous. This is an ebullient and exciting time and promises an exhilarating sense of freedom. The Four of Wands should encourage you to step boldly towards new opportunities. Don't be afraid, things will work out well and you'll feel re-energised and happy as a result of this courageous step.

Fuller Interpretation

Celebration • Freedom from the mundane • Excitement and "buzz" Breaking with routine

This card indicates an opportunity to break free from the mundane and open up new, and probably more "bohemian" possibilities. It's very much about going beyond any boring or conservative limitations. This sense of freedom can be a very thrilling experience and often heralds an exciting and exhilarating change in your life. When you deliberately step out from something that is safe but rather confined, and into something perhaps less permanent but more spontaneous and free, the act can feel very celebratory. So rejoice, you will savour this moment for a long time to come and it may lead to some marvelous opportunities.

Sometimes the Four of Wands does not indicate a significant life change but simply the smaller spontaneous things that happen that make you happy to be alive and feeling energetic and more receptive to interesting new prospects. It may be about the act of doing something slightly outrageous that makes those around you surprised and delighted. This could be as simple as deciding to get a radical new hairstyle or buy a piece of clothing that you would not normally dare to wear, only to discover that it makes you feel like a new person.

Whichever interpretation applies, whether it's a big change or a smaller gesture, if you feel trapped in some way then this card can be taken as encouragement to be unafraid about moving towards new growth and opportunity. Don't worry too much about the reactions of other people, in many ways they will be exhilarated and pleased to see that you have the courage to strike out in unconventional directions.

The picture on this card shows a group of women standing in front of a gateway. They are half playing and half fighting with wands made of flowers. They are in an exhilarated state, pretending to struggle with each other but laughing at the same time. They don't really care what anyone thinks of their behaviour. One of them has broken away and is striding out, confident and radiant, holding a wreath high above her head. Over her is an archway that shows some young children among an abundance of vines. Flowers lie strewn on the ground.

The Tarot of Prague

The image implies not only the courage and confidence needed to take a step into the unknown, but also the joy and sense of playfulness that such an act can bring.

The gateway behind the women is that of the Burgrave's House. In the 16th century, when the King was away the Chief Burgrave would take over the King's duties, freeing the King briefly from his obligations. In a subtle way, then, the gateway symbolises the opportunity to escape from mundane day-to-day duties for a while.

Sources

The young women wrestling with each other are from the Art Nouveau mosaic façade of the entrance to the Lucerna Palace on Vodičkova Street.

The façade is also used for the Four of Cups.

The slightly older woman striding forward with her wreath is from a different, painted façade at Spálená Street, near Karlovo náměstí (Charles Square).

The archway at the top of the card is taken from the lavish red and white painted façade of the inner courtyard of a building in Jilská Street.

The background for the scene is the Jilská Street gate at the Castle. It's a narrow street that suddenly opens out to reveal a glorious panorama of Prague. The smaller doorway directly behind the three girls is the gateway to the Nejvyšší purkrabství (Burgrave's House). Barely visible on the card is the coat of arms of the Burgrave family over the archway.

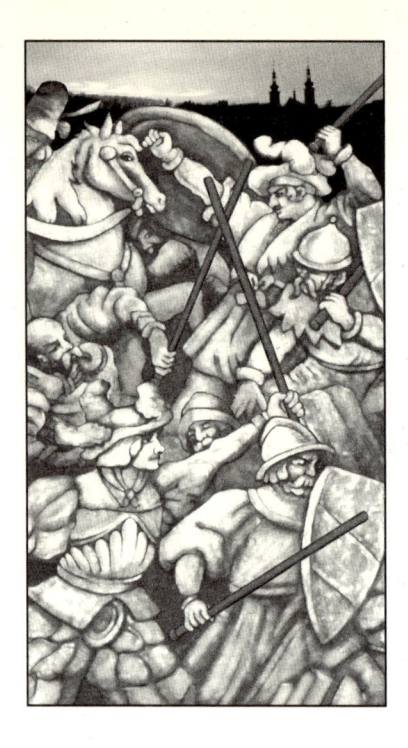

Five of Wands

A group of men are fighting with one another. Their only weapons are staves and shields, so they may not be doing too much real damage to one another. However, they are so tightly packed together that the whole scene is one of chaos and it's hard to make out what's going on. Behind them, the setting sun silhouettes two towers.

Short Interpretation

Sometimes it's the petty irritations in life that can get you down. You may be in for hassles, silly mishaps and perhaps some avoidable misunderstandings and quarrels. Be warned, take things lightly and don't let them get to you. Some days are like this, but see things for what they are: trivial and not worth worrying about.

The Tarot of Prague

Fuller Interpretation

Silly disagreements • Competition • Petty but necessary struggles
Irritations and annoyances • Hassles

There are two main aspects to this card. One is simply about the day-to-day "struggle of life". The other is much more specifically about the silly and irritating things that happen, such as petty quarrels, minor annoyances and irritations, and small accidents and mishaps. You can see how the meaning the card has taken on combines these two overlapping strands. Sometimes when we think about our everyday problems it feels like it is harder to cope with the small things such as a form that has to be filled in, congested streets, the "help line" that puts you on hold for twenty minutes, than the really big issues.

Remember that this card is not about catastrophes; it's about things that are upsetting and irritating. Such petty annoyances may get under your skin but they ultimately aren't that bad when seen in perspective. In many ways we just have to accept the fact that every time we strive towards something better we will encounter obstacles, some of which will be trivial but annoying all the same.

The image on this card shows a group of men who appear to be fighting hard with one another. However, they are not using any lethal weapons, only staves and shields, so the fight may not be as serious as it appears. The overall impression is one of confusion; this is a tussle rather than an organised battle. The indication is that the Five of Wands is about competition and struggles rather than the more grave dangers of all-out warfare or conflict. But as the writer E.M. Forster said, mental "muddle" is often at the root of unhappiness. Try to simplify and clarify your life.

Sources

The background is part of a wall painting showing the battle between the Bohemians and the Turks. The whole painting can be seen on a house on Dukelských hrdinů Street, near Strossmayerovo náměsti, in Prague 7.

[Minor Arcana]

Six of Wands

A happy and relaxed horseman rides across a cobbled street. He holds his hand up in a gesture of peace and victory. He and his horse seem to be almost glowing. Above him, men holding golden wands look down, overseen by an angel who seems to be blessing the scene.

Short Interpretation

This is sometimes called the "victory card". You have been able to accomplish what you set out to do (and more) because of your belief in yourself and in what you are doing. Your optimism and all your hard work have been rewarded. Enjoy this time and celebrate.

Fuller Interpretation

Victory • Recognition of your achievements • Basking in the glory
Pride and self-esteem

The Tarot of Prague

In many ways this card is a lesser version of The Chariot in the Major Arcana. Like The Chariot, it stands for victory and acclaim and can also, in some circumstances, mean that pride and self-satisfaction have gone a little too far, and that it might be better to also show some humility. This card may indicate a victorious outcome to a competitive situation, but it can also simply be about succeeding against the odds or achieving something beyond your expectations. It is very much about success based on real effort, and not simply on luck.

Generally, this is a positive card. In readings, the Six of Wands tends to indicate those points when things are just about to come to fruition and you will see the results of your hard work and be recognised for this success. So enjoy your time in the limelight, but don't let vanity creep in or allow your triumph to go to your head.

The image shows a man riding calmly and triumphantly. Above him are a group of men holding golden staffs. They look lively, but at the same time confident and peaceful. The rider is the focus of the scene and he is bathed in the glow of success. However, he doesn't seem overly proud as there is no particular pomp and ceremony about him. He is happy to ride alone, rather than at the head of a procession.

Watching over the scene is an angel who looks protective and nurturing. He seems to be giving his blessing to this particular victory so we can guess that it was achieved fairly, and without malice or cruelty. In a way this is a picture of an ideal victory, one that can be properly recognised and enjoyed to the full.

Sources

The triumphant rider is a relief from the bronze doors of the West Façade of the St Vitus' Cathedral. These doors are covered in small sculptures showing the lives of Saint Adalbert and Saint Wenceslas.

The angel and the figures holding golden wands are part of the remarkably elaborate and skilful stucco reliefs at the entrances to St James' Church near Ungelt, created by Ottavio Mosto in 1695

For another card that uses part of these reliefs, see The Tower.

SEVEN OF WANDS

A confident-looking man stands on a ledge high above the river. There are wands reaching up to him, as though he is fighting with opponents who can't quite get to him. His own wand is held behind his back, restrained, but at the ready. Behind him is the crowded city, the Castle rising above it.

Short Interpretation

You are winning, but it continues to be a struggle. In times like this you may feel like you are on your own, one against the world, yet maybe in a way this is exhilarating. However, while you have the strength to win this fight, even on your own, consider how long you want to maintain this position. Perhaps you should consider asking for some help, or at least asking yourself if everyone around you should really be treated as an opponent?

The Tarot of Prague

Fuller Interpretation

Struggle • Fierce competition • Determination • "One against the world" • Taking a stand • Choosing with battles to fight

When this card comes up in a reading it indicates a situation in which you feel you are the only one who really understands how to win the current contest. It's the card of the person who feels that they alone are able to keep an action or campaign together. They may complain about doing all the organising, all the communicating, and always being the one to lead the committee, but deep down they love it. It gives a sense of exhilaration and purpose. This card can be very positive if you really are in the position of doing something "against all the odds", as it signifies someone who is a fearless and successful fighter, no matter how strong the opposition ranged against them.

However, this isn't always an affirmative card. We've all met the kind of person who can never ask for help or bear to share their responsibilities because this makes them feel inessential. One example we see in public life is the very charismatic leader who refuses to train or groom a successor. This is fine while the leader is still able to take charge, but when they go, things fall apart.

When the Seven of Wands comes up in a reading, think carefully about the context. Is the card telling you that you can fight and win, or is the message that it's time to think about sharing your commanding position? Is the battle or contest you are engaged in worth all the struggle? If so, then continue to stand firm, but if it doesn't really justify such an isolated personal effort then be prepared either to stand down or to ask for some help in the struggle.

This card shows a man standing high on a ledge, while below him people are wielding wands. He is utterly confident, and even prepared to hold back (his wand is held behind him). However, he looks isolated by his position, even if he is having fun and winning the fight right now. On the front of the ledge below him is a picture of an ancient and forgotten battle. Perhaps the fighter should ask himself whether in retrospect this current fight will be judged as significant or not?

[Minor Arcana]

Sources

The fighting figure with the wand is (perhaps very appropriately) from the "Heart Under" card of the old Bohemian 32-card pack.

The battle scene below him is from the sgraffito façade of the House of the Minute in Old Town Square. It dates from 1600. For more cards that use this façade, see The Lovers, the Seven of Pentacles and the Knight of Wands.

Another scene from the sgraffito decoration on the House of the Minute

The Tarot of Prague

Eight of Wands

Eight wands, each with the head of an animal, are tearing through the air. The animals are creatures of fantasy and imagination. There is a dragon, a unicorn, and various crested snakes and birds, as well as a lion with an ornate mane. Behind them a woman and angel are also falling through the air, but much more calmly. The woman holds an hourglass, a symbol of time passing quickly, and a golden lamp, full of magical possibilities. In the corner, holding a golden ball, is a stork, symbolising alertness, beginnings, new projects and good outcomes. The whole scene is busy and exciting, and full of hope and promise.

Short Interpretation

So many things happening all at once! It's tremendously exciting and all this action gives you vast amounts of energy. You are in the thick of things, so enjoy it, but remember to slow down once in a while and give yourself some time to make decisions. Even with so much going on in your life, and so many thrilling possibilities, you don't have to rush things. Stay alert, and try to remain calm.

Fuller Interpretation

All happening at once • Speed of events • Resolving the issues
The thrill of action

Speed is the essence of the Eight of Wands. It signals actions that are quick and often effective. This card can stand for closure and completion, particularly of projects or business issues that have been lingering unresolved. If you see this card, now may be the time to start sorting everything out and bringing matters to their conclusion.

The Eight of Wands can mean great hope as well as great haste. Sometimes this hope can take the form of news. If so, it is usually about something that is likely to turn out well.

The card shows eight wands flying across space. They all have animal heads, standing for the many possible aspects of action: the courage of the lion, the mythic grace of the unicorn, the fire and strength of the dragon, but also, of course, the deceit and craftiness of the snake. In the current situation, as different types of activities fly around in your world, you may experience any or all of these different aspects. This is exciting, but it may feel uncontrolled. The animal wands are quite wild and you may not feel they can be tamed easily.

However, a calmer scene underlies all this. A woman is falling or floating through the air, but she is utterly at ease with this. She carries two objects: an hourglass and a magic lamp. She can perhaps conjure things from the air, but she can also simply create order by keeping tracking of time. Even as she flies through the air she is, in a sense, able to pace herself and control her impulses. She is accompanied by a cherub holding a candle and a stork holding a golden ball. The cherub is a symbol of light and foresight, while the stork holding the ball is an old symbol of alertness (the ball would fall if the stork fell asleep). The message is that even in all this flying haste, you need to stay alert, maintain your sense of calm, but continue to be aware of what is going on. If you can manage the situation with a clear head it will work out remarkably well, and may well feel quite magical.

The Tarot of Prague

Sources

The eight wands are actually bizarre rain spouts that come from the roof of a palace in Malostranské náměstí. They are so extraordinarily unlikely that very few passers-by actually notice them. In the winter, the water flowing from them sometimes freezes, so that each animal seems to have a long icicle hanging from its mouth.

The background is from the ceiling of the entrance hall of the Lobkowicz Palace in Vlašská Street. This is one of the many Lobkowicz Palaces in Prague. It now houses the German Embassy. It was built between 1703-69 and is said to be based on Bernini's plans for the Louvre (which were never realised). Unfortunately, most of the palace is now closed to the public, but you can get a glimpse of this ceiling when the gates are open.

The ceiling painting in the entrance hall of what is now the German Embassy

[Minor Arcana]

NINE OF WANDS

A tired, yet wary knight stands in front of a castle tower. He is surrounded by wands and holds a particularly large and dangerous-looking one in his hands. A swarm of golden bees buzz around the scene.

Short Interpretation

Like all the Wands, the Nine shows great strength, alertness, and the power to fight through problems. These are great qualities, but from time to time you can be too ready to do battle. Yes, you have successfully tussled with opposition and oppression and this has made you stronger, but don't exhaust yourself. Maybe it's better to relax and let down your guard for a while?

Fuller Interpretation

Battle readiness • A degree of wariness or paranoia • Defensiveness
Hanging in there under pressure • Using your stamina and persistence
Try, try and try again

This card can show a person who, while demonstrating strength, courage and the willingness to keep going against the odds, has slipped into a state of being a little too focused on the next fight and incapable of being at peace. It is good to be guarded and alert, but this card warns that there is a risk that it's possible to form a habit of being too willing to see conflict and to take part in fights. It's a very defensive position, and one that will be exhausting to maintain for too long. Persistent defensiveness can turn into paranoia and a tendency to see everything as a conflict.

However, there is a positive side to this card. In certain circumstances the ability to persist and to keep trying can be very important. When the card appears in a situation that really is one of extended difficulties and demands, then it shows that resilience and stamina are needed to deal with this, although even then there is the warning that this may wear you out if it continues for too long.

The knight in the card is alert, but there is also an air of exhaustion about him. The wands seem to be fencing him in as well as defending him. He is battle-bloodied but unbowed, which is admirable. However, he looks both wary and hostile, as though he might attack at any moment, whether provoked or not. The bees that buzz around him are significant because when a bee stings the result is usually that it kills itself. In other words, there are times when refusing to fight is a better survival tactic. Although this knight is valiant in his defence, he risks losing all if he can't judge when to lay down his arms.

Sources

The tired knight is from a series of wall paintings on the façade of a house in Dukelských hrdinů in Prague. The background is the Nejvyšší purkrabství (Burgrave's House) at Prague Castle, which is situated in a picturesque courtyard near the Golden Lane. It's part of a particularly interesting group of buildings that nowadays are often ignored as visitors hurry to the Lane itself.

[Minor Arcana]

Ten of Wands

A puppet in the shape of a man struggles up a long flight of steps holding a large and heavy bundle of wands. His face is masked and strained, he looks miserably overburdened and, quite literally, stiff and wooden with tiredness. Behind him the city glows with the soft evening light, but he is unaware of this.

Short Interpretation

You are feeling terribly burdened by all the tasks you have taken on: both controlled and stressed. Try to lighten your load (mentally as well as in practical terms). If you let some of your burdens drop you will feel much lighter and happier, and you'll work better and with far greater satisfaction an enjoyment as a result.

Fuller Interpretation

Too many tasks • Weighed down with responsibilities • "a salary man"
Burdens • A slave to your duties

Being burdened by all the responsibilities you have taken on, refusing to say "No" and ending up shouldering too much work and feeling responsible for too many problems, being caught up in a treadmill of overwork, being unable to break free, feeling fettered and controlled, doing things the hard way and getting overwhelmed by the struggle – the Ten of Wands stands for all this and more. It is about being burdened and controlled by others, or simply about being restricted and trapped by too much work and too many responsibilities.

The image shows a puppet figure that has just struggled up some very long and steep steps clutching a bunch of oversized wooden wands. He looks drawn and almost in pain. His face is masked, as though even his facial expressions are repressed by some external control. The image of a puppet is an ideal metaphor for the Ten of Wands as it is, of course, a slave to its master. Puppetry is a tradition in Prague, and there are still many puppet theatres and performances, ranging from the blatantly touristy to some much more serious and subtle productions. It's been pointed out that the whole idea of a man-made "person", whether this is a puppet, a robot or automaton, has been part of Prague for generations:

Prague literature and culture abound in dummies, goylemes [golems], marionettes, wax statues, mechanical dolls and automata
Angelo Ripellino, *Magic Prague*

There is something particularly disturbing about these puppets when they are life-sized because we find ourselves half wondering if they are really just lifeless figures or if they are ordinary people who are under the control of some kind of spell. The word 'robot' is originally a Czech invention that Karel Čapek (in his 1920 play *Rossum's Universal Robots*) derived from *robota*, a word that means the labour an indentured serf has to give to his lord. This meaning is very close to that of the Ten of Wands, which is about realising that you are not free, and have in some way fallen under the spell of a horrible compulsion to work harder and harder and take on more and more.

[Minor Arcana]

When you see this card in a reading, think seriously about how many tasks you have committed yourself to. If you feel imprisoned by your commitments, think about whether you really are trapped or if it is just in your own mind. Sometimes we fall into "workaholism" and almost deliberately weigh ourselves down with work, merely in order to feel that life has some sense. Consider freeing yourself from some of the burdens you are struggling with and how you got into this position in the first place. You don't have to feel like a puppet or an automaton. You can begin to ease up and start feeling more human again.

Sources

The puppet on the card is a near life-sized one that can be found outside a shop in Karlova Street. The steps he is climbing are the steps of the Petřín Hill. They lead from the end of Vlašská Street all the way up the hill, and are an interesting but tiring climb.

Page of Wands

A healthy young person strides forward, firmly holding a wand as though it was a walking staff. His hat is a nest in which a dove roosts. Perched on his shoulder is a laughing cherub, holding aloft a bundle of letters.

Short Interpretation

This card is about opportunity, fresh studies and the beginning of projects. As in all the Page cards, it may also indicate some news or announcements about the exciting and active phase of life that is about to begin. Maybe you will get a message about something that can be enjoyed just for itself, without scepticism. You have tremendous natural enthusiasm and now is the time to put this to good use.

Fuller Interpretation

Eager to get things going • Enthusiasm and originality • Keen activity
News or messages about action

Wands are always about activity, and this card also has all the usual eagerness and enthusiasm associated with Pages. The Page of Wands can indicate the start or announcement of a new undertaking that will require a lot of action. This Page has all the vitality that's needed for such an undertaking, and so success in all such ventures is more than likely. The activity may mean embarking into a new field of creativity or self-expression, or starting something more practical. However, whichever it is, the indication is that it will be something that you can be passionate, confident and excited about. On a more basic level, the card can mean receiving a rather strange or surprising message or letter, or finding a good new friend or ally. Often this will either be someone unexpected, or a person is coming into your life from an unlikely direction.

The image on this card shows a young man (or woman) with a bird's nest on his head. The nest is slightly absurd, which is appropriate because the Page of Wands is never afraid to express himself in an original way (in the original RWS card he wears an odd hat, complete with a feather). As Arthur Waite writes, "his tidings are strange". There is often a slight air of the unexpected about this Page. The nest can also symbolise new beginnings and the hatching of plans and projects, while the dove shows that any action that needs to be taken should be done in a peaceful way; unlike some of the Knights, the Pages in Tarot are not at all inclined to be quick to pick a fight. This Page has an energy that is conducive to co-operation, with none of the watchful or wary aspects of, for example, the Page of Swords.

The angel holding letters is an obvious symbol that this card can indicate messages, letters and communications. However, there is also a more subtle symbolism to this little figure. The angel sits on the Page's shoulder in very much the way that we are used to seeing a child sitting on the shoulder of St Christopher in statues all over the world. This is a gentle reminder that the Page has courage and faithfulness and can be a good guide when starting out on a journey of discovery or a plan of action.

Sources

The Page is based on a statue which is part of a group in a park by the river at Smetanovo nábřeží. The image of the cherub is taken from the Art Nouveau paintings on the wall of the main Prague Post Office in Jindřišská Street, an allegorical series of paintings showing scenes of letters and communication. Vítězslav Karel Mašek painted the original in 1901.

In the background is a view of Old Town Square and the Astronomical Clock Tower.

A close-up of the wall painting inside the main Prague Post Office

[Minor Arcana]

Knight of Wands

A strikingly-beautiful young man rides a white horse high above the rooftops of the city. He holds a wand aloft in one hand. There is a heart on the sleeve of his other arm. In the sky above him there is a complex clock that shows both astronomical and astrological scenes.

Short Interpretation

This person represents someone in your life who is very attractive and full of energy. It is hard to say No to this person, as he or she has an irresistable tendency to always want to "go for it", especially if it's something new. However, this is someone who can also be too sure of themselves, and too certain of their own attractions. The Knight is magnetic, but often thoughtless, and definitely not one to make a commitment. Enjoy his company, but don't get too carried away by his restless charms.

The Tarot of Prague

Fuller Interpretation

A real charmer • A magnetically attractive person • Recklessness "Just do it" • whatever the consequences

The Knight of Wands is very attractive and full of energy, and because of this, hard to resist. He (or she) is a person who tends to "go for it", especially when the challenge is new and exciting. However, he can also be too sure of himself and too certain of his charms. He can be thoughtless, and is unlikely to make a commitment to a relationship or to long-term, painstaking work. He can be reckless and irresponsible, and sometimes loses his temper. He certainly has very little patience with anything he doesn't like.

This card shows a beautiful young man, but he wears his heart on his sleeve and has a general air, perhaps, of being a little too attractive to be entirely trusted. He rides above the rooftops and his feet don't touch the ground. He looks both purposeful and enthusiastic, but also somehow disconnected with the more down-to-earth realities of life. The clock hanging in the sky above him stands both for the simple passing of time, and for the workings of fate. This young hero, lovely as he is, lacks self-control and has very little staying power. In many ways this puts him at the mercy of fate, as he swings restlessly from one thing (or person) to another.

In a reading the Court Cards nearly always stand for actual people, and this card may refer to an attractive but careless person (male or female) in your life. Don't forget however, that it can also refer to the way in which you yourself are behaving. Sometimes it's easy to get so carried away by our own charisma and energy that we forget to be caring and thoughtful towards others.

Sources

The figure is based on a painted façade on the front of the Storch House in Old Town Square. This is a late 19th-century house, but built and painted in neo-Renaissance style. The knight is Saint Wenceslas, and this depiction of him was designed by Bedrich Ohmann (who was also the architect of the house). The clock in the background is the Astronomical Clock (sometimes known as the Astronomical/Astrological Clock) on the Town Hall clock tower.

[Minor Arcana]

More on the Astronomical Clock

The Astronomical Clock was built by Mikulas of Kadan in 1410, then renovated in the 16th century (and again after WWII). It has two faces. The face used here is the older one, and illustrates the scientific knowledge of the time, showing the planets circling the Earth. The clock is known best for its mechanism that strikes on the hour and shows the figures of Christ and the Apostles moving in a procession. When the procession finishes, the figure of Death on one side of the clock turns over his hourglass (for another old Prague rendition of Death with an hourglass, see our Death card) and a cock crows and flaps its wings.

"Death pulled the cord and rang by nodding its head. Other small figures stirred while the cock flapped its wings, and the twelve Apostles glanced impassively down at the street through open windows".
Guillaume Apollinaire

The clock records both time (i.e. the movement of the sun) and the movement of the zodiac:

Over the fixed disc of the astronomical sphere there is a revolving ring with the signs of the zodiac, which make it possible to read in projection the following data: the rising, booth culminations and setting of the various signs of the zodiac, the Sun and the Moon, also sidereal time (the hand with the golden star), Central European Time and also old Czech time (both with the aid of the hand with a little golden hand), the geocentric position of the Sun (indicated by a gold target...and also the planetary hours at a given moment.
Milan Špůrek, *Praga Mysteriousa*

Each June 21, the ghosts of the two dozen Protestant Nationals who were beheaded in Old Town Square in 1621 are reputed to rise from their burial place in the Church of the Holy Saviour and go to Old Town Square where they check that the hands of the Astronomical Clock have not stopped.

The Tarot of Prague

QUEEN OF WANDS

The card shows a happy queen playing with a lively baby boy. She holds a golden wand; he has a set of the golden scales of justice. The boy is smiling, indicating his scales do not hold the threat of retribution, but simply stand for a sense of fair play.

The whole scene is lively, and though grand, also very domestic in tone. This is not an unapproachable or revered Queen. On the contrary, she looks energetic and fun and not at all stiff or formal. Behind her are lush trees, with a castle rising above. A smiling lioness sits in front of the woman and child, perhaps gently protecting them.

Short Interpretation

Warm and approachable, this Queen is very self-assured and deals with people in a confident and straightforward manner. She is full of energy and radiates her vitality and love of life. Sometimes it seems as though she leads a charmed life, but this is probably less about luck and more due to the people around her responding wholeheartedly to such positive and passionate vigour.

Fuller Interpretation

Down-to-earth and straightforward • Energetic • Joie de vivre
Attractive personality • Good at business, in a quirky way
Good humoured

The Queen of Wands is warm and attractive, an approachable figure rather than a majestic, forbidding one. She is the kind of straightforward and self-assured person who is reassuring to be around. Like all the Wands, she signifies energy, in this case of a very healthy and physically fit kind. She also tends to have a strong sexual energy, much more obviously so than the Queens of the other suits. Many people will find her attractive and even magnetic.

Rather oddly, in the RWS version of this card a black cat sits in front of the Queen. Usually this would be a sign of witchcraft (though this Queen is far from the frightening witch of traditional fairy stories, and any suggestion of witchcraft should be taken more in the "white magic", earthy and useful sense), but in fact it's usually interpreted as a sign of protection. In the image on this card the cat has become a big, friendly lioness. The child that the Queen holds in her hands laughs playfully at this animal, which looks and behaves more like a big cat than an intimidating predator.

Like all the Court Cards in this suit, there is a quirky, almost eccentric, creativity about this Queen. While she is very down to earth, she isn't conventional and can sometimes be surprising. She won't always do things in the obvious way, and her imagination and originality can add considerably to her attractions.

The words "Good cheer and let us be joyful" that appear on the bottom of the picture sum up many aspects of the Queen of Wands. The quote is taken, appropriately, from the verse written to celebrate the coronation, in 1619, of Frederick of the Palatinate and Princess Elizabeth of England as King and Queen of Bohemia (the verse was originally written in German, this is the translation given by Frances Yates):

Good cheer, and let us be joyful,
The red dawn of the morn is breaking,
The sun can now be seen,
God turns his face towards us...
Frances Yates, *The Rosicrucian Enlightenment*

Elizabeth had a personality that fits well with this card. She was adored by the English people and considered extremely attractive, intelligent and also rather unconventional. To the English, she became affectionately known as "The Queen of Hearts". In spite of her very difficult situation (she gave birth to her second child during the harsh winter in Prague. He later became famous in the English civil war as the dashing Prince Rupert of the Rhine) she seems to have remained active, cheerful and somewhat philosophical throughout.

Sources

The queen and the baby in her arms are from the façade of a Baroque house in Úvoz Street.

The background shows a view of the Castle and Daliborka Tower looking from the Belvedere (Queen Anne's Palace) across the Stag Moat.

[Minor Arcana]

More about Queen Elizabeth of Bohemia

Frederick, Elector of the Palatinate, and his wife Princess Elizabeth of England (daughter of James I), were crowned King and Queen of Bohemia in the winter of 1619, and became known as the "Winter King and Queen" as their reign was very short, only lasting until the last months of 1620. Their story is actually quite a tragic one, as they accepted the Bohemian crown in some naiveté, not realising the powers ranged against it. They reigned at Prague Castle for less than a year, until their armies were defeated at the Battle of the White Mountain on the outskirts of Prague. This battle not only ended their reign but also started the disastrous Thirty Years' War.

While Frederick and Elizabeth survived their defeat, they were ruined, and had to flee to The Hague, in Holland, with almost nothing. There, the couple set up an impoverished court in exile. Frederick died quite soon after, but Elizabeth continued to run her court, and seems to have commanded enormous respect from all who met her. Frances Yates wrote that "She had a powerful character and she exerted great influence" (*Rosicrucian Enlightenment*).

Elizabeth of Bohemia, who was also known as "The Queen of Hearts"

The Tarot of Prague

King of Wands

A rather portly and flamboyant king stands proudly in front of an elaborately decorated house. He holds two large wands, one is sprouting leaves, and the other has an exuberant vine clambering up it. Behind the king stands one of his senior knights, willing to follow his charismatic leader anywhere. He holds the most eccentric helmet, the crest of which is in the form of a grinning creature in a feathered headdress.

Short Interpretation

Authority combined with action. The King of Wands is charismatic, energetic and often has a good deal of charm and a real sense of showmanship. He is good at communicating with people, and the strength of his willpower often means that people follow him easily. However, this King needs to remember that not everyone can attain his level of action and ability. Sometimes he needs to show more tolerance for lesser mortals!

[Minor Arcana]

Fuller Interpretation

Original and inventive • An inspiring communicator • Authoritative • Charismatic, "a star" • Dares to be different • Acts with panache

The King of Wands is an odd mix of authority and a rather unconventional panache. You might envisage him, for example, as the somewhat imperious but creative master of a theatre company, someone who wields an iron rod of authority but who is also inventive, idiosyncratic and not afraid to buck the norms. The King of Wands is often a bit of a showman, an inspired communicator who may at times exasperate his audience with his absolute certainty about his own right of leadership, but who is also likely to win them over with his power of oratory and style.

The king shown on this card is flamboyant, utterly confident and, even in his late middle-age, positively blossoming with health. The wands that he holds are bursting with life, as is the King himself. Always one to attract and inspire followers, he is shown with one of his faithful knights at his shoulder, a man who in some ways looks almost as colourful and confident as the King himself, but who is content to be lead by his charismatic sovereign. What is meant by the little man/lion on the helmet? Well, he is a symbol both of the King's eccentricity and originality, and also of his authority. In a way, he represents another aspect of the King: odd, showy and fiery, but always in charge.

Sources

The king is taken from a series of wall paintings on the façade of a house in Dukelských hrdinů in Prague (for another card that uses these wall paintings see the Nine of Wands).

The knight holding the strange helmet is from the late 19th-century façade of a house in Karlovo náměstí (Charles Square). The Four of Wands also uses a figure from this façade.

The wonderful, elaborately-decorated house in the background is the House of the Minute, in Staromestské náměstí (Old Town Square).

For other cards that use pictures from the façade of the House of the Minute, see the Seven of Pentacles, the Seven of Wands and The Lovers.

The Tarot of Prague

MINOR ARCANA - CUPS

Cups

The element of Cups is Water, and because of the association between water and both depth and fluidity this suit has come to signify emotions, inner feelings, creativity and aesthetics. Humane and sympathetic, Cups refer to love, affection, sensitivity, intuition and compassion. However, even these sympathetic qualities can have a negative side. There are situations in which Cups have a tendency to be overly fragile or sensitive, or moody and touchy and at times their sensivity may make them too introspective and morose. Cups are focused on inner experience rather than outward action, so while they are emotionally intelligent and aware they are also inclined to be passive, or even apathetic.

If the Cups were artists they would be the Pre-Raphaelites, exquisitely sensitive and concerned with beauty and fine qualities, but also rather self-absorbed, in danger of becoming neurotically over-refined, and highly susceptible to ennui and languor. However, the ability to be responsive to emotions is vital to happiness. Even with the intellect, action and practicality offered by the other suits, life would be empty without the feelings, intuition and creativity that are the qualities of Cups.

At their most positive the Cups are wise, tolerant, and both peaceable and patient with others. The Ace of Cups is a good card to see if you are beginning something that requires creativity and empathy. It is full of life but also indicates a certain calm sense of purpose. The Two of Cups refers to the emotions and feelings in a relationship between two people. It usually shows the beginning of a relationship that will touch you quite deeply. In the Three of Cups this relationship is between a group of people rather than a pair. This is a joyful card about the pleasure of co-operating and sharing. With the Four, however, we see the first signs of the negative aspects of the emotional sensitivity of Cups, as depression and melancholy surface. This card indicates world-weariness and a reluctance to engage with anything or anyone.

The Five of Cups also clearly reveals some of the problematic aspects of the suit. While our life cannot always be full of good things, neither should we slip into believing all is lost each time we experience a setback. This card suggests that a little less brooding and a little more lively engagement with the world will let us see the ups and downs in a more balanced way, instead of swinging between "It's all wonderful" and "All is lost". In the Six, however, the Cups' essential warmth and ability to share come to the fore again. This is a rather strange card with a slightly fairytale quality; it signifies a childlike innocence and trust, reminding us that as children we all were able to openly feel and express our feelings, and that there are times when it's good to remember how to recapture that openness and sense of trust.

The Seven of Cups, like all the Sevens, shows decisions. The Cups are full of imagination and dreams, and this card is about those times when there seems to be a bewildering range of fantastic possibilities. The message is that we need to calmly decide which of these are just fantasies and which are more realistic and useful.

With the Eight, the tension of trying to make decisions has become more of a real struggle. Even when we have built up a great store of good things (friends, companionship, intimacy and shared memories, group creative projects we enjoyed), there may be times when we need to be willing to let it all go and move on to something new. This is not an easy card because it means leaving the easier and lighter aspects of the emotions and moving instead towards a more demanding search for spirituality and a deeper understanding of life.

It is a relief to get to the Nine, which is a typical nine in that it shows the suit's good qualities in a very straightforward and down-to-earth way. This is the "wish card" of the Tarot deck and promises that all of our desires will be fulfilled — as long as they are not too lofty but simply focused on having a straightforward and rather self-indulgent good time.

By the Ten, these wishes have broadened and deepened and become more long term. This card indicates deep emotions and family bonds rather than simple pleasures. In the Ten of Cups, the world is wonderful and there is real joy in the recognition of the gifts that life has brought you.

Court Cards

In the Court Cards of Cups, the primary qualities are about feelings and emotions, although creativity also figures strongly.

The Page of Cups lives in a creative, but also very dreamy and romantic

[Minor Arcana]

world. Although he is studious, his studies are not focused in any practical direction; he loves learning and contemplation for their own sake rather than for any immediate purpose.

The Knight of Cups has great creative potential and a light and joyous enthusiasm for life, but he also suffers from being a bit of a dreamer, albeit a very attractive one. He rarely comes down to earth long enough to make the things he imagines into actual realities. He may, for example, signify the kind of person who is always about to write a great novel or create a great work of art but somehow never quite gets around to it. However, the charm of the Knight is that he is an absolutely happy dreamer, oblivious to the fact that nothing actually gets done, and he is certainly not suffering because of this.

The Queen of Cups manages to balance some practical action with all the seductive dreams and imaginings. She is a wonderful figure in the Minor Arcana, in many ways like a more day-to-day Empress. She manages to be creative, emotional, and full of feeling and sensitivity, but at the same time able to act in the real world. This Queen can put her creative ideas into practice in a responsible and useful way.

The King also shares this practicality, but his sense of responsibility has perhaps gone a little too far for his own happiness. Acutely aware of his duties, he tends to suppress his own emotions and the wilder and more rebellious sides of his creativity so that he can reliably "deliver the goods". He always puts responsibility first, and although at times he dreams of simply dropping job, status and duty and running away to pursue his own artistic impulses, the reality is that it is highly unlikely he ever will.

The overall message of Cups? We can only really enjoy life if we are open to feelings and emotions, those of others as well as our own, but at the same time we have to remember not to ignore our own imagination and intuition. Creativity and feeling need to be balanced with the ability to be practical and to take action, otherwise it's possible to slip into being too much of a "delicate flower". We need to combine our emotions with rationality so that the way we live makes sense *and* feels right.

Ace of Cups

A copper hand, green with verdigris, holds a small, smiling red lion. The lion is rearing up on its hind legs in order to hold aloft a golden cup. A series of bridges over a river can be seen stretching into the distance. Golden yods rain down all around.

Short Interpretation

The beginning of wonderful new emotions and creativity. This is a tremendously exciting time, and you feel as though you are bursting with life. Embrace this glorious sense of energy and innovation and use it to begin something that you will really love, whether this is a new enterprise, a great relationship, or something creative. The world is your oyster right now.

[Minor Arcana]

Fuller Interpretation

Life and energy • A burst of creativity • Accepting love • Pure happiness

The Ace of Cups stands for that exhilarating period at the beginning of a burst of creativity or at the start of a new relationship. The cup on this card indicates a period in which life literally overflows with enthusiasm and energy. It may be a time to lose any fear of intimacy and allow an attraction or relationship to grow, whether it's a full-blown love affair or simply a close and affectionate relationship. Alternatively, it may indicate the beginning of a project or plan that requires a high level of creativity or emotional sensitivity.

In this card a red lion holds a golden cup high over the river basin. The "red lion" was an alchemical term for the Philosopher's Stone. Nicholas Flamel, one of the most famous of all alchemists, explains that this was in part because in the "Great Work" of alchemy the mixture changed colours many times beofre finally becoming the bright red of the final stone.

The life and energy that the Ace of Cups stands for is very much embodied by the idea of the Philosopher's Stone. The creation of the Stone was the aim of the whole process of alchemy as it could not only turn base metal to gold, but could also confer eternal life. For many, however, alchemy was primarily seen as a process of transfiguration and the attainment of happiness and enlightenment rather than the search for gold, riches or artificially prolonged life. The golden 'yods' that are falling around the cup stand for vitality and life, rather than for material riches (*yod* is a Hebrew letter that stands, symbolically, for the hands of mankind and the ability to bring spirit and life-force into the real world).

The Ace of Cups has been linked to the legend of the Holy Grail and some people see in the traditional images on this card a veiled reference to the quest for the Grail. There is, interestingly, a strong link between the Holy Grail and Prague, as some believed the Grail was created from the "lapis ex coelis", a stone that fell from the sky and which was said to have

The Tarot of Prague

created the Bohemian Czech basin where Prague is located. Partly for this reason, the Grail was one of the obsessions of Rudolph II.

Sources

The lion holding a cup is from the house sign of the 15th-century "U Cerveneho Lva" (House of the Red Lion) at 41 Nerudova Street. It is believed that the 17th-century altar-painter Peter Brandl, who was born and lived in the house, modelled this facade.

A striking feature of the lion on the original house sign is the presence of several distinct emblems, including a piece of honeycomb and a cloud, as well as his cup. This makes it likely that it was intended as a specific symbol, probably of Freemasonry. Old Masonic symbols are exceptionally common in the centre of Prague.

The background is a photograph of the Čertovska, or "Devil's Channel", at Kampa Island. The Knights of Malta originally owned Kampa, and in the 12th century this whole area was known as the Jurisdiction of Malta.

Of course, the Knights of Malta and their close associates, the Knights Templar, are both associated in legend with the Grail. The use of their historical area of Prague on this card is therefore appropriate.

The house decoration on Nerudova Street on which the Ace of Cups is based

[Minor Arcana]

Two of Cups

A young man and woman stand with arms entwined on a parapet above Charles Bridge. Below them is a picture of a mermaid with two tails, surrounded by poppies. In the distance is the Malá Strana side of the Vltava river, with the Castle on the horizon.

Short Interpretation

Relationships and partnerships are at the heart of things right now. You are starting a new attachment that may be a friendship or the beginning of a love affair, but it's still the early days and you are just beginning to know and trust the other person. Enjoy this period and don't worry about where it takes you. Whether it turns out to be simple friendship, a good working partnership, or a life-changing passion, it's going to be a relationship that will enrich your life.

Fuller Interpretation

Soul mates • Beginning a relationship • Settling a quarrel
Attraction and friendship

This card usually indicates the beginnings of an important bond with another person. This can be a sexual or romantic attraction and can sometimes point to a wedding or engagement, but it often simply means a close friendship or an important and trusting business or work affiliation that you feel good about.

Because the Two of Cups is always about a positive relationship, it can also stand for peace and healing, and can mean the end of a quarrel, "burying the hatchet", and generally about being willing and able to build bridges and bring about reconciliation.

The image on this card shows a young couple touching hands. Their pose is somewhat formal, suggesting they don't yet have a really established intimacy, although they also radiate respect and affection for one another. The "wateriness" of Cups is very evident in this card. The Charles Bridge and the river form the backdrop to the couple, and a picture of a melusine, a mermaid with two tails, is at their feet. Above them is a Caduceus, the wand of Hermes that traditionally appears on this card. This symbol stands both for peace (heralds and messengers held the sign of the Caduceus up much like we use a white flag now) and for the intertwining of two different aspects or elements. In the context of the Two of Cups, this intertwining is most appropriately interpreted as the coming together of male and female aspects in a harmonious relationship.

The melusine is a subtle symbol. The myth of Melusine (*Roman de Melusine* by Jean d'Arras) is a French medieval tale about a woman who married a gentleman on the strict understanding that he never disturb her while she was bathing on Saturdays. However, one day he broke this trust and discovered that on this one day of the week his wife was, in fact, transformed into a mermaid. She fled, and was never seen again. The melusine, surrounded here by opium poppies, can thus be taken to stand for the need for trust and clear boundaries in a relationship, and also, more mysteriously, for the dreamlike and hidden qualities that we experience as part of romance. It is significant that the word 'romance' comes from the same root as *roman*, an older name for a mythical tale. Perhaps one aspect

[Minor Arcana]

of every new romance is the tendency to create a myth about the other person?

The whole scene on this card is set in the centre of the city, but at the same time slightly apart from it. When we are in an intimate relationship we may feel very much part of the world and more in touch with other people because we are close to one person who touches us deeply. At the same time, we often feel almost as if we are enclosed in a bubble with that person. In one sense, the world flows by in a blur beneath our feet.

Sources

The art deco sculptures are from the front façade of the Czech Cubist-style Trade Court building on Slezska Street in the Vinohrady district of Prague. In the original each figure was associated with a trade or skill, in a style that anticipates Socialist Realism. The woman stood on a ship and the man on a set of cogs and wheels.

The sgraffito parapet is from the rear facade of the 16th-century Schwarzenberg-Lobkowicz Palace (the façade that faces Nerudova and Úvoz streets). High up on this façade there are a number of panels showing a mermaid with two tails (strictly speaking these are not mermaids but *melusines*, a two-tailed mermaid particularly popular in Central Europe). Although on first glance they look like a repeated motif, the expression and the flowers that surround each of them are actually quite different. The one chosen for this card is particularly interesting because her flowers appear to be opium poppies, symbolic of dreams and visions.

The motif of the melusine can be seen all over Prague. The story of Melusine (see above) was an extremely popular myth in the French court, and romantic depictions of this figure are widespread throughout Central Europe. There is an elegant one on a house in Karlova Street that often goes unnoticed in the bustle of tourists. On the King of Cups we have used another particularly sensuous example of a melusine.

More about Charles Bridge

The Charles Bridge was originally known simply as "the stone bridge" and was for centuries the only bridge crossing the Vltava river at Prague. It was commissioned by Charles IV to replace the earlier Judith Bridge after this was destroyed by a flood in 1357. Charles Bridge was begun in the same year, but wasn't completed until 1402. The stonemason in charge was Petr Parler (oddly enough, his name can be translated as "making the stones talk"). The famous statues on the bridge were added at various times over the next centuries. Most date from the 17th and 18th centuries.

There are many legends and beliefs about the Charles Bridge. One tale that still causes amusement is about the time when the bridge was built. The lime for the mortar was mixed with egg to give it strength and so eggs were requested from all over the Czech lands. The village of Velvary, worried about their eggs being broken in transit, are said to have sent theirs hard-boiled. The village has never lived down this story.

There are also various accounts about the bridge having been magically strengthened by having a living animal walled up in it. One variation of this tale is that the souls of the dead wife and unborn child of one of the bridge's building foremen were for many years trapped above the bridge, only to be finally freed when someone crossing the bridge blessed them. Yet another variation on the theme is that there is a magic sword built into the bridge, waiting to be released if Prague is in danger. (For more on this see the Knight of Swords.)

Perhaps of more immediate practical use is the "Bearded Man" relief scupture built into the embankment below the Knights of the Cross monastery. When the river water rises high enough to touch his beard it means that it is about to flood the surrounding streets.

The Charles Bridge is now a major pedestrian thoroughfare. In the summer it is usually crowded with people. Many touch the bronze reliefs at the base of the statue of St John Nepomuk as they cross the bridge, as it is believed this ensures that they will return to Prague. (This relief is shown on the Ten of Pentacles.)

[Minor Arcana]

Three of Cups

Three happy, healthy young women are standing together. One of them is holding up a golden cup as though she is about to make a toast. There are two more cups on the ground. In the background is a painting that shows a group of celebratory angels (or perhaps they are fairies?) and cherubs. At the bottom of the card is a dove, holding the olive branch of peace.

Short Interpretation

Other people are at the centre of your life right now, and it's a very positive thing. You may be enjoying working in a team, or it may be more about experiencing good companionship or mutual trust and support, but one way or another you are in a position where you appreciate how important those around you can be. You should enjoy this sense of harmony and community and let it energise you.

The Tarot of Prague

Fuller Interpretation

Celebration • Co-operation and teamwork • Community
Mutual support

The Three of Cups is essentially about teamwork that is based on emotions rather than strict rationality, in which there is a "gut feeling" that it will work well. When this card comes up in a reading it is an indication that you should rely on the power of friendship, co-operation and every form of teamwork and community. The card also signifies the sense of happy exuberance you can feel when working closely with others. When a co-operation is working really well it can be a source of pleasure and excitement as each side feels both supportive and supported, and you can feel more relaxed simply because you do not have to carry everything on your own shoulders. When you can trust the people around you there is no need to be on your guard or to take on too much so you can really enjoy getting on with the task at hand in a joyful and collaborative way.

The image on this card shows three young women who are happily and animatedly talking. One of them is holding up a golden cup in a toast. They are all dressed and styled in the same way, and look harmonious and comfortable together. Beneath their feet a dove flies over swirling water. This represents both the "watery" and emotional qualities of the Cups suit, and also the peace and harmony that is at the heart of the card. The fairies and cherubs in the background add to the air of celebration and festivity. One seems to be pouring liquid from her jug into the golden cup held aloft — real teamwork!

Sources

The three Art Nouveau-style young women in the foreground are originally from the entrance of a house in Široka in the Josefov part of Old Town. However, in the original there are only two women, one on either side of the door. We took the liberty of photographing one of them from two angles, and then using her twice on this card. The background picture of fairies and cherubs is from the murals in the early 18th century Clam-Galas Palace at the corner of Karlova and Husova streets. The artist was Santin Bossi. The palace is open to the public but this is not always made apparent. If you go past the slightly forbidding façade you will find one of the most beautifully decorated stairways in Prague.

[Minor Arcana]

Four of Cups

A well-dressed young man leans against a tree, wearily gazing at four goblets on the ground in front of him. He seems completely disengaged, his mind obviously elsewhere. Around him his sheep graze unnoticed and untended.

Short Interpretation

You've had it all and now you're sick of it. There are moments in life when we look around at everything we have and it all appears indulgent and too materialistic. Suddenly our possessions look like so much clutter, the fabulous food and drink we once enjoyed seems too rich and unhealthy, and the opportunities surrounding us now feel like traps.

When you fall into this kind of mood, try to find some space and time to think. Ask yourself seriously if this is just a temporary phase of feeling "down", or whether you really do need to cast aside some of the possessions, involvements and material things surrounding you.

Fuller Interpretation

Boredom and tedium • World-weariness • A dull environment
Withdrawal from excesses • Not noticing your blessings

The appearance of the Four of Cups in a reading can indicate an unhealthy degree of self-absorption, and with it a lack of interest in the world and a sense of being "sick of it all". This is really a card about those periods of depression we can all fall into, when we feel sorry for ourselves and are overcome by a feeling of hopelessness. At times like this we risk becoming increasingly apathetic instead of taking action to pull ourselves out of the gloom.

The classic popular remedy for depression is to "get out more", and when this card comes up in a reading it does imply that the querent should indeed make the effort to get out and do something. But this demands more than just going out, socialising and getting more involved in activities. It also means you should get out of the habit of being unhealthily introspective, and stop dwelling on your anxieties.

The young man on this card is a shepherd, a job that is of course very solitary. He seems to have become lost in himself, no longer even taking much interest in the sheep that are his charge. He doesn't see how fortunate he actually is, and instead of appreciating all he has got he has fallen into a sullen state of introspection and dissatisfaction.

The feelings of boredom, pointlessness and self-pity that this card represents can be overcome by putting some energy back into your life, and appreciating what you have, rather than seeing everything as a restriction. All those aspects of life that seem to have lost their flavour, whether they are material, sensual or spiritual, will soon feel worthwhile again if you simply pull yourself out of this spiral of apathy and dreariness. If this young shepherd would only look around him, he might see the beauty of his surroundings and begin to count his blessings.

Sources

The young man is from the lovely Art Nouveau mosaic façade of the Lucerna Palace on Vodičkova Street. The Lucerna Palace is an interesting 1920s entertainment complex. It's particularly well-known because it was owned by the family of Vaclav Havel (who after a lifetime of opposition to the Communist party became the first president of Czechoslovakia after the 1989 Velvet Revolution). Havel is said to have spent much of his time dancing at the Lucerna in his youth. After the 1948 Communist takeover, these buildings were taken from the family and were allowed to become rather run-down. They are now being restored. For another card that uses figures taken from the same façade, see the Four of Wands.

The goblets in front of the young man are from a striking ceramic tile panel in the basement of the Secessionist (Art Nouveau) Obečni dům (Municipal House).

The mosaic façade on which the Four of Cups is based

Five of Cups

A dark figure dressed partly in armour stands in front of an old fortified synagogue. He has one very curious and rather frightening attribute: his face is entirely smooth, without any discernible human features. Yet his stance is not threatening, in fact he looks calm and rather sad. He is the Golem, the legendary being that Rabbi Loew made from the clay of the Vltava river to protect the Jews of the Prague Ghetto. At his feet there are three smashed cups. Behind him but unnoticed are two more cups that are still intact.

Short Interpretation

This is a time of loss, but there are still some good things left. Like all the Fives in the Tarot, the Five of Cups is about struggle. This doesn't mean disaster, but simply indicates a time when there will be difficulties and a sense of defeat. However, while three cups have been shattered, it's important to see that others remain intact. This means that you should acknowl-

[Minor Arcana]

edge the reality of your situation, but also take up what you still have and get on with life. With acceptance and determination, good times will soon come again.

Fuller Interpretation

Loss, but acceptance • Remaining hope • Calm sorrow
Looking on the down side.

Loss and bereavement are central to this card, but it's important to realise that the loss indicated is partial, not total. In a reading, the Five of Cups card does not usually signify loss in the sense of something as serious and absolute as a death, but more likely points to a situation that could eventually be rectified, such as the loss of a job, a relationship or money, or of less tangible things such as losing an opportunity or reputation. The card is also associated with all the regrets and denials that can come with this feeling of bereavement.

It might seem like a sad card, but the Five of Cups actually also carries a message of hope. While three of the cups have been knocked over and their contents spilled (representing all that is gone), two of them still stand. The cups that remain, however, are unnoticed, indicating that in the midst of sorrow it can be hard to look on the brighter side and realise that some good things remain. The picture on this card is reminiscent of the old saying that pessimistic people are those who tend to see a cup as being "half empty" rather than "half full". Sometimes, our perception of the state of affairs can make it appear that things are much worse than they really are.

The statue on this card is generally believed to be a statue of the Golem. (There is some disagreement about this. The true facts about the subject of this statue seems to have been lost over the years.) The Golem is a powerful symbol for this card because his tale is very much about loss and sadness, but is also a tale of hope and the courage to triumph over adverse circumstances.

Sources

The figure in armour with no face is a statue by Ladislav Šaloun. It is one of a pair of statues that stand at the entrance to Josefov, the old Jewish

The Tarot of Prague

quarter of Prague. (The second statue is of Rabbi Loew, which we have used for The Hierophant.) Although it't not absolutely clear who this statue is intended to represent — some guidebooks say it is the "Iron Knight" of Bohemia, others say it is the Golem, and it seems almost impossible to confirm either — the more general opinion now seems to favour it being the Golem, which certainly makes sense as a pairing with the Rabbi.

The Golem was the famous being that Prague's Chief Rabbi, Rabbi Loew, made from the mud of the Vltava to protect the Jews of 16th century Prague. The word 'golem' comes from the Hebrew word *gelem*, meaning raw material. According to legend, since the time of Loew, the Golem has lain lifeless and undisturbed for centuries behind a small, triangular window in the attic of the Old New Synagogue in the Jewish Quarter. He is supposed to be there to this day, ready to awake and protect the Jews again if he is needed.

The statue by Šaloun on which
the Five of Cups is based

[Minor Arcana]

More about the Golem

The Chief Rabbi of Prague, Yehuda Low Ben Bezalel, known as Rabbi Loew, lived in Prague from 1525 to 1609. During this period the Jews were persecuted repeatedly, and there was often terror in the Jewish ghetto. According to the legend, one night in 1580 Rabbi Loew had a dream that suggested a plan of help. It told him to create a strong supernatural being, a Golem, to defend the people of the ghetto.

The next day, Rabbi Loew called two people to help him make the Golem. One account says that these were his wife Edam and his oldest student. Another account claims that they were the disciple Yakob ben Chaim Sasson and the Rabbi's son-in-law, Isaac ben Simon. Instructions for making the Golem were contained in a magical Cabbalistic formula known to the rabbi. The creature was to be composed of the four elements: earth, water, fire and air.

Rabbi Loew was a famed scholar of the Cabbala, and the book he is thought to have used was the Cabbalistic book *Sefer HaYetzera* (*Book of Formation*). This text is partly attributed to Adam, the first man, partly to Abraham, the first patriarch, and partly to Rabbi Akiva, the famous rabbi who lived approximately 2000 years ago. The focus of the book is the creation of the universe and it describes various mystical elements of creation. Among them are the Hebrew words and letters to be used in the process of creation. Because God created the world by uttering vocal commands, the Hebrew words that were uttered have a divine power.

For seven days Rabbi Loew and his helpers prepared themselves spiritually for the task of creating the Golem. On the twentieth day of the Hebrew month of Adar in the Jewish year 5340, at four hours after midnight, they went to the Vltava River in Prague to make the figure out of the clay of the riverbank. It was to be huge (10 feet tall) but with only basic human features on its face.

They made the figure from the clay and began the process of bringing it to life. First, Rabbi Loew's wife (or in some accounts his son-in-law) circled the clay figure seven times and spoke a special mystical phrase. This made the clay become red-hot. The Rabbi then told his disciple to circle the figure seven times and say another mystical phrase. This made the clay figure cool down and become damp. Then unbelievable things began to happen: fingernails started growing, hair covered the body, and eyes appeared in the face.

Finally, the Rabbi himself circled the clay figure seven times. The three of them together then recited Genesis 2:7: "And God breathed into his nostrils the breath of life and man became a living soul." The Rabbi placed a *shem*, a piece of parchment on which was written the name of God, into the creature's mouth and the Golem came to life, opened his eyes and stood up.

Rabbi Loew told the Golem that his name was to be Joseph and that his task was to protect the Jews of the Prague ghetto. He told the Golem to listen only to his personal orders and to do everything he was told. The Golem could hear and see but could not talk, so he simply nodded to show he understood.

For a while, all was quiet in Prague and the Golem worked on mundane day-to-day tasks. As he was not allowed to labour on the Sabbath, the Rabbi would remove the *shem* from his mouth on this day and render him powerless. However, one Sabbath the Rabbi forgot to do this. As a result the Golem began running around wildly, out of control and smashing everything he came across. Household articles, cups and plates, and even furniture were overturned. Cats and chickens were trampled, windows were shattered, and people came running for the Rabbi, who rushed to the wildly rampaging Golem and tore the *shem* from its mouth.

In a different version of the story, we are told that the Golem was indeed needed to defend the Jews of Prague. One day a small child was found dead in the city and was thrown on the road to the ghetto. The Jews were falsely accused of cold-blooded ritual murder, and an angry mob of Praguers carrying torches came to the ghetto looking for revenge. At this point, the Golem reacted. He pushed through the crowd and found the very woman who had killed the child. The terrified woman quickly confessed to the murder and it became clear that the people of the ghetto were innocent.

From then on the Golem searched all carriages and wagons entering the ghetto to make sure that no false and incriminating "evidence" was hidden away. The residents of Prague were frightened because of the Golem's eerie presence, and the accusations against the inhabitants of the ghetto soon stopped. Eventually, the Prague town council issued a decree that declared the accusations against the Jewish community baseless and prohibited them from being repeated in the future. In this version of the story, the decree achieved Rabbi Loew's goal, so he decided to take life away from the Golem.

Both versions of the story of the Golem end in the same way: the Rabbi and his helpers took him to the small attic of the old synagogue, circled around him again, and once more spoke the mystical phrase that had brought the Golem to life, but this time in reverse order. They then wrapped the now lifeless Golem in a *tallit* (prayer shawl) and left him in the attic, where it is believed he remains to this very day.

The Old New Synagogue, the oldest synagogue in Europe

The Tarot of Prague

Six of Cups

Three children sit in front of an ornate and rather "fairytale" turreted house. In front of them there are six common drinking mugs. Two of the children (who actually seem slightly odd in their proportions — are they really children?) are talking and sharing a cup of something. The third child, a girl, sits quietly under an umbrella. She seems to be thinking, not really participating in the general goings-on and secure in her own space.

Short Interpretation

A card about simple goodness, trust and innocence. To some people this simplicity might seem childish or naive, and of course in a treacherous world trusting too much can be dangerous. But don't be afraid to remember what it was to be a child, or even to behave like that once again. If you share openly, whether it is emotional help, a good turn or more material assistance, the rewards can be immense.

[Minor Arcana]

Fuller Interpretation

Childhood memories • Trust and openness • Nostalgia
Giving and receiving

The Six of Cups tells us that simple goodness and openness can seem almost childlike, but this is precisely what makes it so precious; it isn't easy to be as honest and straightforward as a child.

In this card, two of the children seem to be playing at being adults (the boys are perhaps playing at shop). The girl, however, seems to be content to simply be herself. She has created a comfortable space under her umbrella and is relaxed and quietly contemplative. At first glance the scene seems very down-to-earth, just a scene of children playing. But upon closer examination there are some oddities. Firstly, the house in the background looks slightly unworldly; with its turrets and decorations it seems a little like something out of a fairytale. Then too, the proportions of the children are slightly odd, in fact they seem almost like small adults. Are they really children? Or are they grown-ups playing at being child-like? Perhaps both interpretations can be valid, depending on the context of the overall reading in which this card appears.

The Six of Cups can certainly stand for the innocent qualities of childhood that we all still carry within ourselves: simple joys and a clear conscience. This card can also be about nostalgia, playfulness, and indulging in youthful activities, an innocent sort of kindliness such as either giving or receiving help, a gift or a good turn.

Occasionally this card can specifically point toward the birth of a baby, but this is not the usual interpretation.

The Six of Cups is nearly always a good card to see in a reading. It is in complete contrast with, and a challenge to, the scheming, distrust and selfishness often seen around us. However, be aware that it can also warn of being too innocent in a dangerous world. Sometimes this card, if surrounded by "darker cards", can be the small but vulnerable light that shines in an imperfect world. The little patch of protected ground that you create for yourself may not really be able to shade you from all threats, and there are times when innocence can become dangerous naiveté.

However, having said this, the most common meaning for the Six of Cups is the simpler and lighter one of good memories, good friends and good deeds.

Sources

The children in this cup are taken from a frieze painted on a wall in Karoliny Světlé Street in "Nove Mesto" (the New Town).

The very elaborately decorated and turreted Art Nouveau building is on the corner of Pařískà Street and Široká Street, very close to the Maiselová Synagogue.

A section of the late 19th century wall decoration used in the Six of Cups

[Minor Arcana]

SEVEN OF CUPS

A man reaches toward seven cups hanging in the air in front of him. He seems both delighted and enchanted. Each cup contains is a figure of fantasy or desire. These range from a beautiful woman, a castle, and Bacchus (the God of Wine), to kings, a "green man" and the figure of a saint. All look rather out of reach and, indeed, slightly unreal.

Short Interpretation

There are so many choices laid out before you right now that it may feel bewildering. But look carefully: are some of these really just daydreams or fantasies? It may sound a little unromantic, but you may need to work out which of these tantalising possibilities are practical propositions, and which are just tempting illusions.

Fuller Interpretation

Daydreaming • Fantasies • Spoilt for choice • Head in the air

Wishful thinking, but also a kind of creative chaos. The Seven of Cups has all the creativity and emotion of the Cups suit, but it also clearly shows the underlying problem of Cups: it's all very well to have wonderful visions and fantastic dreams, but if you can't focus on a few of these and turn them into realities they all may come to nothing.

The tempting images in the cups, while they are utterly fantastic and, in some cases quite outrageous in conception, are not obviously connected to anything in particular and it's unclear exactly what they are supposed to represent or communicate. They are "fairy fantasies", images that are stimulating and in some cases lovely, but which may not add up to much.

When this card comes up in a reading it suggests that you should think hard about how to actually realise some of your daydreams, or perhaps some of the bewildering array of options that are opening up to you. These may range from very material things such as choices about the job you should take, where you should live, and the subjects you should study, to much more abstract ones. Maybe what you need to think about is whether you value stability over adventure, or if you want to pursue riches rather than spiritual knowledge. Whatever the subject of these decisions (and remember that in many ways the contents of the cups aren't as important as you being clear about what matters to you), the task now is to narrow your focus to only a few and make these real rather than allowing yourself to continue to be bewitched and befuddled by the profusion of options.

Sources

Five of the "fairy favours" springing from the cups are taken from the top cornice of the section of the Clementinum Monastery that faces on to Křižovnická Street. This façade looks classical in style, although, as you can see, on closer inspection it has some very quirky and far from classic touches. It was designed by Brunn in 1850. Because the figures on this cornice are so high up, they are rarely noticed, but in fact they are some of the most eccentric and amusing in Prague.

[Minor Arcana]

The beautiful woman comes from a Secessionist (Art Nouveau) plasterwork decoration above a door at the House of the Three Turks next to the Clementinum in Valentinská Street.

The Castle is from the lavishly carved medieval window of the Old Town Hall in Old Town Square.

The figure of the enchanted man is a Baroque wooden carving from inside the St Vitus' Cathedral. There are two of these figures, very close to the tomb of St John of Nepomuk, and both of them appear to be straining forward to see the silver angels that hang above the tomb. Each carries a small lamp, which is lit from time to time.

Eight of Cups

A hooded and cloaked woman makes her way down a long flight of steps. Behind her, abandoned, lie eight cups. The woman seems thoughtful and sombre, but not entirely unhappy. In fact, her very colourful clothes suggest a rather celebratory mood.

Short Interpretation

Time to move on. You now need to make a physical or psychological move away from a situation that's been going on for far too long. While this can be positive, it may initially be tiring and dispiriting to actually take this step. However, the weariness you feel is actually a sign that you need to change things and get away from what has now become a routine or a fruitless habit. Don't be afraid to take that first step. It will get easier, and one day you will look back and be glad you had the courage to make this change.

[Minor Arcana]

Fuller Interpretation

Moving on • Putting it behind you • Mingled regret and anticipation
First steps in finding yourself

Moving on, even when you know it's necessary, is often hard. We've all had the experience of leaving a job, a place, or a relationship, and though we know we have outgrown it we still find it hard to leave. Sometimes the difficulty of this task manifests itself as a great weariness and we tell ourselves that we will move on but not just yet, not until we feel more energetic. However, this is really a psychological trap. The weariness is probably a sign that you need to act and change things quickly, to extricate yourself from a situation that has become stagnant and unfruitful. This move can be physical or psychological and while the results will be positive, it can also feel tiring and dispiriting to actually have to do it.

The figure on this card is wrapped and hooded, as though she is both preparing herself for a long journey and also, in a sense, trying to slip away unrecognised. Her pose is almost one of mourning, although her bright clothes make it clear that there is also a sense of celebration or gaity about what she is doing.

This woman isn't really at the beginning of the journey, in fact the long, long flight of steps behind her indicates that she has been moving in a definite direction for some time. However, she has only just abandoned the cups, leaving them on the pavement behind her and turning away, about to drop the last one dangling in her hand. Sometimes when we make the final decision to move on the reality is that we have been moving towards this point for a while, without quite recognising it.

Sources

The woman is from one of the spectacular Art Nouveau paintings of saints in the interior of the Church of St Peter and St Paul in Vyšehrad.

The steps she is walking down (called Zámecké schody) lead from the top of Nerudova Street to the Hradčanské náměstí (Castle Square). These stairs lead past the back of the 16th-century Schwarzenberg-Lobowitz Palace, a wonderful building covered entirely in sgraffito decoration. The Two of Cups incorporates the picture of a mermaid from this building.

NINE OF CUPS

A man sits happily in a *hospoda* (a Czech beer hall). The little waiter at his side is there to continually fill his cup. Behind him is a richly-painted screen showing many of the good things of the natural world. On the shelf are nine wine glasses, and at his feet a contented Puss in Boots lounges. All is well!

Short Interpretation

The Nine of Cups is often called the "wish card" because it is about having all our wishes fulfilled, even if in the end these are quite simple. It is a reminder that just having "ordinary" things like good company, great food and drink, and a comfortable place to live can be a wonderful blessing.

[Minor Arcana]

Fuller Interpretation

Earthly pleasures • Simple contentment • Satisfaction and well-being
Having a good time

The "Wish card" is about the fulfilment of all sorts of desires, but mainly of a very down-to-earth or sensual kind. It's about the pleasure of harmless self-indulgence, without any attached guilt. This card may seem a little smug at times, but not in a very serious way. It really is saying "sometimes it's great to just have a good time and relish it". The Nine of Cups may imply a short period of "letting your hair down" while you feel the satisfaction of your wishes being fulfilled, or it may mean a more extended period of pleasure. Whichever it is, enjoy it.

Like all the cards, the interpretation of this card depends on the context. Even the "wish card" can carry a slight warning, and in this case it's simply "be careful what you wish for". Though this card is about getting what you want and enjoying yourself, it doesn't mean that you should throw away all sense of responsibility, or allow yourself to get too full of yourself or complacent. However, if you avoid these pitfalls everything the Nine of Cups promises can be enjoyed fully and deservedly.

The man in this card is sitting in a tavern, but he doesn't look at all like a drunkard; he seems more like a countryman who is accustomed to being outdoors. The tavern is a place for him to relax and to celebrate. There is no dark side to this card and no implication that the man is in any way prone to over-indulge in food or drink. He is merely, at this moment, taking a simple and direct pleasure in his good fortune. The cat lounging at his feet is "Puss in Boots", who in fairytales is the adorable rogue and great lover of the good life. We like Puss because we can identify with him and smile at his outrageously simple and straightforward ambitions. In the Puss in Boots tales he achieves his wishes with cunning, but without actually causing harm to anyone; he just wants to be able to enjoy good food, good company and comfortable surroundings. In the end he gets all this and we are glad to see him living "happily ever after", just as we should be glad to see the simple successes that the "wish card" signifies.

The presence of Puss in Boots also reminds us that there is a saying that there are times when we should be "selfish as a cat", i.e. not harmfully or deeply selfish, but simply self-seeking in the sense of being like an innocent animal that just enjoys sensual gratification. There is nothing wrong with these simple, earthly pleasures if we indulge in them occasionally and honestly. There are times, after all, when we all benefit from being uncomplicated about enjoying the comforts of life.

Sources

The image of the man in the tavern is taken from a group of folk-style paintings on the façade of a house on the corner of Valentinská and Veleslavínova. They all show ordinary scenes of happy family life. The little waiter is from the wall of one of the inner courtyards in the U Fleků beer hall. In the original he is holding up his tray to a woman who appears to have just taken a plump roasted chicken from the oven, and the scene is reminiscent of one from a Germanic fairytale.

The painted panels in the background are very old panels that used to be on the ceiling of the Vrtbovská Palace. They were moved in order to better preserve them, and are now in the entrance hall which visitors pass through to enter the famous Vrtbovská Baroque gardens.

The "Puss in Boots" (who we just had to include) can be found far above the street as part of a façade in Karlova Street situated just by the House of the Golden Well (see the Ten of Swords). He is part of a particularly well-executed Art Nouveau group on the house.

Ten of Cups

A family is together in the gardens of a fine-looking house. They seem very loving, and glad to share their happiness with one another. Above them is a garland of flowers and golden leaves. Below them stand ten wine cups.

Short interpretation

There is tremendous joy in your home and family life and you feel well off and content. The happiness that comes from things close to home, like close family and long-term relationships, can often be more fulfilling than new or spectacular pleasures. Recognise the deep joy of your domestic tranquillity; its value can't be overestimated.

The Tarot of Prague

Fuller Interpretation

"Wonderful world" • Sheer joy in life • Family and domestic happiness

This card is about happiness and good fortune in all things, but especially in familial and domestic areas. It's about being well-off in a material sense, but more than that it's also about finding contentment and harmony, and a general sense of peace and well-being.

It can also stand for any family event and for improved family relationships. It's about the happiness that comes from close, long-term relationships, and also the conscious appreciation of that happiness.

The image in this card shows a large family, grandfather, parents and children, all smiling and apparently at ease with one another. They seem both happy and relaxed to be together. Around them are the sunny gardens of a palatial mansion. They are not particularly richly dressed, so it isn't clear whether they are the owners of the house or simply pleased to be there for the moment. However, while not obviously rich, this family does look comfortable. All are well, if not lavishly, dressed, and the children are positively blooming with health.

Sources

This family is taken from the series of wall paintings on the façade of the 19th century Wiehluv dům, a richly-decorated house on the corner of Vodičková Street and Wenceslas Square.

The gardens in the background are those of the Wallenstein Palace. The colonnaded building in the garden is the famous Salla Terrena (a type of garden room popular in the Renaissance). Prague Castle can be seen in the far distance.

Page of Cups

A youthful figure stands on a platform in the centre of the river. In the water at her feet a little mermaid frolics and holds up a wreath of water flowers. However, the Page gazes at his cup, apparently oblivious to her.

Short Interpretation

This is a good time to channel your emotions and creativity in a light-hearted way, especially if you are at the beginning of a project or relationship. What you are starting may not be profound or earth shattering, but it will feel poetic, romantic and very sweet. Taking a rather carefree approach to new things can be enjoyable sometimes and it may let you use your strong imagination and sense of humour to the full. So by all means be reflective and thoughtful in what you are doing, but also be a little playful. The results will be none the worse for it.

Fuller Interpretation

Creative imagination • Untroubled sensitivity • Psychic abilities
Intimacy and imagination • Reflection and study

The Page is always more light-hearted than the other Court Cards. While some of this simply comes from youth and a slightly child-like approach to life, it can also manifest itself as a rather gauche but attractive enthusiasm. Like all the Cups, the Page of Cups is emotional and intuitive, often in response to another person, but perhaps, as in the case of this card, as part of a new project. He is unafraid to experience emotion and to show it. He is also very responsive to beauty and to the arts in general, and in matters of creativity this aspect of the Page will be particularly noticeable, probably pointing towards involvement in an artistic project, in collaboration with other people.

It is a card of sensitivity, intuition and intimacy, and also of enthusiasm in studies and learning. It doesn't have quite the rounded creative achievement of the Queen of Cups, and in terms of work, studies or projects it may imply something romantic, touching and passionate, though perhaps not profound. Of course, in many projects (and, for that matter, relationships), seriousness and profound meanings are not appropriate, and the Page is often an excellent card to see when you are undertaking something you want to be meaningful and to have a real artistic quality, and yet still be enjoyable in a light-hearted and sociable way.

As with all the Page cards, this card may indicate messages or news. In the case of the Page of Cups, this news is likely to relate to artistic or studious projects, though possibly these will be of an enjoyable but rather minor kind.

The picture on this card shows a Page who is slightly other-worldly and dreamy. The rock he stands on actually seems to be floating rather than firmly grounded (the mermaid's tail goes clear under the rock and out on the other side) which may symbolise that the Page is himself a little ungrounded. The mermaid herself signfies the rather poetic and romantic aspects of the Page. He seems to half-ignore her, however, caught up instead in rapturous contemplation of his golden cup.

[Minor Arcana]

Sources

The statue is from a group of statues on an early 18th-century plague column in Hradčanské náměstí (Castle Square) by Ferdinand Brokoff. Another statue from this column has been used for the Six of Pentacles.

The mermaid is from a painting in the Salla Terrena (a lavish garden room popular among wealthy families in the Renaissance) in the Wallenstein Gardens in Malá Strana.

One of three panels showing mermaids at the Wallenstein Palace's Sala Terrena

Knight of Cups

This Knight rides a horse high above the rooftops of old Prague. He is happy, but possibly oblivious to the fact that his horse is asleep (or even unconscious?). Floating above his cup is a shining golden face surrounded by rays of light. The whole image has the unreality of a dream, but this dreamer is enjoying himself and doesn't particularly want to wake up.

Short Interpretation

You are a dreamer, but happily so. Perhaps that's fine, but remember that it's easy to dream your life away, riding high above everything without ever really connecting. Maybe it's time to come down to earth for a while and put those dreams and imaginings into practice?

[Minor Arcana]

Fuller Interpretation

Lost in fantasy • Lack of commitment • The Happy Dreamer
Head in the clouds

The creativity and imagination associated with Cups make the Knight of Cups a very attractive figure. However, while he is both amusing and stimulating to be around, his weakness lies in his constant dreaminess and detachment from the world. He is somewhat escapist, adores flights of fantasy, and finds it difficult to ever come back down to earth. He is very given to building castles in the sky, which is charming, but very frustrating at times for those around him.

As a colleague he is likely to be stimulating and full of imagination, but ineffectual when it comes to practical matters. As a lover, he may seem passionate and lovely to be around, but he probably won't commit in a practical way to anything or anyone, and may sometimes be rather narcissistic and caught up in his own individual dreams.

While the knight on this card is flying happily above the rooftops of a fairytale snowy Prague, he doesn't seem to have noticed that his horse is asleep, or, even worse, unconscious. There is something thrillingly fantastic about the image, but where is the knight really headed? If he can come gently to land, while retaining some of his ability to make flights of the imagination, then he may be able to achieve a more successful and productive balance in his life.

The king's sleeping or dead horse is a reference to the connections that are occasionally drawn between this card and the Death card (for instance Rachel Pollack goes into this resemblance in some detail in her book *Seventy Eight Degrees of Wisdom*). There is a sense in which, like Death, the Knight of Cups is about loss of identity. However, in the Knight's case, it's a matter of someone who loses himself in fantasy, and this is rather different from the more dramatic loss of identity and self that is implied by the Death card.

The radiant golden face hovering above his cup is a more positive symbol that signifies not only the knight's visionary aspects, but also the fact that his visions are beautiful, even if they tend to remain on a higher plane and are never quite brought to any real fruition.

Sources

There are a lot of statues of "good" King Wenceslas in Prague, but this wild modern one by David Černy is a favourite. It currently hangs in the Lucerna, a Secession-style shopping passage off Wenceslas Square. King Wenceslas is very much a symbol of Prague, and in the days of the "Prague Spring" liberation movement the old statue of the King on Wenceslas Square was a rallying point for peaceful protest until the communist government surrounded it with bushes to keep people from laying flowers there. The source of our Knight of Cups therefore signifies joyful freedom and liberation.

The knight's cup is from the sign of a 16th-century goldsmith's house at 16 Nerudova Street. The sign dates from 1682, but the beautiful gilding was added in the 18th century.

David Černý's sculpture at the Lucerna Palace

[Minor Arcana]

Queen of Cups

The Queen is looking calmly into her cup. She is dressed in quite elaborate and archaic clothes, giving her an ageless and rather "fairy tale" appearance. Beneath her feet are a merman and merchild, a link to the element of water associated with Cups but also an indicator of family and community. In the background are the river and the waterfront towers of the buildings that line the bank.

Short Interpretation

The Queen of Cups signifies a rare and wonderful balance between intellect, creativity and the emotions. When this Queen is in your life she can bring tremendous gifts of imagination and vision that can actually be put to productive use. Perhaps she is sometimes a little too dreamy, but her poetic and creative abilities are so strong that she is in no danger of being lost in her reveries and she will always be able to turn dreams into reality.

Fuller Interpretation

Warm and caring intelligence • Creative action and accomplishment • Imagination and achievement • Sense *and* sensibility

Creative and intellectual harmony and balance is at the heart of this card. The Queens of the Tarot are in many ways the most balanced of the Court Cards, and this Queen is the most balanced, successful and harmonious of them all. Loving and loveable, she is arguably the most positive card of the Minor Arcana and can be interpreted as a more down-to-earth version of the joyful dancer shown in The World card of the Major Arcana. The Queen is able to strike a balance between the dreaminess and passivity of the Knight of Cups and the self-disciplined repression of the King. She alone manages to be compassionate, sensitive and considerate of the feelings of other, while still remaining capable of taking creative action and making a real impact. At the same time, she is in touch with the more psychic, spiritual and intuitive aspects of life, though in a less awesome or detached way than the High Priestess. This Queen is very much part of life and happily involved in it.

There is a strong contrast between the "lightness" and relaxation of the Queen in this card and the rather stiff and buttoned-up appearance of her King. Though she looks rather other-worldly and slightly "fey" she doesn't seem unapproachable.

The Merman and merchild at her feet signify two aspects of the Queen. One is her general harmony with water, the element of Cups. The other is her connection with children, family and community.

Sources

This image is taken from the 1701 statue of "St Barbara between St Catherine and St Elizabeth" by Jan Brokoff and Ferdinand Maximilian Brokoff on the Charles Bridge. The background scene is the Old Town bank of the river. The shells are from the Baroque Vrtbovská garden, which has a theme of seashells and mermaids throughout its statuary.

The Merman and merchild are from the staircase of the Troja Chateau. Troja was built in the late 17th century as a magnificent country residence for Count Sternberg (it is now in the Prague suburbs but was originally surrounded by parkland and vineyards.)

[Minor Arcana]

King of Cups

He sits on a platform on the river. Though his face is warm and kind, he looks rather tightly dressed and seems to be holding himself in. He ignores the seductive mermaid with two tails that frolics next to his throne.

Short Interpretation

You are dutiful, mature and sensible, but perhaps you're not entirely comfortable with your responsibilities? Maybe you'd like to break out, throw caution to the winds for a while and be a bit more creative? At heart, you'll always put responsibility before self-expression, and this is no bad thing. Just don't forget to pursue your own dreams from time to time. In the end, not everything depends on you.

Fuller Interpretation

Bowing to your responsibilities • Repressed imagination
Controlled creativity • Deciding to put head before heart

Like all the Kings, the King of Cups is mature and responsible, with considerable accomplishments to his name. However, he is not entirely comfortable in his role as a respectable conservative in society. While he maintains self-discipline and dignity, in many ways he would rather be cavorting with the mermaids.

He has not lost his creativity (it is still very much alive and kicking), but because he has chosen to channel it towards more upstanding and socially responsible activities he at times feels restricted and frustrated. This is a King who can seem "super straight-laced" simply because he knows that if he let go even a little he might quickly revert to a kind of madcap artistry and rebelliousness. Usually, he is a likeable enough character, who is simply very aware of his role and his responsibility. However, in some circumstances he can be troubled and troubling, and his severe self-repression may manifest itself as anger and resentment. In these cases, it becomes important for the King to forget duty, even briefly, and pursue his own dreams and emotions.

Like all the Cups, the meaning of the King changes somewhat when he is directly associated with the arts. In that context, he can stand for a mature talent who has achieved recognition and a respectable place in society. An example of this kind of King would be the artist or musician who, after a wild and outrageous youth, later finds himself bestowed with honorary degrees and a place on the board of a worthy arts institution.

In the image on this card, the King is literally rather buttoned-up. He is dressed properly, and even quite stylishly, but he gives the impression that he doesn't feel very comfortable. He holds his cup stiffly, showing that even when he is allowing himself to be creative and emotional, he never relaxes and forgets his responsibilities. A mermaid cavorts in the water in front of him. She is actually a melusine, the two-tailed mermaid popular in medieval courtly romances who, so the story goes, wed a human man. She represents wild romance, and the call of something untamed and unearthly. However, the King studiously ignores her seductive presence and stays firmly pinned to his throne, showing an iron resolve to put head and duty before heart and impulse.

[Minor Arcana]

Sources

The King himself is from our old Bohemian deck. In the original he is, appropriately enough, the "Hearts King".

His cup is from a door sign in Nerudova Street, very close to the sign of the red lion with a cup used in the Ace of Cups.

The melusine (a mermaid with two tales) in the water beside him is from a group of magical figures on Smetanovo nábřeží. The original composition also includes a dwarf, a cow, an eagle, a lion (all used on The World card), a dragon and a sphinx. For other cards taken from these statues, see the Six of Swords and the Page of Wands.

For more on the myth of the melusine, see the Two of Cups.

The scene in the background is a view of the Old Town end of the Charles Bridge.

The "King of Hearts" from the traditional Bohemian 32-card pack

The Tarot of Prague

MINOR ARCANA - SWORDS

Swords

The Swords' element is Air, and this suit is associated with all aspects of the mind, primarily the intellect and the ability to be analytical, dispassionate and reasonable. Swords demonstrate honesty, objectivity, fairness and, on occasion, a fair amount of sharp wit. However, the suit does have a distinctly negative side. Swords can be so cool and logical that they become insensitive and thoughtless. They tend to be very self-assured and confident that they are right, to the extent of being opinionated and dismissive of any differing points of view and this means they can often be confrontational.

If the Swords were artists they would be Constructivists: very challenging on the intellectual and analytical level, but unconcerned with, or even hostile to, sensual or emotional pleasures and frequently determined to be controversial and argumentative.

It is the ability to think concisely and with razor-sharp precision that makes Swords such a strong suit. However, though many people seem to value intellect above all else, a balance must be achieved between the intellect of Swords and the emotions, ability to act, and practicality of the other suits. Swords is often seen as the "bad" suit of the Tarot, and it does indeed contain more cards with a potentially negative reading than any represented by the other suits. However, the interpretation of most of the cards does very much depend on context. Even the rather dreaded Three and Ten of Swords are not entirely bad or doom-laden.

The Ace of Swords is an exceptionally good card to see if you are starting something that requires logic and learning. It is at once incisive and energetic. The Two of Swords is about balancing and controlling the emotions. Like all the Twos, it shows that though things are stable now, this will soon begin to change. Holding emotions at bay in this way cannot be continued for long. In the Three of Swords the delicate balance has been lost, and sorrow and even despair have set in. This is a difficult card, though it does carry the implied advice that the best way to deal with sorrow is to accept it and wait for happier times to come. The appearance of the Four of Swords indicates the need to rest and recuperate, and to temporarily withdraw from the passion and intensity of life. This is a respite from the restless intellect, activity and (at times) the disturbing emotions of the Swords.

As in the other suits, the Five very clearly reveals problematic aspects of Swords. The inclination to attack any situation head-on (present in many of the Swords cards) can result in the humiliating defeat signified by the Five of Swords. In this situation the best recourse may simply be to slink away and retreat.

The Six of Swords shows another quiet period, though one that is much more troubled than that seen in the Four. It indicates the undertaking of a difficult journey, during which it's important to be as calm as possible. The journey may simply be a physical move to somewhere unfamiliar, or it may be much more psychological in nature. Whatever its form, to successfully complete this journey requires calmness, resignation and acceptance. Like many of the Sixes, this is an odd card, said to carry a message of silence and change.

Sevens are about decisions, and in the case of the Seven of Swords the problem is that the decisions are hasty and not thought through. This card can stand for a sudden burst of revenge, or some petty nastiness, or simply a rash action that irritates everyone but achieves nothing. It isn't a card of enormous import or weight, but rather of silliness, stupidity and annoying trivial attempts to draw attention to oneself.

With the Eight, the tension of having to make a decision has become a struggle against paralysis in order to take control and to act. All the Eights are about moving on, but in the Eight of Swords a self-imposed prison prevents the necessary first steps from being taken. The seemingly impregnable walls of this prison are psychological rather than real, but to escape you first you need to be willing to see the true situation, rather than blinding yourself to it.

The Nine is typically a very down-to-earth distillation of the suit's qualities, and as this is Swords these qualities are troubling. The situation shown in this card is that of nightmarish despair which may rather histrionic. Like all the Swords, there is a sense that much of this trouble exists in the mind. Applying just a bit of cool, rational thinking can conquer this despair. The swords that seem to be threatening may not strike at all if this calm approach is taken.

By the Ten, the sense of threat and despair has become something more real. This card often shows a situation in which the very lowest point of a

[Minor Arcana]

difficult situation has been reached. As with all the Swords, the reference may primarily be to a psychological state rather than a physical event. However, in the Ten, unlike the Nine, this doesn't usually point to a hysterical or overstated reaction to events, but a real moment of being under attack or anguish. As this is Swords the implication is that the best way to get through this is by applying calm, logical thought or deep meditation, rather than by taking any specific action.

Court Cards

In Swords, the qualities of Court Cards are applied to the intellect and reason. The energy of the Page is to a large degree directed towards being watchful and alert. This Page is vigilant and, uncharacteristically for Pages, conscientious and responsible beyond his years; but he may also be secretive and at times too guarded.

The Knight of Swords, however, certainly doesn't wait and watch. He is all action and courage. He has a tendency to charge in, as the saying goes, "where angels fear to tread", and when a situation calls for incisive action he is always able to provide it. However, he has no sense of restraint or tact and will sometimes see conflict where none is intended.

The Queen of Swords is altogether less frenzied and more thoughtful. Like all the Queens, she manages to balance the negatives and the positives, which in the case of Swords means balancing the rather harmful inclination toward physical and mental conflict, with the helpful ability to apply intelligence and rationality. The Queen of Swords has experienced trouble in her life, and may well have been involved in fighting and struggle at some points. However, she has come through this with added self-confidence and wisdom gleaned from these experiences. As the clear thinker and clear speaker of Swords, she will always give you straightforward and sound advice, even if it may hurt to hear the truth.

The King shares his Queen's mental agility and incisiveness, but this is turned less towards his immediate friends and colleagues and more towards the formal and ordered facets of the community around him. He is very much judge and stern authority, always fair, but not always kind. He has tremendous command and authority, and will exert this in the way he thinks best, regardless of popular opinion.

The overall message of Swords is that incisive, intelligent thinking is vital – life can't be based entirely on intuition and emotions. However, the down side is that this kind of intense thinking can turn inward and become rather neurotic. If intellect is to be truly positive it needs to be active and outward-looking, like Wands, and also must be balanced with some sound common sense such as that provided by Pentacles and also with the emotional sensitivity of Cups.

ACE OF SWORDS

An armoured hand holds a straight sword wreathed in a crown and golden leaves. The red roofs of the old city below stretch into the distance. Golden 'yods' hang in the air around the blade.

Short Interpretation

The Ace of Swords is the supreme card of new intellectual pursuits. Using your mind incisively and with real clarity is a huge advantage in life. There is a danger, however, of focusing on this as a way of keeping your emotions in check. Try to balance your intellectual power with some sensitivity. The richest achievements are usually the result of a blend of rationality and feeling.

Fuller Interpretation

Intellect • A new opportunity for learning and developing your mind
Bravery and courage • Force – sometimes to excess • Triumph

The Ace of Swords points to opportunities requiring mental and intellectual strength. There may be a new situation that demands analysis, logic and reason, or perhaps there is an opportunity to develop the mind. Whichever it is, this card implies that the opportunity will be seized with tremendous strength and forcefulness, and pursued with courage.

For the most part this is good, and the Ace of Swords is a great card to see if you are about to launch into a fresh activity that demands intellectual effort, or if you are going to champion a cause that requires some clear thinking. However, bear in mind that this card is so forceful that it can imply excessive dominance. Like most Swords, the Ace can be double-edged. Make sure that you don't pursue your goals with such force and focus that you cut out other people.

The image on this card shows an armoured hand. It implies strength, but also perhaps some hardness and a willingness to fight. The sword is topped by a glowing crown signifying triumph, and also by golden leaves and *yods* (a Hebrew symbol used in the traditional RWS cards to indicate vigour and the life force) to show the sheer, irresistible vitality of this Ace.

In this picture the whole city seems to be spread out for the taking. However, any triumph will not be through violence but through the power of incisive thought. Curiously, though this card shows a sword, in many ways the message is that the pen is mightier than the sword; in other words, that intellect will often achieve more than physical force.

Sources

The armoured hand is from a suit of armour outside an antique shop in Josefov (the old Jewish quarter). The crown is from the front of a Baroque house that is now the U Krála Karle Hotel in Úvoz Street, and the beautiful bunches of golden grapes are from a decoration on a Baroque house in Prokopská Street, both in Malá Strana.

The background is also Malá Strana, showing the red-tiled roofs of this quarter seen from rooftop height at the top of Nerudova Street.

Two of Swords

A blindfolded woman stands on a riverbank. She holds two swords above her head in a gesture that is perhaps defensive, perhaps defiant. Her feet look solidly planted, but this is not a stance she can hold forever. Sooner or later she will have to lower the heavy swords. Sitting in front of her is a very anxious-looking lion wearing a crown that appears to be slipping from his head.

Short Interpretation

Right now you just want to keep the world out. You refuse to see what's around you, or to have anything to do with it. You'd rather put up a barrier against emotions than acknowledge what you feel and make the necessary difficult decisions. This position may feel safe, but you can't maintain it forever. Maybe it's time to start getting involved again? If you take off the blindfold and let down your defensive shield you could be having a lot more fun.

Fuller Interpretation

Blocking out the world • Keeping yourself safe – at least for a while • Anxiety and defensiveness • Refusing to face up to things
Putting up barriers

Perhaps appropriately, this card has two, rather different, potential meanings. The first is about managing to achieve concord, harmony and balance in difficult or threatening circumstances. The second, which is more negative with respect to social and human affairs (and more typical of Swords) is that of blocked or repressed emotions, feeling psychologically trapped, and of not facing reality and closing one's eyes to the truth.

The appropriate interpretation in a reading will very much depend on the underlying situation. The indication may be that a person who looks very much in control of a difficult situation is in fact feeling the strain. While the barrier made by the two swords is effective, it's hard to maintain this stance and sooner or later it will simply be too much of an effort.

The woman in this card stands with her feet firmly planted on the banks of a river. In many ways she is exposed to the world, but she holds up her swords defiantly as if to ward off anyone who might approach her. She looks triumphant and strong, but she is blindfolded, so there is also an impression that she is in some ways a victim or captive. Her hands, however, are not tied, and she could easily remove this blindfold if only she could bring herself to first lay down her swords.

In front of her is a lion, looking extremely worried. Although he wears a crown he does not look as though he has any authority. In fact, he looks a little helpless. He represents the aspects of this card that are about anxiety and psychological defensiveness. The lion is actually strong, possessing both physical strength and a powerful status, but he is paralysed by angst.

In many ways, the image on the card is reminiscent of the Eight of Swords, in which a similarly blindfolded woman is trapped within a circle of swords. In the Two, however, the woman is more active and less of a victim. She has chosen to put up a barrier between herself and the world. In some situations this is valid; there are times when you must defend yourself in order to maintain control and keep yourself safe. However, the

[Minor Arcana]

main point to remember here is that if you try to maintain your defences or control for too long it will leave you worn out, anxious and, perhaps, powerless. You need to judge when the time is right to lower the barrier, look truthfully at your situation, and decide what to do next.

Sources

The woman is from an old photograph of the murals on the walls of the main Prague Post Office in Jindřišska Street. Vitězlav Karel Mašek (1865-1927) created these murals. The original paintings are all about postal, transport and telegraphic services. We added the swords to the woman, who originally held the shield of the city of Prague in her hands.

The background is the embankment at the Charles Bridge on the Old Town side of the Vltava.

The anxious lion is one of our favourites of the many Prague lions. He is from the stucco façade of the House of the Golden Well in Karlova Street. It dates from 1714, which is when the last major plague epidemic in Bohemia and Austria finally ended. The façade is believed to have been a thanks-giving for the end of the plague — however, the expressions of the two lions that form part of the group imply that much anxiety remained. For another card taken from this façade, see the Ten of Swords.

The Tarot of Prague

Three of Swords

Three swords pierce a heart that is held aloft by three cherubs. In the background are the roofs of the Old Town. The scene is dark and the light has a greenish tinge – there seems to be a storm brewing.

Short Interpretation

There is only one way to deal with heartbreak, and that's to accept it and realise that even the most violent emotional storms blow themselves out. It may sound trite, but it really is better to have loved and lost than never to have loved at all.

[Minor Arcana]

Fuller Interpretation

Heartbreak • Grief over a loved one • Being stabbed in the back
Pain and sorrow

This card is not a happy one and has few redeeming features. It signifies terrible heartache and sorrow, probably concerning a loved one. Because of the swords, this card is sometimes taken to indicate an actual illness or death, but in fact this would be an unusual interpretation. It's much more likely to point towards betrayal by someone you trusted. Remember, however, that it doesn't always indicate your own loss, it can occasionally mean that it is your behaviour that has brought sorrow to someone else.

Take this card as a warning when it comes up in a reading. Sometimes it is there as a strong indication that you need to look around to see what's happening. Is someone cheating on your business? Is your close friend or partner letting you down behind your back? Sometimes it's so painful to see such betrayal that we avoid looking until it's too late. Face up to things bravely and you may be able to prevent the worst from happening.

In this image, three cherubs hold a pierced heart. These cherubs remind us that in love, betrayal is one of the risks we must accept. However, to most of us it is a risk worth taking. Yes, we may be terribly hurt sometimes, but even if this happens it shouldn't prevent us from being willing to give our heart and our trust again. The worst, lasting damage that betrayal can do is to make us too bitter to love again. Don't let this happen. Even if you are hurt, get over it and accept it, and don't let it rock your fundamental belief in people.

Sources

The statue of the cherubs and the heart can be found on the Charles Bridge. We coloured the heart red; in the original it is weathered stone. The rooftops are those of the group of buildings around the Clementinum and Karlova Street in the Old Town. Particularly prominent is the large cupola of the Church of St. Francis Seraphim, which is inside the Clementinum, the former Jesuit monastery and library complex.

Four of Swords

Two wooden effigies, a man and a woman, lie against a stone wall. Above them four swords are at rest. In the wall there is one window, through which one can see a monk who seems to be giving a rather stern blessing. The scene is one of silence and withdrawal, but it isn't unhappy, merely quiet and a little sombre.

Short Interpretation

This is a time to stop fighting and simply withdraw, rest quietly, and recuperate. When the time comes to get involved in things again, you will feel healthier and more energised because you took this quiet period of retreat.

[Minor Arcana]

Fuller Interpretation

Time out from the fray • Rest and recuperation • A pause to reflect
Mental silence and stillness

No matter how much it's in your nature to be active, there are times when the best action is actually to take a break, get away from what is going on around you, and give yourself a chance to recuperate. Whether this involves meditating deeply about the situation, or simply pausing to reflect and take stock, it will leave you in a much better position to act effectively later.

If you give yourself some downtime to prepare emotionally and physically for a testing time ahead it can often make a huge difference to your eventual success in meeting the challenge. So take some time out, enjoy this period of contemplation and stillness, and later when you re-enter the fray you will be refreshed and recharged.

The image in this card shows a man and woman lying down with arms crossed on their chests. They look very like the effigies from medieval tombs, but if you look closer their expressions are actually quite lively. They seem merely to be resting. The stained glass window showing a monk indicates that whole scene is set in a church, or a religious place. This is not so much a reference to spirituality as to meditation. Churches are quiet spaces for contemplation. For centuries they were also places of asylum, affording temporary refuge from troubled times.

Sources

The two figures were found on the door of a small Baroque villa just beside the Čertovska, or "Devil's Channel", on Kampa Island. This building was badly affected by the devastating 2002 floods, and if you look carefully you can see some cracks in the woodcarvings caused by their being under water for some time.

The wall is actually one of the walls of the older of the two Charles Bridge towers at Malá Strana. The tower dates from the 14th century, and the stone has some beautiful scars and signs of its age.

The window is part of an Art Nouveau stained glass window in St Vitus' Cathedral by Alfons Mucha. It is a gorgeous example of his style.

Five of Swords

Three soldiers are disgraced. Their fight with a dragon has been laughably unsuccessful and they slink away as the dragon shouts and breaths smoke after them. Five of their swords have been tried and have failed, and the triumphant dragon now possesses them all. If you look closely you can see that the soldiers wear white feathers on their helmets, an emblem of their disgrace.

Short Interpretation

Acting out of self-interest is definitely necessary sometimes, but be careful: if it becomes simply selfish and narrow, then it's time to step back and try to see things in a more communal and co-operative way. If all you can see is your own point of view and interests, you will quickly feel hostile and isolated, and this could even lead to acts of deceit and betrayal. Try to find a "win-win" solution that is good both for you and others.

[Minor Arcana]

Fuller Interpretation

Meanness and sneakiness • Defeat by dubious means • Selfishness
Dishonour

This card can imply that there are times when it is necessary to be selfish and act in your own interests, but it also carries a strong warning that if taken too far, that selfishness can become hostile, self-defeating, and can lead to a narrow view of the world, and to self-interested, deceitful and dishonourable behaviour.

The dragon has often been associated in Europe with cunning and slyness, as well as with fieriness. In Western mythology it's a beast that is as likely to overcome its adversaries by deceit as by brute force. It is also famously solitary and greedy. The dragon is a strong creature that usually wins its battles, but it has a reputation for being miserly and xenophobic, even towards others of its own kind. It also has a habit of gloating over its ill-gotten hoard of gold. This is appropriate as this card implies not just a deceitful act, but also the tendency to gloat over getting "one up" on other people.

All this perhaps explains, in part, why the dragon in Christian and pre-Christian iconography is often used as a symbol of sin. Time and again, medieval and Renaissance sculptors showed saints treading dragons underfoot as an allegory of the need to overcome sin and sinful thought and behaviour. Our dragon is green with emerald eyes, to specifically indicate jealousy and envy.

This card shows a scene in which no one has really come out the better. The soldiers, presumably sent to kill the dragon, have lost almost all of their swords and are now running away ignominiously. The once proud crests on their helmets have been transformed into the white feathers of the coward. They don't even have enough courage to retreat openly, but instead are trying to both tiptoe and hurry at the same time, a laughable sight. They look the epitome of disgrace.

The dragon is ineffectually breathing out smoke. It looks frightening and victorious, but what has it really gained? Only a few swords, which, when held in its claws look like ludicrous toys.

The Tarot of Prague

Sources

The beautiful but angry dragon is from a 1902 mural of "St George and the Dragon" on the courtyard walls at "U Fleků", which is one of the most famous beer halls in Prague. The Nine of Cups shows another figure, a little boy, from U Fleků. The Devil card is also partly based on the same wall paintings.

The three, shifty soldiers running away are from much older (mid-1500s) sgraffito pictures on the Martinic Palace, on the corner of Kanovnická Street. In the original they are part of a picture showing a scene from the life of St Joseph. For more cards that show pictures from these sgraffiti, see the Seven of Swords, The Devil and Strength.

The background shows the Petřín Lookout Tower (Petřínska rozhledna) This is a 60 metre high scaled-down copy of the Eiffel Tower, built in 1891 on the occasion of the Jubilee Exhibition in Prague. It was closed to the public for many years but was finally opened again in March 2002 after major reconstruction.

The original "George and the Dragon" wall painting at U Fleků

[Minor Arcana]

Six of Swords

A woman sits on a raft that is being guided to shore by a hooded man. She looks thoughtfully at the two children who she holds in her arms. On the water a swan floats peacefully – it seems as though the place where they will land will be tranquil and calm. In the background, a water wheel turns.

Short Interpretation

One of the strangest cards of the Tarot, the Six of Swords points towards the need for quiet and calm while passing through a time of sorrow, difficulty or transition. Unlike most of the Swords (except the Four), it is a card of silence and inaction. Any activity at this time should be mental or intellectual, rather than physical. The journey you are taking is very much a passage through a period in your life. You will travel through this and come to your journey's end safely, but at the moment it's important to be peaceful and remain serene and unafraid.

The Tarot of Prague

Fuller Interpretation

Taking a journey, maybe a mental one • Feeling blue
Going quietly though a troubled time • Acceptance of difficulties

This is a rather ambiguous card that has two possible meanings. The first and most typical is about feeling low, or having an attack of the 'blues'. Usually this depression is nothing severe, but it still leaves you with little emotion or energy to do anything. If you are feeling generally listless, sometimes just sitting back and accepting a quiet lull in your life is better than trying to struggle against the situation.

The alternate meaning of this card points to travel and transition. On one level this could be a simple journey, such as taking a business trip, but it could be something more violent and less voluntary, such as being uprooted from one's home. Because of the unsettled aspect of Swords, it is more likely to mean some sort of imposed and stressful trip rather than something joyful like a holiday. At a deeper level, the journey indicated can be a journey of the mind or soul; a transition to a different state of being. Read in this way, this card can be a little like the Judgement card in the Major Arcana, although the transition that it indicates is not so much a complete rebirth as it is of simply moving into a different period in your life. In other words, the result will be significant, but not necessarily life-transforming.

An air of stillness and poignant beauty hangs over the picture. The man pushing the raft along is going about his task quietly. He is hooded and his face is hidden. He is a little reminiscent of Charon, the silent ferryman from Greek myth who took souls across the river Styx to the Underworld. The symbolic figure of the ferryman is wide-spread, appearing in Irish, Norse and Japanese myths, as well as Greek and Roman. There is obviously something deeply archetypal about the image of a person being ferried over a river. It seems to represent transition and "crossing over" in quite a universal way.

The woman and children in the boat look thoughtful and rather sad. Where are they going? It's impossible to guess, but this looks like a journey that is more about psychological need than practical necessity. The woman takes nothing with her except the children who she obviously cares for deeply. They seem to have no baggage and not even any visible

[Minor Arcana]

provisions. However, the swan floating behind them is a symbol of both gracefulness and peace. The overall image suggests the woman and her children will continue to travel quietly, wherever their journey takes them, and will accept their destination with good grace. The water wheel that can be seen in the distance is a reminder of the wheel of fortune and signifies the twists and turns of fate.

Sources

The man poling a raft is from the group of statues at Smetanovo nábřeží. For other cards that draw on this group of statues, see The World, the Page of Wands and The Hermit.

The graceful woman and children are from the Jan Hus memorial by Ladislav Šaloun. It is prominently situated in Old Town Square and is often the site for vigils and peaceful demonstrations.

The waterwheel on the Devil's Stream in the Kampa district

Seven of Swords

A man tiptoes away from a huddle of buildings, laughing to himself and holding an armful of swords. Everything is quiet, and the action seems to be taking place early in the morning or at twilight. In the background, a figure is seen making off with a door. The whole scene looks like a bit of sneaky theft rather than serious looting, and there is something faintly ludicrous about it, especially about the man sneaking off with the door.

Short Interpretation

Sometimes just rushing off on your own and acting without thinking things through is just not effective. It might be momentarily satisfying, but what does it really achieve? Next time, how about asking for some advice and assistance before you race off on some hare-brained scheme? Your friends are actually there to help, if only you'd let them.

[Minor Arcana]

Fuller Interpretation

Acting alone • A silly, spur-of-the-moment act • A small revenge "Why on earth did I do that?"

This card shows someone running away after doing something somewhat ineffectual or silly. It's very much about the type of situation in which something is done in the style of the 'lone hero', when a bit of planning and teamwork would actually have been much better. The card can sometimes refer to a dishonourable act (which may be the root cause of the reluctance to involve others), or it can simply be an act done on the spur of the moment, perhaps more as a gesture than as a real attempt to achieve anything effective.

The image on this card shows a man smiling as he tiptoes away with some stolen swords. The camp from which he probably took them is in the distance. Behind him another man can be seen sneaking off with a door. The motive for the thefts seems to have been revenge rather than material gain. Neither man is stealing anything of any real value. Both of their actions seem like futile, slightly silly gestures of defiance rather than something likely to be effective.

This card is closely associated with the Five of Swords, though that card is much more clearly about dishonour and selfishness rather than rashness.

Sources

The man with the swords is taken from the Czech Taroky. In the original, he is the Knight of Bells.

The background scene is part of a series of sgraffito panels at the Martinic Palace, located at the beginning of Novy Svět, on the corner of Kanovnická Street. This scene is from the set of panels in the inner courtyard of the palace which illustrate the myth of Hercules. While no one seems quite sure anymore of the exact meaning of each panel, it is likely that the one we have used depicts the task of cleaning the Aegean Stables, which Hercules accomplished by removing the stable doors and diverting a river through the whole complex.

Hercules is also known for defeating Cerberus, the three-headed dog that guards the Underworld. This may be the root of the local legend that if you walk past the Martinic Palace between 11 and 12 at night, a fiery, black dog may follow you. However, according to the story, the dog can go no farther than the Loreto Chapel that stands a couple of hundred yards away. When you reach that point it will leave you to vanish back into the night.

The sgraffito picture that forms part of a "Labours of Hercules" series at the Martinic Palace

[Minor Arcana]

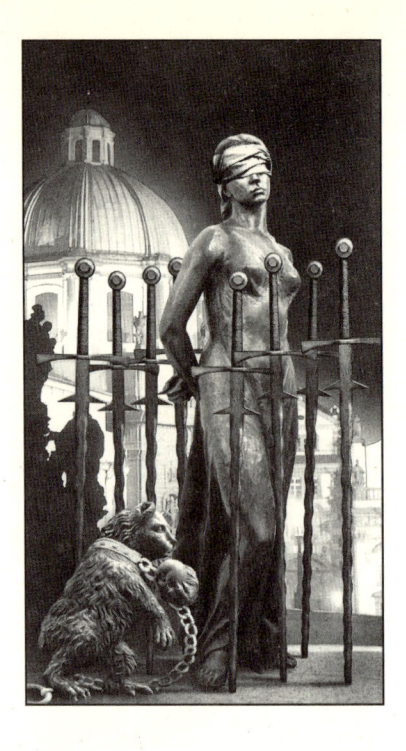

Eight of Swords

A woman stands behind a barrier of swords. It's night-time and she seems alone. Her eyes are bound and on first glance she looks quite helpless. However, look again and you can see that her arms may not actually be bound. Perhaps all she really has to do is remove her hands from behind her back, pull off her blindfold and move away? The bear at her feet has already taken up his ball and chain and begun to walk off. Perhaps she should follow?

Short Interpretation

You feel completely hemmed in, unable to see a way out. But in reality the things around you that seem like impassable barriers may not be that hard to get around. Just take off your blindfold, look around you, and work out how to begin to break down the wall. Escape is probably in your own hands, so begin to believe that you have the power to make that break if you want to.

Fuller Interpretation

Feeling trapped • Letting circumstances control you • Frozen into immobility • Refusing to help yourself

Feeling hemmed in and trapped is sometimes more in the mind than an actual physical state. Many of us remain in a grim or depressing situation because we feel there is no escape from it. We can find many reasons not to make a move. We may use financial responsibilities as an excuse: "I hate this job, but I have to pay the mortgage." Or maybe we appeal to excuses like education or age: "I would love to change my situation, but I'm too old/young/uneducated/uneduated/inexperienced/afraid." Whatever the apparent reason, it's important to consider how much of a restriction these justifications really are. Is it honestly so impossible to get out of this state of affairs? Are you convincing yourself you are trapped simply because making a change seems frightening or difficult?

The woman in this card looks completely trapped and surrounded by swords, but she probably isn't imprisoned at all. Her hands are behind her back, but are they actually bound? Perhaps all she needs to do is remove her blindfold and free herself.

The little bear indicates that liberation is often in your own hands. His chain has been loosed from its fastenings and he has taken up his burden (it looks like an iron ball, but in fact it's an apple, an old symbol that signifies life) and is happily walking off. The message is that often we have the power to break free from a situation in which we feel trapped and ensnared, but to do so takes effort.

Sources

The woman with her eyes bound is from a statue at the main post office in Jindřišska Street.

The swords themselves are based on those made by an armoury shop in Prague. The bear is from the door sign of a Baroque house on Mostecká Street.

The background is a night view of the Old Town end of the Charles Bridge.

Nine of Swords

A young woman has thrown herself against a cold stone, and she lies there prostrate and weeping. On the front of the stone there is a grim-looking death's head. The nine swords behind her form what looks like the bars of a cage. The whole scene, while strangely elegant, seems to be one of utter despair. However, above the woman there is a very different image that she may not be aware of: an old man has raised his sword above his head, prepared to strike an unseen victim, but a smiling angel has taken hold of his blade, calmly preventing the deed.

Short Interpretation

This is a time of anxiety, nightmares and many fears, but things often look blackest when you're actually almost through the worst period. This isn't to deny what you are feeling, but remember that the darkest hour really is just before the dawn – and a brighter future may lie just ahead.

The Tarot of Prague

Fuller Interpretation

Severe anxiety • Nightmares and black thoughts • Hysteria – seeing the worst side • Despair and disappointment

This card is undoubtedly one of the darkest of the deck. It shows a woman prostrate with despair, and all around her are images of death and swords. She seems literally trapped by anguish and hopelessness. However, the dreamlike image above her shows another possibility. A man lifts his sword in anger, about to strike, but a serene angel gently holds back the blade. This angel indicates that a calm, rational response is possible even in all this darkness, anger and despair.

It's often said of the Nine of Swords that it shows a bad situation that is perceived as a tragedy but which in fact is not. In other words, like all the Swords, it is as much about mental processes and the intellect as it is about the physical realities of the situation. Arthur Waite says of the figure on the RWS version of this card that "She is one who knows no sorrow which is like unto hers", and the sense here is of someone who is possibly indulging in despair and self-pity, perhaps even as a way of seeking attention.

In our card, the girl who is crying has beautifully coiffured hair and is elegantly dressed. This, and her dramatic pose, implies that there may be an element of performance to this scene. At the same time, she seems unable to pull herself out of this frenzied grief; the swords are caging her in. The scene above her (perhaps part of her less conscious imaginings or dreams?) suggests something rather different. The angel in this image is notable for being absolutely calm. She is almost sleepily preventing the violent act, suggesting that if we can approach a seemingly black situation with inner calmness, with a sense of peace and forgiveness, then the horrors symbolised by the swords may suddenly seem less serious, and may actually be prevented. Instead of giving way to anger and hysteria, we should quietly and confidently use our intellect to try to find non-violent resolutions. In the words of the current Dalai Lama: "to give in to hatred is always to lose".

[Minor Arcana]

Sources

The weeping girl is part of a 19th century gravestone in Vyšehrad Cemetery. The stone with the death's head symbol is much older. It is a carving on the statue of St Francis Borgia on the Charles Bridge. Ferdinand Brokoff was the sculptor and it dates from 1710.

The beautiful scene of the angel and the angry man is one of the powerful chiaroscuro paintings in Ungelt, just behind the Týn Church. It probably depicts the story of Abraham and Isaac.

For other cards that feature these chiaroscuro paintings, see the Three of Cups and The Magician.

The chiaroscuro wall painting from which we took the background image for the Nine of Swords

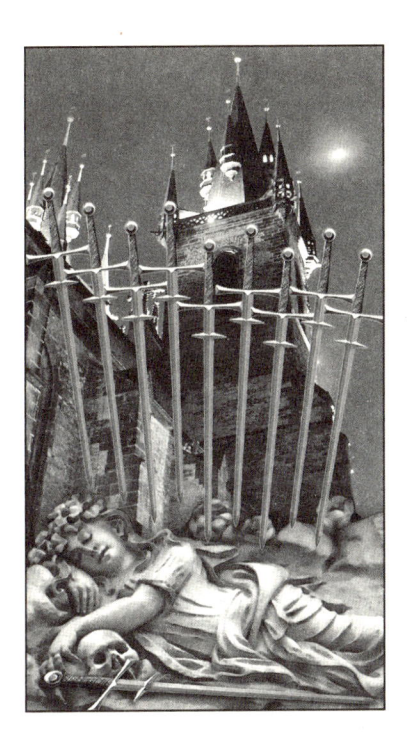

Ten of Swords.

It's evening. A beautiful, deathly pale, young girl lies with her arm resting on a grinning skull. A sword has fallen from her hand. Nine more swords are flying through the air around her. Lovely, but rather livid, white graveyard flowers surround the scene, and two Gothic towers loom above the girl, their turret lights beginning to twinkle in the growing darkness.

Short Interpretation

Like all the Tens in Tarot, this is the fullest expression of the suit, so the Ten of Swords refers to the worst aspects of conflict, and can indicate that the thing that was most dreaded has actually happened, leaving you in much pain and distress. However, there is a milder interpretation that says that Swords are also about the intellect and mental processes, and the situation may not be as bad as it feels. Perhaps it is partly in the mind? If you assess what has happened rationally, you may find you can live through this disaster more calmly than you first thought possible.

[Minor Arcana]

Fuller Interpretation

The lowest point • Pain and sadness • Mental dissolution

Though the usual interpretation of the Ten of Swords is undeniably that it speaks of pain and of hitting a very low point, there is also the suggestion that some of the misfortune exists solely in the mind. The Tens in general usually signify the characteristics of the suit being at their most extreme (in the case of Cups this is extreme happiness and contentment, in the case of Pentacles, extreme good fortune, and in Wands, the simple extreme of taking on too much). In Swords, the suit characteristics are about the intellect and incision, and also the tendency to become involved in conflict, and these combine at their most pronounced in the Ten to indicate a mixture of anger and mental anguish.

This card can often be interpreted as meaning that the person laid low may have been brought to this state by his or her own mind as much as by anything external. When Aleister Crowley described this card as the "death of the intellect" (*The Book of Thoth*), this may be in part what he meant. Just as the Ten of Wands shows someone overwhelmed by a profusion of tasks and actions, the Ten of Swords can be interpreted as someone overwhelmed by the impossibility of finding a rational answer to all of life's questions.

The figure in this card is as white as death, and she appears to be lying in a churchyard, but she is not dead, only sleeping and dreaming. However, something real has happened; the skull under her fingers can't be denied. The swords falling through the air are menacing. Are they real swords that will soon kill her? Or are they "mental swords", and is the perceived threat primarily in her mind?

It's important to notice that in this image the relationship between the girl and the death's head is unclear. Is she victim or perpetrator? Is the sword near her hand her own? In spite of her angelic beauty, is it possible that at some point she gave way to anger and violent impulse? When you see this card in a reading, remember that it can be about something done to you, but that in some circumstances it can also stand for something you have brought upon yourself through your own actions. Regardless of the interpretation, the indication is that it's important not to fall into a "martyr" mentality. Swords may be falling around you, but at some point you will wake up and look back on all this and see it as a nightmare that is now over. It will pass.

Although this card indicates the low point, this also means that at least things can't get any worse. While it isn't a comforting card to see in a reading, it should reassure us that the situation should soon begin to improve. There is also a clear message that you have to pick yourself up, take responsibility for your own actions, and begin to take steps toward recovery if happiness is to return.

Sources

The sleeping young girl with a skull is from the unusual stucco façade of the House of the Golden Well in Karlova Street. This dates from 1714, at the tail end of the last major plague epidemic that devastated Bohemia and Austria. In the original sculpture the skull symbolises the many people who died as the plague devastated the region repeatedly from the 11th to the 18th century. The lion used in the Two of Swords is also from this façade.

The looming towers are those of the Gothic Týn Church. The courtyard behind the Týn Church was supposedly the scene of a real murder centuries ago. A Turkish merchant apparently killed his sweetheart for unexplained reasons. However, wracked by guilt over the deed his ghost (recognisable by the turban it wears) still wanders around Týn Court carrying his former lover's head in a jewellery box.

[Minor Arcana]

Page of Swords

A young woman stands before Prague, as though on guard. At her side is the shield of the city. She wears the eyes of a peacock and carries her sword upright. A seabird soars past her. Although the image is one of watchfulness, this is not a dark scene. There is warmth as well as vigilance in the expression of the Page.

Short Interpretation

You are full of energy, enthusiasm and cleverness, but you find it hard to let your guard down, and because of your vigilance you sometimes stand aloof and observe the world instead of taking part. Of course there are times when it's better to wait and watch, but there are also moments for stepping down from your pillar and getting some hands-on experience of real life.

The Tarot of Prague

Fuller Interpretation

Being on the alert • Bravery and watchfulness • A clever and acute sense of vision • Observing the situation • Seeing the prospects

When the Page of Swords appears in a reading, it is important to remember that there are two rather distinct ways in which the card can be interpreted. The first is that of being on the alert for both threats and opportunities, the second is, more positively, about guardianship.

The Page is honest, clever and brave, and deals with challenges well, but at times he may tend to be overly cautious and inclined to stand aside to wait and watch in case any of the prospects he sees turn out to be just too problematic. In fact, because of the tensions present in many Swords cards, even the apparently promising opportunities he sees may lead to some difficulties and challenges, and are unlikely to be straightforward or entirely easy. It's true that in many unfamiliar situations there is a need for vigilance or closer examination before taking action, however, it's also important not to get into the habit of always being cautious or on the alert. Sometimes it simply isn't necessary. This card tells us to ask ourselves how necessary our vigilance really is. Should we be more on our guard, or perhaps less? This card can often act as a signal to increase one's level of wariness, but in some situations it can actually imply that one is being too suspicious and it might be a good thing to let down the guard a little.

The Page wears the eyes of a peacock on his armour, indicating he is ever watchful. However, the peacock is also known for its pride, and in the Page pride sometimes manifests itself as a sort of clever vengefulness. He will always notice if he has been slighted, and it's impossible to pull the wool over his eyes. In one way this is good, but the Page can perhaps be too quick to exact revenge for such incidents.

The other aspect of this Page — and a more positive one — is that of someone who acts as a guardian. In this situation, his alertness is an entirely good quality. We have chosen to use a statue of Bruncvik to represent him, because he is the hero who permanently watches over Prague, always ready to awake and draw his magic sword to defend the city in times of trouble.

In many ways, the Page can be seen as someone who is a good friend and

[Minor Arcana]

a bad enemy. He will watch over you and defend you, but he will take action if you attack him in any way. In some ways, he is a person to be a little wary of, but also someone whose dexterity, acuteness and alertness are admirable when put to appropriate use.

Sources

The figure of the Page is based on the 1884 statue of Bruncvik by Ludvik Simek, which guards the Charles Bridge on the Malá Strana side of the river. Bruncvik was a chivalric hero who travelled the seas for seven years, during which time he was joined bz a brave lion. Both eventually returned to Bohemia, and in their honour a picture of the lion was placed on the Bohemian coat of arms (where it still is). The sword of Bruncvik is now supposed to be buried in the Charles Bridge. Like Arthur's Excalibur, it is a magic sword, ready to protect the country and to come to its aid in times of trouble.

In the Prague floods of 2002, the rising waters rose around this statue, which stands alone in the river beside the bridge. This seemed to provide an archetypal image of bravery in adversity.

Knight of Swords

An armoured knight sits astride a rearing horse. The knight holds his sword unsheathed and at the ready, and the horse, wearing an iron spike on its head, neighs belligerently and seems about to charge forward. Behind them the black towers of a cathedral are outlined against a dark and threatening sky.

Short Interpretation

Action is a great thing, but first try to think about the effect it will have on other people. Sometimes you can be too impulsive and keen to take risks. Your decisions are rational and often correct, but dashing into things precipitously can have some unpredictable consequences in terms of how others will react. Look before you leap – and try to be a little more compassionate.

[Minor Arcana]

Fuller Interpretation

Rushing in where angels fear to tread • Acting first, thinking later
Self-assurance and keen intellect • "I know I'm right" • Battle lust
Feelings don't matter

The Knight of Swords is terribly inclined to rush in and assert himself, even when this can upset or offend others. The trouble is, he is always absolutely sure he's right, and what is even more frustrating for those around him is that, in purely intellectual terms, he often is. However, this focus on the intellect and logic means he doesn't really concern himself with the possible emotional consequences of his actions. This can make him seem terribly highhanded and insensitive, so he is often someone who is respected rather than liked.

The picture on this card shows a knight charging at full tilt with drawn sword. He is completely armoured and also arrayed with plumed helmet and billowing cloak. He looks utterly confident. Even his horse seems belligerent and ready for battle; it is iron-shod and carries a spike on its head. It bears a passing resemblance to a unicorn, but actually, this horse is the unicorn's absolute opposite – not pure and gentle, but virile and aggressive. The whole picture shows someone who cannot be argued with or opposed. It's likely that this knight will always get his way, and that he will rarely pause to listen to any differing opinions. Although he is clever, he is not interested in finding negotiated and peaceful solutions. His answer to most problems will be to use force.

Sources

The picture of the knight is taken from a fresco on the ceiling of the Great Hall of the Wallenstein Palace. In the original, Duke Wallenstein is depicted as Mars, driving a chariot pulled by four armoured horses. We changed this to show the Duke astride one of the horses.

In the background is St Vitus' Cathedral, its Gothic towers soaring towards a stormy sky. This is the view of the cathedral from the top of the Stag Moat.

The Tarot of Prague

Queen of Swords

A graceful but sad-looking woman stands on a snowy hillside. She holds a sword and an open book. Beneath her feet is a winged lion. Behind her rise the two towers of a monastery.

Short interpretation
You've experienced some sorrows in your life, but you have come through these bad times with your usual great courage and you have acquired a great deal of wisdom. Now you can see the world clearly, and many of the people in your life look to you for your strength and understanding.

Fuller Interpretation

An inability to "suffer fools gladly" • Some sadness in life • Shrewdness based on experience • A balance between experience and intellect
Wit and wisdom

[Minor Arcana]

The Queen of Swords has grace and a stern beauty, but she is not an altogether happy figure. She has seen some sadness in her life and may even, at times, have been through mourning and loss. However, her enormous mental strength enabled her to persevere and she has gained tremendous wisdom as a result of her experiences. She is an intellectual, but unlike the King of Swords she has no tendency to be over-reliant on her powers of reasoning. She draws equally on both her "book learning" and the knowledge gained from the challenges of life.

She is astute, and she also possesses a sharp wit. Instead of allowing herself to become bitter, this queen has put all her good and bad experiences down to life's rich tapestry. She has become a mature personality, forthright and continually honest, and she has learnt not to take things too seriously. If you need some straight advice, she is an excellent person to turn to. However, while she can seem very witty with words, and in some ways quite light and airy, don't forget the basis of her strength. She is not someone who will take kindly to foolish questions or behaviour, and she can be positively cutting if she sees irresponsibility or sloppy thinking. Enjoy her company, but treat her with respect.

The queen shown on this card is both fine-looking and thoughtful. She holds her sword delicately, but with poise and balance. She gazes straight into the eyes of the viewer, with a slight questioning tilt to her head, as though making an honest, or maybe even an unnervingly frank appraisal. She carries a book, signifying her intellect and learning, and also holds a sword. At her feet is a winged lion. In one sense this animal is a little like the lion who stands at the feet of the Queen of Wands, but, while the Wands' lion is friendly and almost huggable, this beast is far less approachable; a creature of myth rather than of reality. While the Queen and her lion are warmly and brightly coloured, the scene behind them is snowy and white. This Queen has been through some cold and hostile experiences, but she has managed to emerge full of vitality and, if you approach her with intelligence and sensitivity, she can offer a good deal of warmth and sound advice.

Sources

The Queen is taken from an early medieval illuminated manuscript in the collection of the Strahov Library. The original showed St Catherine of

Alexandria. St Catherine was known for being beautiful, of noble birth, and of an unusually high intelligence — all qualities that make her similar to the Queen of Swords. The lion is from a slightly later manuscript. In the original, he sat at the foot of a saintly scribe and was probably a sign for St Mark the Apostle (for more on the significance of the winged lion, see the interpretation of The World card.)

The background shows a snowy scene of Petřín Park and, in the distance, the twin towers of the Strahov Monastery, where the library is housed.

The early medieval manuscript from which the figure of the Queen of Swords was taken

[Minor Arcana]

King of Swords

A king sits in a formal posture, holding a large, burnished sword and a golden hawk. Behind him is the magnificent figure of a winged angel brandishing a huge sword which has just struck down a tree around which a serpent is coiled. The words "mane, thegel, phares" are written on the angel's girdle.

Short Interpretation

The King of Swords shows a keen ability to analyse every situation, and puts this to use in maintaining his authority. If uncontrolled, his realism can slide into materialism and a love of power, but he can also be a strong defender of justice and truth. If this King is in your life, make sure that his intelligence is put to good use and does not become dominating.

The Tarot of Prague

Fuller Interpretation

Keen intelligence • Judgement and command • War-like and destructive • Clever but domineering • Fair, but vengeful at times Firm friend, implacable enemy

Like all the Swords, the King is intelligent and intellectual, but in the case of this card some negative and occasionally even violent aspects can overshadow the positive side of his acuity. When he is in a situation of authority the King of Swords can be a wise, calculating and brave leader, a source of great strength in times of trouble, and a faithful friend. But he is also inclined to be proud and domineering and will sometimes turn to violence or destructiveness to get his way. Arthur Waite described this King as someone who wields "the power of life and death, in virtue of his office".

The King of Swords is driven by pure intellect, and it is just this that makes him brilliant but also uncompromising. He will always have a rationale to support his demand that his decisions be followed without question. He takes great pride in his power of reasoning, and finds it almost impossible to imagine that other forms of decision-making, perhaps more influenced by emotional or practical considerations, could possibly outweigh his intellectual judgement.

In many ways, this makes him akin to The Emperor of the Major Arcana. The fact that there are some similarities between the image of this card and of The Emperor is therefore entirely appropriate. However, the difference between the two is that while The Emperor is an archetype of rationality, the King of Swords is much more about the real world use of rationalism and intellect to maintain power and authority. To make this clearer, The Emperor might represent the principle of logic and intellect, but the King of Swords is much more likely to stand for an actual personality who is driven by such principles.

The king in the foreground looks calm, controlled and rather formal, the image of a strong but fair ruler. In addition to his sword, he also holds a hawk, a symbol of keen sight and of swift attack. Behind him there is an image of a beautiful but terrifying figure brandishing a huge sword. This is an avenging angel who has just struck down a tree wrapped in the coils of a snake — the tree of pride and false knowledge. Around his waist is a

[Minor Arcana]

banner with the words words "mane, thegel, phares". These are the words that, according to the biblical Book of Daniel, were written by a mysterious hand on the wall at Belshazzar's feast. The words foretold the fall of Babylon, which came just at the point when Belshazzar became overconfident in his power and his absolute domination. The cut tree actually comes from the earlier dream of King Nebuchadnezzar. This dream foretold that he would be "cut down" because of his sin of immense pride.

Sources

The seated King is from the front of the Powder Tower situated at the beginning of the old "Royal Route". The statues on this tower depict the Kings of Bohemia and were created by Čapek, Seeling and Šimek in the late 19th century.

The magnificent Art Nouveau angel is from a tomb at Vyšehrad cemetery. The words on the banner are there in the original. Their meaning is:

Mane: God hath numbered thy kingdom and ended it.
Thegel: Thou art weighed in the balance and found wanting.
Phares: Thy kingdom is divided and will be given to the Medes and Persians.

MINOR ARCANA - PENTACLES

Pentacles

The suit of Pentacles is associated with the element Earth, and is characterised as pragmatic, grounded and connected with the everyday. This is the practical and earthy suit of the Tarot, and perhaps the most comforting and easy to understand.

This suit concerns all material things, including money, and for this reason a querent can sometimes almost feel insulted at seeing a lot of Pentacles in their spread. They may feel it implies that they are very materialistc but in fact, while some of the cards do refer directly to money, most are more generally about the pragmatic realities of life. While not very glamorous or thrilling, Pentacles are warm, friendly, and down-to-earth. They often signify practical and manual skills and can also stand for competency and reliability. However, even these good qualities may have a negative side. There are situations in which Pentacles can be too materialistic or hard-headed, and their pragmatism can at times become a bit dull and lacking in imagination. It's impossible to say who the Pentacles would be if they were artists, because they never would be. However, we can think of Pentacles as the craftsmen of the world. It's true to say that craft can attain the level of art, but in a manner that has some practical application and that displays obvious manual and technical skill.

The Pentacles are in some ways the "salt of the earth". This can make them sound rather unglamorous, and they are certainly not the romantics of the Tarot. However, without them the intellect of Swords, the energy and action of Wands, and the emotional sensitivity of Cups would remain ungrounded. Pentacles bring it all down to earth and give our lives a solid foundation.

The Ace of Pentacles is definitely the card you want to see if you are beginning a project that calls for common sense and business acumen. It promises the beginning of an enterprise that will thrive if you are willing to put in solid effort. The Two of Pentacles is about the way in which these practical matters need to be juggled and organised. This card represents the kind of person who actually enjoys answering the phone while filling in a form, and at the same time keeping an eye on their computer screen. These sorts of jugglers are invaluable in a business, especially in the early stages of a "start-up".

The Three of Pentacles is quite different. It's about mastery and professionalism in a practical field. It can refer to manual craftsmanship, or to the qualified and accomplished practitioner in any specialisation. It also tends to indicate the ability to work with and learn from others in a team in order to master a skill.

With the Four, however, the first signs of the slightly more negative, overly materialistic aspects of Pentacles do begin to appear. This card signifies a tendency to hang on too tightly to material goods, a trait that may actually hold you back. It's important sometimes to keep what you've got, but it's equally important to recognise that there are times when you should let go.

The problematic aspects of the suit become much clearer with the Five. This indicates a lack of material comfort, and a helplessness and blindness when it comes to dealing with the practical necessities of life. It often points to a situation in which people need help, but don't quite know where to turn to get it. The relationship between the material and practical sides of life has become muddled and out of control. The Five is often an unhappy and uncomfortable card.

The Six, however, offers the beginning of a solution. This card is about charity: the ability to both give and accept help when necessary. Like the other Sixes in the Tarot, this is a somewhat strange card. It can be very positive when it refers to charity that is given and received honestly and with good intentions. But this meaning can also be read in a negative way if the implication is that either the giver or the recipient is not entirely well-meaning. Sometimes the main reason we give charity is to make ourselves feel good, and on the other hand we may at times take charity when we are perfectly capable of helping ourselves.

The Seven indicates a point where a decision has to be made. This card is about quietly mulling over the options, and carefully considering what comes next. It has an aura of achievement and practicality, and it's clear that the plans indicated will be realistic and not anything "pie in the sky".

With the Eight comes the need for struggle and effort, but with Pentacles this struggle is a very practical one rather than some sort of inner turmoil. This card represents apprenticeship and the need to work hard, perhaps for many years, to gain the skills you desire. Whether you are learning a language, getting a qualification, or acquiring a manual or artistic skill, the Eight is about the the need to apply yourself, work hard, and be patient. After all, attaining mastery of a skill takes time.

The Nine of Pentacles shows the suit's good qualities in a very straightforward way. This card is about simple material contentment and prosperity. The woman on this card has "made it", probably through common sense and hard work as much as anything. She also seems to have an aesthetic sensibility, a reminder that being practical does not stop us from appreciating beauty; indeed, one way of bringing something beautiful into our lives is through the practicalities of craftsmanship and artistic skills.

The Ten, as the culmination of Pentacles, at first seems simply to indicate prosperity. However, this card is not entirely straightforward and has some shades of meaning that are not always easy to interpret. It is sometimes read as signifying that in all this down-to-earth practicality there is a danger of ignoring some of the sheer magic of life. Unlike most of the Pentacles, this card carries an odd sense of "otherness", maybe warning us that life cannot be lived in a totally matter-of-fact way and still be wholly satisfying.

Court Cards

In Pentacles, the qualities of the Court Cards manifest themselves in a very down-to-earth way. The Page is about new opportunities for projects and tasks, and in this case these projects will demand hard work but may well lead to prosperity and material gain. In the Knight of Pentacles the enthusiasm of the Page gives way to a rather exaggerated sense of responsibility. For the Knight, projects have to be pursued with a dogged persistence. This can make him rather stubborn or, on occasion, obsessive. In his allegiance to duty and practicality he often entirely forgets about the need for enthusiasm and pleasure in the work.

The Queen of Pentacles is an altogether lighter and happier character. Like all the Queens, she manages to balance the suit's qualities — in this case the Pentacles tendency towards "workaholism" and materialism and the more positive traits of practicality and skill. The Queen is also a worker, but she loves her work, which is likely to be of a rather sensual nature, and often specifically oriented towards making others comfortable and happy.

She will always invite you in and cook a superb meal, and she will apparently do this effortlessly and often with great joy.

The King also shares this practicality, but with a less balanced sense of his own needs. Instead, he worries about his dependants and the community around him. He is probably the consummate businessman and provider, and a real rock to lean on. However, he smiles less often than the Queen and will often drive himself harder than he would really like, simply because he feels that it's his responsibility to do so.

In summary, Pentacles tell us that we need to be prepared to be hard-working, practical and sensible if we are to achieve much in life. But these qualities needn't be seen as boring or dull – after all, most of the arts require exactly the kind of practice and skill that Pentacles represent.

A final note. There has been considerable debate about whether this suit should properly be called 'Coins' or 'Pentacles'. Until the Rider Waite Smith tarot of 1909-12, it was known as Coins. Arthur Waite, a member of the Golden Dawn occult society, seems to have changed it to Pentacles to make it fit in better with the Golden Dawn magic rituals. We decided not to choose the name Coins as it can tend to make the suit seem too focused on money. For us, *Pentacles* better encapsulates the idea of "the magic of everyday things" that is central to these cards.

[Minor Arcana]

Ace of Pentacles

A hand holds a disc with the smiling face of the sun on it. In the background one can see a golden road leading up through a stone archway to gardens beyond. Above the gardens are a pretty tower and a castle, shining in the sunlight.

Short Interpretation

There are new opportunities in material or practical matters. Don't just dream about what could be, it's time to keep your feet on the ground and start projects or enterprises that will lead to wealth (which may be more than just monetary), security and real happiness.

Fuller Interpretation

A practical opportunity • Prosperity on its way
Great joy from everyday matters

Like all the Aces, this card is about beginnings and opportunities. Being the Ace of Pentacles, these opportunities are likely to be in areas involving money, material comforts, or worldly issues. This indicates that there may be a chance to begin to be very productive in a particularly "real world" way. It may be about a process that will lead to financial prosperity, or it may be about wealth other than the strictly material kind. It could indicate that you will gain something that increases your standard of living, even if it doesn't have a definite financial value. Any magic in this card is of a very ordinary kind − it's about finding happiness from down-to-earth comforts, a good environment, and a feeling of security. But this shouldn't in any way diminish the importance of the Ace of Pentacles: sometimes these quite ordinary things can bring enormous joy.

The image on this card shows a hand holding a disc on which there is a smiling sun radiating optimism and energy. In the background, a golden pathway leads through a stone archway and up a flight of steps towards a castle and gardens. This shows that you stand at the beginning of a new and wonderful path, but the steep steps indicate that you may have to put some effort into realising the opportunity you've been given. There are two towers within reach, a smaller one, in the garden itself, and a much larger one that is part of the castle on the hill. Perhaps you will only get as far as the smaller tower − symbolising a lessser goal − or maybe you will reach your ideal, symbolised by the castle itself. It may not matter either way, as even the lesser achievement will be very worthwhile. The prospects are sunny, so follow the golden path that lies before you.

Sources

The background of the Ace of Pentacles is an old stone pathway and wall in Petřín Park. This park is ancient and beautiful, and many vague legends are associated with it (there are supposed to be fairies living there, and it's certainly atmospheric enough to make you half believe this). We were told one New Year's Day that if you walk through the particular stone archway shown on this card you can leave your old life behind and begin a new and better one − this seemed very appropriate to the Ace of Pentacles.

In the background is the Malá Furstenberská Garden (the small Furstenberg Garden) at the Castle. The Daliborka Tower can be seen in the distance.

[Minor Arcana]

Two of Pentacles

A young man juggles two discs, each of which shows the glowing face of the sun. His pose is awkward but he seems to be enjoying himself. Behind him lies the river, with an old house and tower rearing up on the far bank.

Short Interpretation

This is the person who feels they always have to "spin the plates", juggling many things at once. However, while they may sometimes moan about this, they really do enjoy a sense of keeping all the balls in the air, and are very good at doing so. When this card appears it indicates that you should trust your instincts because right now you really can manage many things simultaneously. Relax, and appreciate the joy you get out of being busy, even if it may occasionally feel like a lot to manage at once.

Fuller Interpretation

Partnerships and relationships • Having fun • Trusting your instincts
Finding a balance between positive and negative • Juggling things

Appropriately enough, this card actually has two contradictory meanings which you may have to manage to balance when interpreting it. It is about juggling and "keeping the plates spinning" (though not in a pressured sense), and about fun and recreation. But it can also mean news or that some obstacles are rearing up, bringing trouble and agitation. The key to working out which interpretation should predominate in a reading is to look at the querent's situation. The Two of Pentacles may come up when someone is managing to juggle a lot of things at once and is actually enjoying doing so (the exact opposite of the Ten of Wands, which indicates someone who is simply weighed down by too many tasks).

This card can be similar to The Fool in some aspects. It doesn't have the spiritual sense of the "wise fool" of the Major Arcana, but in a lighter and slighter way it is similar to the more worldly aspects of The Fool. It refers to the "foolishness" of letting go a bit, having fun, and being flexible. In juggling, if you think or worry too much about what you are doing, everything becomes difficult and the plates or balls will fall to the ground. So you simply have to let your instincts take over. By staying relaxed, you keep everything in balance and enjoy what you are doing.

The image on this card shows a very bright young man who seems utterly unperturbed that he is juggling two discs with smiling suns on them. His feet are firmly planted on the ground, and even though the position of his arms make it clear that what he is doing is in some ways awkward and difficult, he looks at ease and confident.

Sources

The young man is adapted from the "Acorn Over" figure (originally holding swords) on the Bohemian deck of cards. The two discs he is juggling are two roundels from the door of the Church of St Peter and St Paul at Vyšehrad. The buildings in the background are part of a complex (which includes the Smetana Museum) on the Old Town bank of the Vltava, just by the Charles Bridge at Novotného lávka. Nowadays they form an odd mix of a café, a nightclub, and a museum.

[Minor Arcana]

Three of Pentacles

A man in Baroque dress stands outside a theatre. He is, of course, Mozart, and the theatre is the Estates Theatre, where the opera *Don Giovanni* was first performed. Above him is a sign showing three violins and three pentacles.

Short Interpretation

The Three of Pentacles shows not merely achievement, but perhaps even fame, renown and glory in your chosen skill or profession. This has not been achieved overnight, but is the result of hard work, commitment, planning and teamwork. Now that the level of accomplishment has been recognised, remember how many people contributed to it and take pride in what's been achieved.

Fuller Interpretation

Skill and craftsmanship • Attainment • Being famed for your abilities
Being justifiably proud of your work • The Maestro

Above all, this card stands for accomplishment through teamwork. It may indicate a trade or skilled labour, especially if it involves teamwork and planning, or it may mean skills in more artistic pursuits. Regardless of the particular field of achievement, it is likely to demand technical skill such as that needed by a musician, a highly-trained painter, or a classical dancer. This is not a card of effortless talent. It very much implies that even with the kind of innate genius of a Mozart, real mastery can only be achieved through commitment and hard work.

This card is thus often about a very high level of competence, but also sometimes stands for fame, renown and glory achieved through hard work. It's important to recognise that while this is the card of the "maestro", it is never about the solitary genius. The Three of Pentacles always carries the recognition that even when an achievement looks like the work of an individual, many other people have contributed.

The image on the Rider Waite Smith version of the Three of Pentacles shows a mason at work in a church or cathedral. We decided to change this a little and use the idea of craftsmanship and skill in music rather than in masonry. Music has played a particularly important role in the cultural history of Prague, and we simply couldn't leave Mozart out of the deck as he is so closely associated with the city. In fact, Mozart was an enthusiastic Freemason, so in an indirect way the original reference to masonry has been retained. He is shown here in front of the Estates Theatre, which is where his opera *Don Giovanni* was first performed. At the time, Mozart had fled Vienna, finding it rather pompous and stuffy, and come to Prague. The day after the opera's first performance, Mozart was delighted to hear a street sweeper whistling an aria from it. To him, this was how opera should be — accessible and enjoyed by everyone.

The Estates Theatre therefore symbolises two aspects of this card; the fame and renown of Mozart himself, but also the teamwork, planning and

[Minor Arcana]

consummate skill needed to perform an opera. It also reminds us of the importance of a good audience. They are part of the team, too.

Sources

We drew the face of Mozart. It is based on a famous portrait by Barbara Kraft.

The background is the Stavovské Divadlo (Estates Theatre) which was built by Count Nostitz in 1783.

The three violins are from a house sign in Prague. Local myth has it that they mark the house where three crazed fiddlers ascend from Hell each night to play a Czech mazurka, only to vanish back to the underworld before dawn. The historical facts, however, tell a different story. In the 17th century the house was the studio of a family of traditional master-craftsman puppet-makers. One member of the family began to make violins for the musicians of the Loreto Chapel. The sign was therefore put up to indicate this trade. It dates from around 1700.

More on Mozart in Prague

Wolfgang Amadeus Mozart first came to Prague in January 1787. He stayed with Count Thun at Thun Palace, Thunovská 14 (now the British Embassy), and also at the House at the Golden Angel at Celetná 29 in the Old Town. After conducting an enthusiastically received performance of *The Marriage of Figaro*, he made the famous remark that "My Praguers understand me". In a letter to his friend Gottfried von Jacquin, he described a ball where people danced to arrangements of the music from *Figaro*: "because here there is talk of only one thing – Figaro; nothing is heard, played, sung or whistled but Figaro; no opera seen but Figaro, and again Figaro..." Mozart returned to Prague in the autumn of that year, this time bringing his wife with him. He stayed at The House of the Three Small Golden Lions in central Prague, then moved to Villa Bertramka. His time was spent time writing the opera *Don Giovanni*, and its first performance was in Prague at the Stavovské Divadlo (Estates Theatre), on 29 October 1787.

The last time Mozart came to Prague was in 1791, when he was commissioned to write an opera for the coronation of King Leopold II of Bohemia. The result, *La Clemenza di Tito*, was composed in just eighteen days at Villa Bertramka. During this stay Mozart is known to have attended the masonic lodge Zur Wahrheit und Einigkeit (Truth and Unity) where his cantata *Die Maurerfreude* was performed. Mozart went back to Vienna to work on *Die Zauberfloete* (The Magic Flute), and died there on 5 December 1791. The Czechs were the only people who honoured his memory, with a special mass held in the St Nicholas Church in Malá Strana, where Mozart had on one occasion played the organ.

There are many stories about Mozart's various visits to Prague. One of the most interesting is about the meeting between Mozart and Casanova at the Bretfield Palace at 33 Nerudova Street in 1787. Certainly, they were both in Prague at the time and they were both also freemasons, so the meeting is entirely probable. It is even thought that Casanova attended the premier of *Don Giovanni*. If so, then nothing could have been more appropriate as the opera is thought to be partly based on episodes from Casanova's life.

Four of Pentacles

A rather solid-looking man holds a large stone pentacle. He gazes at it, very absorbed. Beneath his feet are two more pentacles, and another is tucked into his robe. The richly-carved door behind him has several threatening faces of devils on it, one of which seems almost about to bite him on the shoulder, but he is seemingly oblivious to this.

Short Interpretation

Mine, mine, mine! This card is about wanting to hold on too tightly to what you have, possibly to the extent of being greedy and acquisitive, and saving your money rather than spending it. This can also apply to power, and wanting to be in charge and insisting on having things your way even when you know that this is selfish. But remember that by refusing change and preferring to consolidate your position, you may be missing out on new opportunities.

The Tarot of Prague

Fuller Interpretation

Sitting tight • Keeping hold • Saving and being frugal • Meanness and miserliness

The Four of Pentacles shows a man holding on too tightly to his possessions. Although this usually refers to material property or money, it may indicate someone who insists on holding on to power. The implication is that if you sit too tight you may feel safe, but you risk closing yourself off to opportunities and to new possibilities or collaborations.

In certain readings this card can be more positive and can stand for a person who is sensibly protecting what they have, maybe by being frugal or by saving — there are times when it makes sense to hold on to what you have.

The image shows a man who seems very preoccupied with his large stone pentacles. One is even tucked safely under his robe, but it looks like this could be uncomfortable. He sits with his back to a large carved door so he doesn't see the carvings of aggressive little demons (he also doesn't notice the one that is actually next to his feet). Holding on to possessions can be done to excess, or for reasons of miserliness rather than sensible frugality. The lurking demons remind us of the dangers that such meanness brings: it can leave one open to out-of-control materialism and selfishness, as represented by The Devil card. Although the Four of Pentacles is not nearly as much of a warning as The Devil when it comes up in readings, it is worth remembering that it can in some ways symbolise the "thin end of the wedge" as far as selfishness is concerned.

Sources

The man holding the pentacles is from a façade in Pohořelec. Originally, he was displaying a biblical text to the Virgin Mary. The door behind him is the wonderfully decorative Gothic door of the former Town Hall in Old Town Square. It is believed to be extremely old, dating from the time of Vladislav II (1140-58), although obviously it has been carefully restored many times. The little demon holding two shields or pentacles (tucked into the right-hand corner of the card) is taken from our old Bohemian playing cards.

[Minor Arcana]

Five of Pentacles

A despairing woman holds out her crying baby. Both child and mother seem blind to anything around them. Snow is falling and beginning to lie on the pair and on the church behind them. The impression is of intense cold and equally intense misery.

Short Interpretation

When you are struggling you can feel very alone. You may be battling an illness, or a downturn in your work or financial situation, and the situation may seem very unfair or even hopeless. However, help is at hand if you look for it. Don't be too proud or independent to ask for some assistance. You may not need to struggle alone.

Fuller Interpretation

The need to look for help • Money worries
Being worn down • A struggle • Closeness in hard times

This card often shows up in times of trouble, such as the loss of money or a job. It implies a struggle to make ends meet financially, and this can result in a feeling of immense tiredness and general ill health. The card can also indicate chronic illness, or on-going worries and anxieties other than financial.

The image shows a weeping woman and child. Snow is falling on them and the scene seems to be one of utter despair. In fact, the woman cannot see that there is a church right behind her. In her misery she can see nothing but her own situation, and she has turned inwards rather than looking for the spiritual or material assistance that might in fact be close at hand.

Either she and her child have been shut out and rejected, or the mother does not feel inclined or confident enough to ask for help. Either way, the situation is one of isolation and exclusion, without support or aid. But the implication of this card is that no matter how exhausting and hopeless your situation, it is always worth seeking help. When the Five of Pentacles appears you should remember that your current difficulties may be long-term, but they won't last forever.

There is a secondary meaning in this card, one which gives hope. The mother and child obviously love one another, showing that in times of difficulty we can often hold closely to someone we love. One good thing about hardship is that it can sometimes bring people closer together if they feel true commitment to one another "for better or worse".

Sources

The church is at Náměstí Míru in Vinohrady (formerly the site of the vineyards of the Castle). The photograph was taken during a snowstorm just before Christmas.

The woman and child are a detail from a statue of St Ivo on Charles Bridge. It was done by Matthias Braun in 1711. In the original, this woman is called "the widow".

Six of Pentacles

A serious young woman is handing bread to two beggars crouching at her feet. She is richly and warmly clothed, while the two recipients are almost naked. The group is in front of a church. If you look closely you can just make out that the carving at the top of one of the pillars shows a devilish figure forcing bread into the mouth of a young man.

Short Interpretation

It is good to give and to receive charity, as long as it is done sincerely and in the right spirit. If you are the giver, be generous. Don't give just to make yourself feel better; make sure that what you do will really make a difference. If you are the recipient, appreciate the gift and try not to be resentful. At its best, charity is a way of sharing and should bring joy to all those involved.

Fuller Interpretation

Charity • Social responsibility • Giving and receiving

Charity has always been central to our ideas of goodness. As the saying goes "It is better to give than to receive". But charity also has some more problematic associations in the modern age. We are often very reluctant to accept charity, as it can seem humiliating. The motives behind giving to charity are also sometimes suspect, and people who donate are sometimes perceived to be doing so more out of a desire to show off or to foster a sense of indebtedness, than genuinely to help.

This card asks us to think about all these aspects of charity. Traditionally this card has shown a hierarchy, with the person who gives standing over and above those who receive. Yet ideally one should give charity in a spirit of equality. It's crucial to respect the person you give charity to, and not to expect them to "look up" to you as a result. It's also important to give what people really need. Aid agencies all make this point: the wrong form of help can be worse than no help at all. As giver, you need to be humble enough to listen to people when they tell you what would really be the best way to offer assistance.

The image on this card shows a calm and well-dressed woman giving bread to two semi-naked beggars. She looks beautiful, generous, and not at all haughty (unlike the man on the traditional RWS image of this card). However, look closely at the image and some questions arise. She is warmly clothed, as though the weather is cold, so the men must be freezing. Is she really giving them what they most need? Would warm clothing make more sense? There is also a picturesque quality about her pose. Perhaps she is a bit too conscious of her own image as a "caring person". However, it really does depend on how you want to interpret this picture. One might assume that she is simply giving what she has at the moment, and doing so with generosity and respect. It depends on your perspective.

The background is a church (of course religious communities of all kinds are usually closely associated with charity and caring for the vulnerable). High up on one of the church pillars is a small sculpture. You can just make out that this shows a devil forcing bread into the mouth of a reluctant and scared young man. This nasty little tableau can be seen as a

[Minor Arcana]

contrast to the much gentler scene below, or it can be taken as a warning and commentary on it. Perhaps the message is that what may begin as genuine charity can quickly become a self-serving imposition on other people if it is not really done from the best of motives. In the end, the good that charity does often depends not just on what you give but also on the spirit in which it is given.

Sources

The statue of the bountiful lady is one of the charitable figures shown on a group of statues in the square in front of Prague Castle. All the figures relate to charity or to missionary activities. In the original statue this lady was handing bread to only one man (we added another from a different scene in this group). Perhaps it's a coincidence, but this particular square is still a favourite spot for beggars.

The demonic figure forcing bread into the mouth of a young man can be found inside St Vitus' Cathedral at one of the entrances to the Wenceslas Chapel. The background is a view of the exterior of St Vitus' Cathedral.

This strange pair of gargoyles is high on a pillar inside St Vitus' Cathedral

The Tarot of Prague

Seven of Pentacles

A man rests on his staff and gazes at the golden fruit on the tree in front of him. At his feet is his flock; behind him the city can be seen through the early morning mist. On the arch above, two figures, Temperance and Prudence, look down benevolently.

Short Interpretation

It's time to take satisfaction in a job well done. Yes, you're tired, but it's a good feeling that comes with a warm glow of satisfaction. What you've built is now strong enough to continue to grow without needing every bit of your attention. So stop for a minute and give yourself time to look back at what you've done. Your sense of attainment and of having achieved something is well deserved.

[Minor Arcana]

Fuller Interpretation

Reflecting on a job well done • A pause for planning • An opportunity to rethink tactics • Finding sensible strategies

Time to stop for a minute, reflect on what's been achieved, and see where you stand. Sometimes this card is simply about pausing to take stock and enjoy some of the fruits of your labour, and maybe even rest for a bit. At other times, though, this break is more active, and the card is also about considering change, thinking out the next moves, being able to question what you've done, and generally being able to stand back and make some decisions.

It has been called the 'Time Out' card. However, unlike some cards, it doesn't signal momentous change but is more likely to mean that you are being offered an opportunity to readjust your tactics and strategy.

The image on this card shows a herdsman with his flock. He is at rest, leaning on his staff and gazing at the seven gold pentacles on the tree in front of him. They represent what he has achieved, the "fruit of his labours". Behind him is a slightly misty vista of Prague rooftops and the castle. They rise up almost like a vision, and perhaps they exist as much in his imagination as in reality.

On the arch above are two of the classical Virtues: Prudence, who looks in two directions at once, and Temperance, who calmly pours water from her jug. These two are the muses of this scene. They indicate that the decisions are being made with care and moderation. There is nothing extreme about the meaning of this image. While the herdsman may be taking some time to conjure up visions of his possible future, these are carefully thought through and practical in their nature. This card is therefore quite different from the Seven of Cups, in which the options are fanciful and unreal. In the Seven of Pentacles, the possibilities are sensible, weighed with care and consideration, and entirely realistic.

On the panel between the two Virtues is the word 'Praha', the Czech name for Prague. It is believed that the word 'praha' is derived from *prah* which means 'threshold'. This card shows a person reflecting on what's been done in order to make careful decisions about the next step. The word 'Praha' therefore serves to indicate that the next steps will lead across a threshold and into something both different and better. The decisions represented by the card will not feel like momentous ones; after all, they are fundamentally about material and practical matters rather than higher issues. However, if the opportunity to take stock is done with real concentration and common sense, the outcome may be that you begin to see far more possibilities than you at first expected.

Sources

The herdsman is taken from one of the sgraffito panels at the House of the Minute in Old Town Square. It dates from 1600. For other cards that show decorations from this house, see The King of Wands, The Lovers and the Seven of Wands.

The figures of Temperance and Prudence are from the sgraffito decoration on the Míčovna (Ball Games Court) at the Castle. Boniface Wolmut created these beautiful decorations between 1567 and 1569.

The familiar 78-card deck includes only three of the four cardinal virtues: Temperance, Strength and Justice. Prudence is absent (a few of the more uncommon types of tarot deck, such as the Florentine Minchiate, do include Prudence). The reason for this has been much debated. All sorts of explanations for this have been suggested, but none have been totally convincing. We decided simply to include Prudence, albeit in a minor role. She is shown in the traditional manner, with her principle face looking in one direction, and a second, which is bearded, looking the opposite way.

[Minor Arcana]

Eight of Pentacles

The card shows a wrought-iron balcony high above the town. Various traditional trades are depicted. These include a baker, a blacksmith, a washerwoman and a knife sharpener.

In the centre is a very decorative depiction of the Black Sun. The buildings and roofs of the crowded city stretch out behind the balcony.

Short Interpretation

Work, work, work. It can be hard going, but once you've achieved a high level of skill and knowledge it will be worth it. Keep going, focus on what you're doing, pay attention to it, and be patient. When you are qualified you'll be proud that you stuck it out, and you'll take a real pride and pleasure in realising how much you are capable of.

The Tarot of Prague

Fuller Interpretation

Apprenticeship and craftsmanship • The rewards of hard work
Satisfaction in a job well done • Learning a skill

This can indicate a time of great diligence and focus. It's very much about hard work, developing your skill, and paying attention to details. It means being painstaking, 'dotting the "i"s and crossing the "t"s,' and generally being patient enough to check all the fine details. It's about getting things right through care and concentration.

It's also about the pleasure in mastering a skill, particularly a very practical one. While learning how to do something is a hard and tedious path, it's also a tremendously rewarding process.

The Black Sun in the centre of the railings on this card is part of the original ironwork. It is an interesting symbol to find in this context, as its meaning in alchemy is 'transformation'. Usually, we think of transformation as a spiritual process. However, the presence of the symbol here stands for a more down-to-earth type of transformation: that brought about by the skill of the artisan, who can transform ordinary materials into something both useful and beautiful. Perhaps it also stands for the transformation of the apprentice into a master (or mistress) of their chosen craft or profession.

Sources

This card shows the balcony of a Baroque house in Tržiště Ulice (Market Street). We've altered the layout so that all the metal figures can be seen. Each figure represents a trade or skill. The Black Sun is part of the original ironwork.

The view visible behind it is of part of Malá Strana, one of the oldest districts of Prague and traditionally home to many artisans.

[Minor Arcana]

Nine of Pentacles

Flowers and rich decorations surround a golden-haired woman. She is holding a gold disc in one hand. There is a picture of a beehive with gilded bees behind her, and a golden sun, moon, and more discs hang above it. A kingfisher is perched on the woman's other hand.

Short Interpretation

The Nine of Pentacles is the card of material prosperity. But it isn't just about acquiring money or possessions, it's about reaching some kind of security and maturity. There can be tremendous pleasure in simply knowing that you have finally arrived at a stable and comfortable point in your life, especially when this was the result of your own efforts. So look around at the good things and good times that are now yours, and enjoy what you have achieved. You deserve it.

Fuller Interpretation

Prosperity • A comfortable life • Refinement • Self-reliance
Material success

The picture is one of civilised refinement. The Nine of Pentacles isn't a particularly exciting or adventurous card, but it is very positive, indicating the attainment of a comfortable and maybe even enviable lifestyle. It's also about being in control and able to act with independence and self-confidence. It can indicate an escape from the coarse or vulgar, and the adoption of a more cultured and refined approach to life. The Nine of Pentacles is always a picture of tact, diplomacy and calm maturity.

The image on this card shows a prosperous woman standing in front of a gilded background. The beehive behind her signifies industriousness, the making of a home, and also, because of the richness of honey, it stands for the good things in life (honey was the only available sweetener for centuries and so carried far more significance than it has now).

The reason for the presence of a kingfisher is that it was the symbol of the Guild of Barbers and Bath-keepers in Prague. A visit to the baths was, of course, a refined and luxurious pastime in medieval times, so the presence of this symbolic bird stands for both refinement and also the domestication and taming of the wild. In reality it's almost impossible to tame a kingfisher so it is striking to see it perched quietly on this woman's hand.

Sources

The golden beehive with a sun and moon is from the top of a building in the street called "28 října" at the Old Town end of Wenceslas Square. It is a symbol related to Freemasonry, standing for industry and co-operation.

The mosaic with golden rain, flowers and *yods* (a Hebrew letter that stands for life and energy) comes from an Art Nouveau-style tomb in Vyšehrad cemetery.

The lady herself is taken from a late 18th-century statue in Celetná Street. The kingfisher that sits on her wrist is one of several kingfisher emblems on the Old Town Charles Bridge Tower. They were probably put there during the reign of Wenceslas IV (1361-1419) – he was famously a most enthusiastic patron of the baths in Prague.

[Minor Arcana]

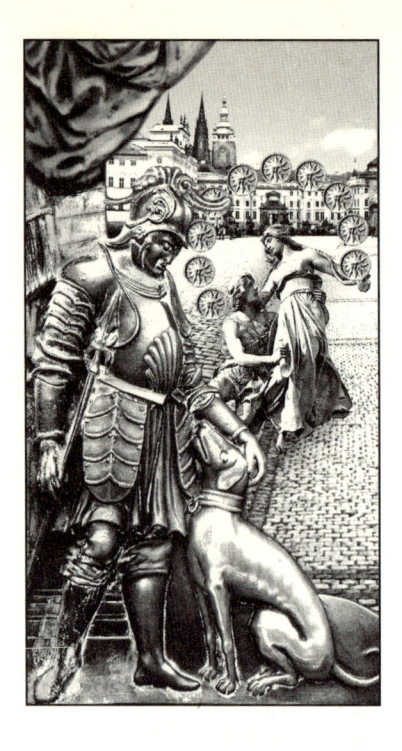

Ten of Pentacles

A happy couple, the man and woman totally absorbed in one another, are standing in a market square. The woman is almost dancing with happiness. Above them, ten pentacles form an arc, which both closes off and protects their world. In the foreground there is a very different scene. An old man in armour strokes a dog. Both seem pensive, almost sad, and yet they glow with a rich, golden light.

Short Interpretation

This is the card of conservative achievement. It is about attaining sensible and down-to-earth goals, probably in business or other material matters. However, it can also imply that there is something more magical "outside the walls" of your immediate business or domestic environment. Make sure that in your well-deserved comfort you are not becoming too self-absorbed to pay attention to the more spiritual sides of life.

Fuller Interpretation

Affluence and material well-being • Permanence • Convention and some closure of the imagination • "Magic at the gate"

On the one hand, the Ten of Pentacles is simply about the aura of affluence and well-being that can surround success in business. It is a conservative card and very much about maintaining a state of well-being so that it becomes a permanent fact. It's about working towards a sustainable goal and arriving at a lasting prosperity and contentment.

However, there is another potential reading of this card, and it may seem that it contradicts the first. The old man outside the gate (who is clearly not part of the successful and self-contained world of the happy couple) is a symbol of the higher things that have been ignored and, to some extent, shut out. Many successful business people neglect — and even disdain — matters of the spirit, ethics or aesthetics. The Ten of Pentacles can warn us that in the midst of material success we should still recognise that these more intangible aspects of life should not be ignored. While securing a comfortable situation is a perfectly sensible thing to do, there is the danger of closing off your imagination. We all know couples that seem happy, almost smug, but at the same time are like sleepwalkers. It's possible to be so focused on very localised domestic and career successes that you allow yourself to slip into a routine. Time goes by and you never look up and see the wonder of the wider world. You forget how to take a risk — and how to dream.

This card can be quite difficult to interpret accurately as it has some rather complex layers of meaning, so it's particularly important to look carefully at the context in which it appears. What other cards are around it? What is the situation of the querent? By asking yourself this it will become easier to choose the best interpretation of the situation.

The image on this card shows contrasting scenes: a happily self-absorbed couple is in the background; and a much older, more thoughtful man pats a dog in the foreground. While this composition does largely follow the traditional Rider Waite Smith scheme for this card, this is an instance in which knowing the particular significance of the source image we chose will add a lot to your understanding of the potential interpretation. The man and dog in the foreground are taken from bronze plaques on the

[Minor Arcana]

pedestal of the statue of St John Nepomuk on the Charles Bridge. St John was a martyr who was killed by being thrown off the bridge, and it is popularly believed that these bronzes are magical. If you touch them it will ensure that you will return to Prague, and it may even grant you an additional wish. In the hustle and bustle of the Charles Bridge during tourist season, it's interesting to watch visitors turn aside from the stalls and the street performers and take a moment to touch this pedestal. In fact, the legend is that the magic part of the picture is actually the scene that shows the body of the saint being thrown into the river. However, almost everyone chooses to touch the little scene of the saint patting his dog as well. (The dog has become polished by all the hands that have rubbed him over the years.) It provides an experience that feels literally like a moment of being in touch with the possibility of magic. Remember then that the message of the Ten of Pentacles is that while we enjoy our happiness and achievement we should never forget to look up from our immediate concerns from time to time and recognise a higher force.

Sources

The couple in the background are taken from a statue of Šarka and Ctirad at Vyšehrad Castle.

The bronze plaques in front of the statue of St John Nepomuk on the Charles Bridge are by Jan Brokoff, and date from 1683.

The bronze relief of St John Nepomuk on the Charles Bridge

The Tarot of Prague

Page of Pentacles

A young man (or could it be a boyish young woman?) stands in a library in front of a shelf of heavy tomes, smiling distractedly at a miniature castle he is holding. He is wearing rich robes that look very comfortable, but which are so voluminous and trailing that it must be difficult to move quickly in them. A large pentacle is propped on the bookshelf behind him.

Short Interpretation

This Page is studious and serious, and so focused on his studies and intellectual pursuits that he can sometimes think of little else. This total involvement and absorption in work can be wonderfully effective, and doing something for its own sake is much more fulfilling than working for money or status. Relish what you are doing, but don't forget to look up now and then to see what else is happening in the world. There may be an opportunity at hand for some material advance – don't miss it!

[Minor Arcana]

Fuller Interpretation

Being practical and effective • An opportunity to be prosperous
Studying and learning

Like all the Pentacles, the Page is essentially practical, and like all the Pages, the card points to the arrival of a message or news. However, this Page is also very studious and so focused on learning, and on doing things he loves simply for their own sake, that he sometimes forgets to act. He is essentially a rather unworldly figure (at least in Pentacles terms), and the sense of enthusiasm and energy shared by all the Pages is, in his case, very much focused on his own rather esoteric projects.

However, oddly enough, even while this figure doesn't really bother to think about material things, he may well represent an opportunity to attain more wealth, security or some material achievement. The castle is, after all, a symbol of prosperity and status. While the Page may like the castle more as an object of study, he may also suddenly see this other aspect of what it represents, and – his practical side coming to the fore – may choose to seize the opportunity that lies in his hand. While he takes no notice of the books behind him, they are in reality also concerned with prosperity and knowledge, as they are in fact the old registers of property ownership in the country.

The Page, then, is at first sight a slightly contradictory figure: studious but inherently practical, unworldly but almost guaranteed to be given some opportunities for material gain. He can be interpreted as that phase in life (perhaps while a student) in which an essentially grounded person has the opportunity to be dreamier and more involved in his studies simply because he loves it. However, this Page will not grow up to be The Hermit. Rather than devoting his life to study he will quite soon turn to more practical and businesslike matters and may eventually surprise his fellow students by turning into a figure more like the King of Pentacles – still learned, but essentially focused on the business of business.

Sources

The image of the Page is from the painted façade of a house at Dukelských hrdinů Street, near Strossmayerovo náměsti, in Prague 7.

The bookcase is in the "New Land Registry Hall" at the Old Royal Palace. It's part of a small but remarkable collection of books that record details of land ownership. All are marked with numbers and symbols on the spine, rather than titles. No one quite knows why this is, but it's believed to be because the servants in charge of the books were illiterate, and so needed distinctive signs in order to tell one from the other.

The original 19th-century mosaic on which the Page of Pentacles was based

[Minor Arcana]

Knight of Pentacles

A young knight sits astride a heavy horse. They are not moving. The horse's head is bowed, the young man seems to be gazing at nothing in particular, and even the dog with them is still. The towers of a gothic church are behind them.

Short Interpretation

So you dot all the "i"s and you cross all the "t"s and you've always made sure that everything is done in exactly the right way – and where has it got you? You've been so busy being absolutely correct and sticking to the same old formula that you're in danger of completely losing any sense of inspiration or sparkle. Maybe this absolutely methodical way of doing things is right for you. But perhaps, just for once, you should let your hair down, let everything go hang, do something wild and have fun! You'll feel much better for it.

Fuller Interpretation

Methodical to the point of obsession • Sensible and solid
Predictable and faithful • Patient • "Not seeing the wood for the trees"

This Knight is thoroughly solid. He can be obstinate and stubborn, but on the other hand he is never flighty or fickle. He is thorough and even obsessive, particularly when it comes to details. While the Eight of Pentacles shows the importance of being methodical and careful when developing a skill, the Knight is an example of someone who has let attention to detail get out of hand, he's become a person who is completely stuck into a predictable way of doing things. This is because he insists on always doing everything in a familiar and safe way, and has forgotten how to apply innovation or initiative.

In a reading, the interpretation of the Knight is of course very influenced by the cards surrounding it. Ask yourself if this fixation on tying up all the loose ends is a good thing. Maybe it is, but if all this dedication and diligence isn't really necessary it may become a habit that traps you, preventing you from achieving the big things simply because you are so busy looking at the details.

In the image on this card, the knight has all that he needs, he is young, he has a powerful horse and a faithful dog, and yet there is an aura of greyness and immobility about him. The pentacle in his hand is a wonderful thing, a sun with twelve rays, yet he gazes past it as though he isn't really interested in it. He can only see the smaller, practical things in life, and is blind to the bigger, more magnificent ones. His pose looks uncomfortable, and his armour seems constricting. Even his dog look as though it is being held back and is "hangdog" and depressed.

It's significant that the towers behind the Knight are those of the Týn Church. Like many of the oldest churches and cathedrals in Europe, the Týn took centuries to build. It is a reminder of the patience and faith that is sometimes needed to complete drawn-out and intricate tasks. It's important to bear in mind that while the Knight of Pentacles usually signifies the need to be more adventurous, there are times when it indicates that a methodical and painstaking approach may be the only way to complete your mission. You just have to be able to judge whether you are sometimes losing sight of the overall aim and getting lost in minutiae.

[Minor Arcana]

Sources

The Knight is taken from the Art Nouveau mosaic on the façade of the the Municipal House (Obecní dům). The mosaic was designed by Karel Spillar and is called "Homage to Prague". The whole building is famous for being a superb example of Czech Secessionism ("Secession" is the Central European term for the style that was called "Art Nouveau" in France). For another example of a card based on the Obecní dům mosaic, see The Empress.

The background shows the two towers of the Týn Church in Old Town Square. They can also been seen (from a different angle) in the Ten of Swords.

The rather hunched dog is from the base of an Art Nouveau bronze door that leads into one of the Vodičkova Street entrances of the Lucerna Palace.

The Tarot of Prague

Queen of Pentacles

A woman is firmly seated against the background of a small, cosy-looking street where the streetlamps are glowing softly. She is smiling at the pentacle in one of her hands. In her other hand she is holding a cornucopia overflowing with fruits. Her crown is a castle, and a friendly little little cherub and ram stand companionably at her feet.

Short Interpretation

Practical magic! The Queen of Pentacles makes magic from the most ordinary things: good friendship, a beautifully-cooked meal served with generosity, a stunning garden produced by years of love and care. Her house is not "designer perfect", but hers is a home that you always enjoy and in which you often want to spend time. This ability to touch other people and to make them feel happier every time is actually very rare, so when we come across it, it's truly magical.

[Minor Arcana]

Fuller Interpretation

Generous and sharing • Naturally intelligent and sensible
Nurturing and kind • Hardworking, practical

The Queen of Pentacles is gentle, nurturing, and down-to-earth. She is also generous and sensible, good with animals and children, and welcoming and caring to anyone who comes to her door. Maybe a little like everyone's ideal of the perfect maternal figure? She is the symbol of trustworthiness, so you can tell her your secrets without worry, and receive a lot of support and warmth in return.

However, while she is generous and good with people, she isn't an extrovert or partygoer. In fact, this Queen is inwardly quite shy and quiet, preferring to work hard but without drawing attention to her efforts. Sometimes her natural reserve can develop into a kind of inward-looking melancholy or moodiness. However, her natural practicality means that she can usually quickly shake off these moods and get back to her more normal state of focusing on others.

The image on this card shows a woman dressed in warmly coloured clothes and crowned with a little castle. She immediately brings to mind the phrase "my home is my castle", but for this Queen it is more a case of her power and status coming from domestic matters. The cornucopia of fruits in her hand underlines her generosity and abundance towards others. In many ways, just as the King of Swords is a little like a worldly Emperor, so the Queen of Pentacles is a more approachable and much less sacred version of The Empress. Like the Empress, she is also associated with children, as symbolised by the little cherub who plays in front of her. The inclusion of the ram is primarily a symbol of the natural world that this Queen is so at ease with, however it also serves as a nod to the original RWS card in which a ram's head (a reference to the zodiacal sign of Aries) is shown on the Queen's throne.

The Arthur Waite interpretation says of this Queen that, "she contemplates her symbol and may see worlds therein". It was this that made us set this card in the Nový Svět ("New World") district next to Prague castle. Not only is it a New World (or at least was in the 15th century), it is also a place that has a very domestic, small-scale beauty. Nový Svět isn't full of palaces, but it has charming cottage-like houses and small winding cobbled lanes. Its beauty isn't spectacular, but it's both touching and appealingly domestic, and fits in well with the domestic magic of the Queen of Pentacles.

Sources

The Queen is taken from one of the figures on the base of the statue of Charles IV at Křižovnické náměstí, the small square that stands at the Old Town end of Charles Bridge.

The street behind her is one of the few that make up the tiny district of Nový Svět near Prague Castle.

The cherub and ram are from the front of a house in Národní Třida. All the signs of the zodiac are shown in a glorious blue and gold colour-scheme.

The original sign of Aries, part of a façade that shows all twelve signs of the zodiac

[Minor Arcana]

The King of Pentacles

A serious but calm man sits holding an open book. He is entirely golden, bringing to mind the myth of King Midas who turned all he touched into gold. On the open page of the book there is a golden pentacle in the shape of the sun. The man's robes are covered in flowers, but in spite of this he looks flat, and rather formal and strict. At his feet are two more bulls, again in gold. Behind him lie the towers of the Charles Bridge.

Short Interpretation

In many ways the King of Pentacles is the ultimate "grown-up": successful in his business and professional life, and a rock to his family. He isn't adventurous, but can be surprisingly courageous if necessary, and when it comes to rational or intellectual matters he will always defend his beliefs. He appears cold, and even a little "flat" emotionally, but those close to him know he is in touch with the warmer and more natural sides of life. The heart of gold is there, it's just buried under a very stiff outer shell.

Fuller Interpretation

The business person • "Head of the family" • A strong belief in what's right • A typical accountant • Sensible to the point of being boring

The King of Pentacles shares the authority of all of the kings in the Tarot. Mature and keenly aware of his responsibilities, he may at first seem a little forbidding and somewhat boring. He is very successful in business, but probably more for the sake of his family and dependants than because he himself is particularly materialistic. He will always put duty first, and while this may mean that he has had to somewhat neglect his own love of study and learning, it also means that he is an absolute rock to his family and a dependable provider.

The King is depicted as being golden and glowing, and at the same time "flat" and stiff. This sums up the contradictions of this card. The King of Pentacles certainly has the "Midas touch" with money. He is a natural businessman and a great provider. However, he can also be so practical and sensible that there is no room left for emotion. In this respect he is a little like the stereotype of an accountant; someone rather dull, and so concerned with facts, figures and finance that there is no time for fun or frivolity. He is certainly dependable, but there may be times when you wish he could also be a little more rounded as a character, and able to let his hair down and have fun at least once in a while.

The King of Pentacles is always associated with Taurus, the bull. Like a bull, he has stamina and willpower. However, like a bull he can also be stubborn, particularly when his beliefs are challenged, and in such a situation he may display an unexpected courage. In a reading, it is worth remembering these qualities of the King, and not focusing solely on his rather dull and materialistic aspects.

Sources

The King of Pentacles is based on a cast metal plaque in the Clementinum, the old Jesuit complex and library beside the Charles Bridge.

The bulls (a traditional symbol in this card) are taken from a staircase in Prague Castle.

The background shows the Malá Strana towers of the Charles Bridge.

Tarot Readings

Tarot Readings

Tarot readings *do* work for many people. If you try, you'll probably be surprised just how enlightening a good reading can be. So does this mean that the Tarot is magic, or a mystical way to tell the future? Some people believe it is, but many more think that the Tarot is simply a very vivid and compelling way of looking at where you are now, and visualising your possible actions and options. Seen like this, Tarot is not so much a way to foretell the future as a method of helping you to get fresh insights that will let you take control and responsibility for shaping your own fate.

The very visual nature of the cards makes them an excellent way of sparking creative insights into situations — literally letting you see things in an entirely new way. A good reading can be very effective at getting a person to look at things afresh. Sometimes facts that are hard to face are easier to think about through the medium of the cards. A reading can lay things down in very graphic terms that make it hard to avoid realities, but also have the advantage of not feeling too confrontational. Imagine, for example, how hard it would be to hear a friend tell you that you are being materialistic and neglectful of the more emotional or spiritual sides of life, and harder still to listen to someone saying you that you are prone to addictive behaviour. But if The Devil and, say, the Four of Pentacles came up prominently in a reading, it might make admitting the truth of your behaviour easier, simply because a reading feels more objective and less personal than a friend's comments ever can. Many people say that the cards can be incredibly blunt, but it's interesting that they usually report this without resentment — and often with a great deal of gratitude about what they have learned about themselves.

Of course, this doesn't just apply to negative indications from the cards. Many of us find it surprisingly hard to recognise and take pride in our own abilities and good qualities. Again, a Tarot reading can be a great way of coming to see this. Learning to acknowledge and appreciate good things about ourselves is an important step in building a better future.

Another positive aspect of the Tarot is that most of the cards have potential interpretations that are about possible options and ways forward. The Tarot isn't at all fatalistic but is very much about making your own destiny. As the saying goes — the best way to predict the future is to create it. A good reading doesn't just say "this is your situation", it also suggests what you can do next, whether this is capitalising on good events or dealing well with bad ones.

How can you learn to read the cards effectively? The first thing to say is that there are now many books and online courses available. There are also some excellent online forums and chat rooms in which you can exchange information and, in some cases, even exchange free readings as a way of learning through practice. This book will give you the basics, but good reading comes through practice; you'll find that the more you read with the cards, the more your confidence in your own insight and intuition will grow.

There are three main deck systems that people follow for readings. The first is based on the old "Marseilles"-type decks. The long history behind these sis appealing for some, but many people find that the fact that the "minors" (which in these old decks should properly be called the "pips") are like ordinary playing cards, rather than being illustrated with symbolic pictures, can make their meanings hard for a beginner to learn.

A more popular, and much more recent system is based on the "Thoth" tarot designed by Aleister Crowley and Lady Frieda Harris in the 1940s (though not published until 1969). Some people find Crowley's associations with black magic make them wary of using this tarot system, in spite of the fact that the Thoth is not, in itself, a particularly "dark" deck. In the Thoth deck the Minor Arcana Court Cards are fully illustrated, and the other suit cards employ some significant colour and styling, rather than having full pictures to illustrate their meaning, so they are reasonably easy to learn.

Most beginners' courses and books use a symbolic system that is that based on the "Rider Waite Smith" (also called the Rider Waite or the Waite Smith) deck. This deck was originally published in 1909 by followers of the Golden Dawn esoteric society. As an early deck intended primarily for divination (rather than for playing card games) it was very influential. The fact that the RWS Minor Arcana cards are fully illustrated is a great help to beginners, and indeed for many experienced readers this continues to add a useful range of nuances to possible interpretations.

The *Tarot of Prague* is based on the symbols and meanings used in Rider

Waite Smith, so it is a fairly easy deck for a beginner. However, it still incorporates enough twists and variations on the RWS tradition to stimulate a more experienced reader.

In this book there are "short interpretations" of each card, and these are a good, simple way of getting started. The key words and key phrases at the beginning of the "Fuller Interpretations" sections are also a quick way to get a feel for each card. Using these you can give reasonably accurate readings the minute you take the cards out of their cover. However, it really is worth going beyond these summaries and learning to read the much fuller range and depth of meanings that the cards offer.

Learning the cards

There are many approaches to learning Tarot, but of course the first step is very simple: get to know the cards and the range of meanings. At first, this can look like a daunting task. There are, after all, 78 cards, and each has a number of possible interpretations depending on where they appear in a reading and the question being asked. However, it actually isn't as difficult as it might seem.

Firstly, the principle meanings of the Major Arcana often relate very closely to their names (though the names shouldn't be taken too literally, e.g. the Death card is not usually about physical death at all). As these twenty-two cards are very distinct from each other, and have very separate and clear meanings, it isn't too hard to acquire a basic understanding of all of them. Many people learning the Tarot initially limit their readings to these twenty-two cards, and it's perfectly valid to do this. Although you won't get such subtle or wide-ranging readings as you would from using the whole deck, the essential essence of the Tarot is contained in the Major Arcana, so you can expect quite coherent and meaningful readings with these alone.

Don't be too daunted by the fifty-six Minor Arcana cards. The easiest way to familiarise yourself with them is to remember that they are grouped in various ways. Firstly, each suit has particular characteristics that apply to all the cards in that suit (summaries of these are given at the beginning of each suit). You will also find that cards with the same number will have some similarities. These can be very briefly outlined as follows:

[Tarot Readings]

King..... Social responsibility. Power and authority. Success, maturity, discipline.
Queen.. Shows the qualities of the suit in a very essential way. Creativity, roundedness and a real world wisdom.
Knight. Drive, forcefulness, responsibility to others. Issues around action, inaction and impetuosity.
Page..... Exploration, study, enthusiasm, risk-taking, beginnings, news and messages.
10......... Completion, for better or worse. Ending a phase or an activity in preparation for going beyond it.
9........... Making compromises. Struggle, burdens. Growth and maturation through experience - good and bad.
8........... Issues around movement, speed and change. Collecting ideas and tasks.
7........... Victory, recognition, individuality and choices.
6........... Old habits. Communication and social responsibilities.
5........... Loss, conflict, challenges, hard choices.
4........... Structure, stability. Balancing security against risks, or excitement against safety.
3........... A strong expression of the element - this can be good or bad. Cooperation or conflict.
2........... Union, balance. Taking decisions. Dealing with emotional forces.
Ace...... Showing the basic quality of the suit. Energy. Beginnings and new possibilities. Creativity, forcefulness (usually in a good way).

Keeping a tarot journal

One interesting way of learning is to keep a journal. This is very simple, just a matter of writing down some notes about the spreads you've tried so that you can review your progress and also recording your thoughts on individual cards. You will see that over time your understanding of the "standard" meanings will improve and, just as importantly, that you will begin to develop your own intuitive interpretations. Good readings depend a great deal on being able to see a coherent pattern in the spread. You will gradually learn how to choose from the range of possible meanings so that the readings make sense and feel "right".

Another good way of practising is to draw one card each day (or once every few days if time is tight) and simply meditate on it, writing down your thoughts as you go. Again, you will find that if you do this regularly, over a period of time your knowledge of each card will deepen and this adds tremendously to the potential depth and subtlety of readings.

As the *Tarot of Prague* is such a narrative deck, you may find it helpful to look at each card as though it is the illustration from a story. Imagine this story, its situations, characters, how it begins and ends. This may help give some fresh insights into the meaning of the spread and deepen your intuition about the possible range of interpretations of each card.

Remember that the journal is a learning tool, not something that has to be presented to others, so it doesn't have to be beautifully written. Work in the way that makes most sense to you. If you want to sketch, scribble or add pictures to your journal, that's great. Equally, there are no right or wrong physical forms for the journal — you can use a cheap notebook or a very special and lavishly decorated book, you can throw it into your bag or keep it wrapped in a precious fabric on a special shelf. It doesn't matter what you choose, as long as it feels evocative and meaningful to you.

Spreads

There are many tarot "spreads", or ways of laying out the cards for a reading. Some of these, like the Celtic Cross, are traditional and widely used, while others are much more recent and less well known. It's fair to say that spreads fall in and out of fashion, with one becoming popular for a time only to be superseded by another. However, personal preference also plays a part and you may find that you relate better to some than others. You shouldn't feel you have to use the "classic" spreads. Also try not to limit your use of spreads by allowing yourself to believe that, for whatever reason, you are only able to work with certain types of spread. There are no hard and fast rules. There are many spreads in use so why not try and use new ones from time to time?

The only way to decide which spreads work for you is to try some out. If you are interested in seeing the wide range of spreads in use, the online Tarot forums are a good place to start. Many of them have whole sections in which spreads, old and new, are discussed. To get you started, though, at the end of this section I've given some examples of spreads that are popular, and one that is specially devised for use with the *Tarot of Prague*.

One last thing to say about spreads is that there is absolutely nothing wrong with inventing your own; it's often a very creative and interesting exercise to do this and it can be particularly insightful to devise spreads that deal with specific issues like work, relationships or family. The old traditional spreads have been well tested, and they tend to work well and give useful readings. However, there is nothing magical about them and if, over time, you decide that your own personal spreads work better for you, well, why not? Whatever you feel comfortable with will probably, in the end, give you the best readings.

The use of a significator

Many readers start each reading by asking the *querent* (the person asking the question) to choose a *significator*. This is simply a card from the pack that represents the querent at the moment. There are many ways of doing this. Some readers will simply ask the querent to pick a card at random, or choose a card that seems suitable. However, the most common method is to take out all the twelve male Court Cards if your querent is a man or boy, or all the female Court Cards if it's a woman or girl. (In most RWS packs this means only the four queens, though in the *Tarot of Prague* you have the option of also including the Page cards as they are intentionally gender-neutral in appearance.) The querent is asked to look at these and choose the one that they feel fits them *at this particular time*.

You can, if you like, modify this method. Sometimes it seems appropriate to take out only the Page cards for a boy, the Knights for a young or early middle-aged man, and the Kings for an older man. Similarly of course, this means that you can select the (androgynous) Page cards for a girl or a young woman, and the Queens for an older woman. Personally, I prefer not to age-stereotype in this way, but many readers would disagree.

You will most likely have noticed that one big issue in all this is that it can all seem rather gender biased. After all, in a reading the Tarot cards should not be taken to refer to a person of any particular gender, regardless of the person shown in the picture (e.g. the Magician and Hermit can refer to a woman, the Empress and High Priestess to a man). So why should the significator card be chosen only from the Court Cards that show a particular gender? It's a good question, and an interesting example of the way in which modern thinking is now questioning some of the traditions of the Tarot. In fact it's entirely acceptable (and nowadays the practice of many readers) simply to pull all sixteen of the Court Cards out of the pack and present these to the querent, with instructions to choose one based only on intuition, rather than by whether the card happens to show a man or a woman. This often produces interesting results, and certainly gives the querent a good range of images from which to choose.

Although the significator takes no explicit part in most readings, it is well worth taking a moment or two to think about which card the querent has chosen, and perhaps to discuss it with them. This can give some very useful insights into their particular concerns, and especially into how they see themselves in their current situation.

How to begin a reading

After the querent has chosen their significator, put the other cards carefully back into the pack. Shuffle the cards well. Place the significator on the table so that it is clearly visible and hand the pack to the querent. Ask him/her to quietly focus on the significator and think hard about their question. It sometimes helps if you point to the significator card and calmly say something like "This is you. Please look hard at yourself and focus on your question." Ask them to gently shuffle the cards while they do this. Explain that they should keep shuffling until they feel the time is right to stop. At this point, ask them to cut the pack into three stacks and place each stack on the table. Pick these up in whatever order feels right to you (don't shuffle again) and lay out the cards.

Some general aspects of reading

The main issue in any reading is to be able to recognise and express patterns. These can come up in a number of ways. I've seen spreads that are mostly composed of a single suit, or that contain a high proportion of Major Arcana cards, three of the four Aces, or an unlikely number of nines and tens. All these can be read as being significant. When you first look at a spread you may sometimes get the feeling that it is just a jumble of cards and doesn't make any sense at all. But look again, and begin to search for patterns. It can be quite surprising how these can leap forward and suddenly reveal some significance that was not apparent at first.

[Tarot Readings]

Reversals

One subject that I haven't mentioned yet is "reversals" — cards that fall upside down in a spread. Some readers simply read these as though they are normal, right-side up cards, other readers will apply a "reversed" meaning. As the whole subject of reversals is a complicated one, they are not dealt with in this book. Personally, I think reversals can add a tremendous amount to some readings, and though they may initially seem complicated (the exact interpretation of a reversal is often even less clear cut than that of a normal card) it is worth learning how to read them. As it is really a subject in its own right, any quick explanation of reversed meanings here would probably be misleading. However, *The Complete Book of Tarot Reversals* by Mary Greer and Barbara Moore is an excellent book on the subject. This goes into detail about how to incorporate reversals into readings. Greer describes these as providing "an opportunity to reach below logic and lead us into the realm of potentials and underlying causes where everything is connected and Magic happens."

Of course the various online forums also often have interesting and thoughtful discussion threads on this topic and are another good place to both begin and to further develop your insights into using reversals.

Traditional Spreads - The Celtic Cross

The Celtic Cross is one of the oldest and most widely used spreads. It was first mentioned in Waite's *Pictorial Key to the Tarot* and it is now widely believed to have been devised by W.B Yeats, the Irish poet and play-write, who like Waite was a member of the Golden Dawn.

Ironically, because the Celtic Cross has been so popular, it can be a confusing spread to learn, as you may come across different variations of it that have evolved over the years. The one we give here is a good basic way of using the Celtic Cross. At ten cards (or eleven if you count the significator) it is quite a large spread, so perhaps it isn't an ideal one to start on, although I must admit that it's the one I decided to learn on, and it does have the advantage of extending your skills and intuition in a very enlightening way.

The cards of the Celtic Cross are laid out as shown here. Their basic meanings are:

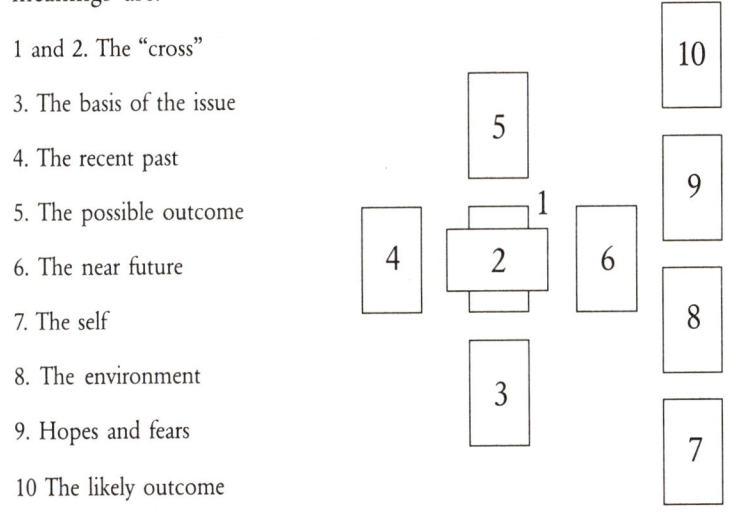

1 and 2. The "cross"

3. The basis of the issue

4. The recent past

5. The possible outcome

6. The near future

7. The self

8. The environment

9. Hopes and fears

10 The likely outcome

Traditionally this spread uses a significator. This is chosen first and put down on the table, and Card 1 is then laid directly on top of it. Because of this, Card 1 is often called the "cover" card. However, personally I prefer being able to see the significator throughout the reading because it can act as a useful indication of how the querent may currently see himself or herself, so I usually put the significator on the table at some distance from the spread (as shown).

[Tarot Readings]

Whether or not you choose to incorporate the significator, the "cross" can often be seen as a microcosm of the whole reading. It gives two separate aspects of the answer to the basic question asked. *Card 1* stands for the general situation. It's very much about the querent, so it's also sometimes described as being the inner aspect of the situation. *Card 2* (which by the way is always read as right way up, never as a reversal, even if it falls upside down) shows the opposing or reinforcing influence. It can also be read as the outer aspect of the situation. If this seems rather confusing or contradictory, then think of it this way: Card 1 is the most basic and innermost aspect of the situation underlying the question and so sometimes it can reveal the real query behind the apparent one. For example if a freelancer asks a question phrased as "will I get some work over the next six months?" Card 1 may reveal that the real concern is a much more fundamental one about security and professional choices. Card 2 tends to show the more obvious and outward aspect of this, which can either oppose or reinforce the first card.

The other cards are rather more straightforward. *Card 3*, the basis of the issue, is an event that has helped bring about the current situation. It's worth remembering that this event may be in the past, or it may be a factor that is on-going. Whichever it is, it is likely to reveal, sometimes in quite a surprising way, the circumstances or stimulus that lies behind the present state of affairs. It is worth remembering that this can be something as obvious and immediate as an actual event that is the cause of the current situation, or it can indicate a much longer term and more subtle set of underlying influences.

Card 4, the recent past, also shows a past event, but one that is now fading in importance. Usually it should be regarded as something that should simply be acknowledged and let go. The querent should now be moving on from whatever is shown in this card.

Card 5, the possible outcome, is more problematic. The most important point to understand about tarot readings is that they are not predictive. The tarot reader who says, "This is what will happen to you" is probably talking nonsense. The possible outcome is just that, a possibility. When it shows an undesirable outcome, you should look to the rest of the reading to gain insights into ways to avoid it. When it's good, think about how to make this possible outcome really happen. Either way, one of the main things to consider in this card is whether it supports or opposes Card 10, the more likely outcome. In some readings, these two cards are quite different, and the reading is clearly saying that there is a choice between two divergent paths. In others, the possible and likely outcomes may reinforce one another. In this case, the reading can seem much more "fated" though in fact, there is still nothing inevitable about this outcome and the rest of the reading may give pointers about how to achieve or steer clear of it.

Card 6 shows the near future. This is straightforward but remember that it is the near future as it specifically relates to the particular question being asked.

In a reading you may find that *Card 7* is often almost laughably accurate and can give some real insights. It simply shows the querent's self - as they are in their current circumstances. It is often at its most revealing when considered together with *Card 8*, which shows the environment. Between them, these cards can tell you a lot about someone's state of mind and the realities of their situation. Remember that the environment can refer to broad social, economic and political factors, as well as to much more personal matters like work and home life or the people of influence in the background. It really depends on the particular factors that are important to the querent in their particular situation.

Card 9, representing hopes and fears, is another of those cards that can sometimes reveal the real anxieties or wishes beneath the apparent question. Again, this card is often very easy to interpret, but even when it seems obvious it's worth spending a little time to work out what it can tell about the whole spectrum of aspiration and anxiety from the querent's viewpoint.

Finally, *Card 10* shows the most likely outcome. Of course, remember again that in any reading the "outcome" card or cards are never absolutely predictive. The whole point of tarot readings is that after considering your situation and your possible actions, you can actively make a difference to your future. So try not to let the querent hang on to this final card as though it's the answer to the whole the reading. Like all the cards in a spread, it should not be seen in isolation, but very much as part of the overall pattern.

As I've already said, the Celtic Cross it can be particularly useful to see how this "outcome" card relates to Card 5, the "possible outcome". Sometimes the two will really seem to reinforce one another, other times they will be very different. When they reinforce each other it may indicate that this outcome is more likely to come about, and the querent should think about the consequences of this. Is the outcome a desired one? If not, what actions or options in the current situation could make this less likely to happen? Can anything be changed to affect the situation more positively?

When the "outcome" and "possible outcome" are very different from one another the element of choice may be more apparent. Which is the best outcome? What can the reading tell you about achieving this? How can you avoid going down the other path?

The Three-card Spread

This is a very good beginner's spread as it is simple and straightforward. However, its use isn't just limited to beginners. Many people continue to use this spread, often as an "everyday" spread, finding its quickness and clarity very appealing.

The cards are simply laid out in a row. Their basic significance is:

1. The situation underlying the question
2. Problems, or issues that may hinder
3. Opportunities, or things that may help

The Five-card spread

This gives a little more detail than the three-card spread. It can be a good spread to use if you want to do a fairly quick reading that still covers most of the important information about a situation.

The cards are usually just put in a row, horizontally or vertically, as you prefer:

1. Factors in the past
2. Issues in the present
3. Hidden or unconscious influences that should be considered
4. Advice, possible actions
5. Probable outcome

With both these spreads, one of the major advantages of their simplicity is that you have a lot of opportunity to look at each card. Go slowly. You can choose to lay all the cards face-up immediately, or you can lay them face down and turn them over one after the other, but whichever way you choose, look at each card carefully in turn, and also look at the whole spread once all the cards are face up. Take your time and don't feel you have to begin the reading immediately. Sometimes the meaning will jump out at you right away, but at other times you may need to quietly consider different possibilities before coming to any interpretation.

The Prague "Threshold" Spread

The word Prague (*Praha* in Czech) means threshold. When the city was founded, Queen Libuše is supposed to have said that she could envision a great fortress whose glory would reach to the sky. She commanded that the castle that was to be built be given the symbolic name "Prague" (Praha) from the Czech word for "the threshold" (*prah*) as this indicated that even great lords would have to stoop before it. The Prague "threshold" spread is a fairly simple five-card spread that I devised especially for use with the *Tarot of Prague*. It is designed to give insight when you are on the threshold of a significant change in your life.

1. Where you are now. The current situation

2. What lies on the other side of the gateway, i.e. the outcome of this step.

3 and 5. Issues you need to consider or actions you need to take (the two pillars of this gateway).

The left-hand card (3) is more likely to refer to mental or intellectual processes.

The right-hand card (5) refers more to actions.

4. The influence that lies over the steps you are taking (the lintel of the door).

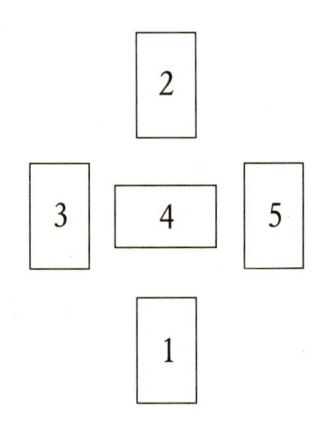

The first thing to consider with this spread is what it can tell you about how your present situation relates to the possible outcome. Is the outcome what you desire? Are there good things about your current position? Should you take this step or consider it further? Then, by looking at the "gateway" cards you can see two aspects, mental (internal) and active (external) that play a part, and also the broad influences that are significant.

Example of a reading using the Threshold spread.

The querent, a woman in late middle-age with a background as an author and teacher, was on the verge of starting an online commentary column and wanted to know whether this would be successful, what advice she should follow and what issues should be taken into account.

This reading was done at a distance, so the querent did not take part in a dialogue, however their response to the emailed reading report was "Spot on. I only wish I could be this clear about everything in my life!"

The spread was as shown:

1. The Fool
2. The Magician
3. Four of Cups
4. Ten of Cups
5. Knight of Swords (reversed)

Looking at the general pattern of the spread. It's often a good idea to start by taking a look at the entire spread to see if it feels as though it's answering the question. In the case of this spread, the fact that the current situation card is The Fool and the outcome The Magician seems entirely appropriate. Also, the Four of Cups is certainly about a psychological state and the Knight of Swords indicates action. All in all then, this spread obviously fits the question. It looks both strong and clear.

Coming to the detailed interpretation, The Fool is an interesting card to see when you are just about to start on a new enterprise. It shows someone stepping into the unknown happily and with a simple faith. So it looks as though you are going into this new enterprise because it feels right rather than because you've done a lot of logical analysis. Because of this you may be feeling that it's a real leap in the dark, and perhaps you're wondering if you are being a bit foolish or naďve in taking this step? However, the message of The Fool is that things should work out fine.

Looking at the next card, the "outcome", we see The Magician, which is a great card to see here, especially when you are beginning something that needs creativity and a certain "spark". It means that the result is likely to be very positive. The Magician takes pure energy out of the air, and makes it into something real on this earth. This actually made me smile, because

[Tarot Readings]

it's so very appropriate as a metaphor for what you're doing – starting an online column. After all, in your column you'll be using a digital medium, which is pure energy, to express your thoughts. In a sense, it's all coming out of thin air. Yet the result will be a column that will be real and tangible for readers.

There's an important point that I want to bring up about both The Fool and The Magician. As Major Arcana cards, they tend to be particularly strong in meaning and thus indicate that something really quite significant is taking place as you make this step. But more than that, they are both cards that imply that actions are taken effortlessly. The Fool doesn't think about what he's going to do, or put work into planning and analysis. He simply steps out, and takes his path with *joie de vivre* and a simple belief that all will be well. Similarly, The Magician does not work at his magic, he performs it in a flash, literally with a wave of his wand. Unlike The Fool, The Magician is focused and powerful, but one thing they have in common is that like The Fool, The Magician doesn't need to labour hard over what he does - in a sense he is simply a channel for what happens.

So the overall message that you should take from this, oddly enough, is that what you are about to do shouldn't feel like hard work. Stop doing background research such as looking at spreadsheets and analysing the potential audience. Simply take the first steps – even if others think what you are doing is mad – and keep the whole thing, in a sense, effortless. Once you have this column up and running it shouldn't feel like drudgery, it should be enjoyable and easy; just draw on your vast reserve of knowledge and your ability to inspire and charm with your ideas.

Looking at the other three cards, there is some really clear advice here. Firstly, the Four of Cups is in the position of "mental processes that you need to consider". This card is about boredom, disillusionment, and a general lack of interest in life. It indicates that you may be in a state of depression and "navel-gazing" right now. Perhaps you feel so fed up with the current situation that you wonder if it's really worth starting on this new project? Maybe you feel a bit sorry for yourself and half think that it makes more sense to just "opt out" and do nothing? Well, you should resist this way of thinking. The "outcome" card says that you will end up by doing something wonderful that will make you incredibly energised.

So you really do need to pull yourself out of this current dangerous state of gloominess and get on with things.

The Knight of Swords (reversed) is significant in the position of "actions to think about". The Knight is fundamentally about charging into action in an aggressive way. He is brave and a bit wild and tends to direct his energies outwards, without much inward reflection. The fact that this card is reversed seems to me significant in this reading. The conventional interpretation for the reversed meaning of the Knight (the one given by Waite in *The Pictorial Key*) is that it indicates an exaggeration of the wild and careless aspects. However, I'm not so sure that this fits here and I'd say that considering the overall spread, the message is more likely to be that you are lacking, rather than exaggerating, some of the characteristics of the Knight. Perhaps you should be a little more courageous about what you're doing? Perhaps you need to exhibit more confidence in your own abilities, even if this does mean that you need to take some assertive action – which is I'd guess something you normally find hard to do?

As an aside it's worth pointing out that while all cards have to be interpreted very much in context, this may be particularly true of reversed cards. You can see how the "classic", and brief, reversed meaning given by Waite doesn't quite fit in this reading. It's necessary to look at it in a slightly different way, and then it suddenly makes sense. One of the reasons I don't give quick summarised meanings for reversed cards in this book is that they might well mislead. It really is advisable to read and learn in-depth before tackling reversals.

Finally, we should look at the Ten of Cups in the position of "the influence that lies over" this step in your life. This card signifies emotional happiness, usually of a domestic kind. It's important to point out that, unlike the Ten of Pentacles, this is not primarily about material good fortune. The family traditionally shown on this card may or may not be well off in a financial sense, but they are indisputably happy. What does this mean for you? I think it suggests that your strong family life will be an important influence on what you are doing. Okay, this next step might feel much less secure than a "proper" job, and some people may even tell you that it's silly, but your home life will provide the support you need. One of the implications may be that you should draw on this in your column, so perhaps you should let your domestic life appear in your writing in some way?

[Tarot Readings]

BIBLIOGRAPHY

Carter, Angela. *Burning Your Boats, Collected Short Stories*. London: Vintage, 1996.
Crowley, Aleister. *The Book of Thoth*. Samuel Weiser Inc., 1999.
Decker (Ronald), Depaulis (Thierry) and Dummett (Michael). *A Wicked Pack of Cards*. Duckworth 2002.
Demetz, Peter. *Prague in Black and Gold*. London: Penguin Books, 1997.
Kadlec, František. *Golden Lane*. Prague: Správa Pražského hradu, 1999.
Hoeller, Stephan. A. *The Royal Road: A Manual of Kabalistic Meditations on the Tarot*, USA: Theosophical Publishing House, 1975
Kaplan, Stuart. *The Encyclopaedia of Tarot*. Volume 2, Stamford: US Games Systems 2002
Kaplan, Stuart. *The Encyclopaedia of Tarot*. Volume 3, Stamford: US Games Systems 2002
Lovecraft H.P. *The Case of Charles Dexter Ward*. Weird Tales, 1941
Meyrink, Gustav. *The Golem*. Prague: Vitalis, 2003
Neruda, Jan. *Malá Strana Stories*. Prague: Vitalis, 1999
Neubert, Karel., Ivo Kořán, and Miloš Suchomel. *Charles Bridge*. Prague: Gallery of the City of Prague 1991.
Pollack, Rachel. *Seventy-Eight Degrees of Wisdom*. London: Thorsons, 1997.
Porter, Tim. *Prague Art and History*. Flow East Ltd, 1995.
Prague Everyman Guide. Everyman, 2001.
Prague Historical Monuments and Culture. Prague: Pražská Informacní Služba, 2001.
Baštová (Markéta), Cvachová (Teresie). *The Loreto. A guide for The pilgrimage Site*. Prague: Order of the Friars Capuchin, 2001
Propp, Vladimir. *Morphology of the Folktale*. Texas: University of Texas Press, 2001 second edition.
Ripellino, Angelo Maria. *Magic Prague*. London: Picador, 1995.
Roob, Alexander. *Alchemy and Mysticism*. Koln: Taschen, 1996.
Špůrek, Milan. *Praga Mysteriosa*. Prague: Krásná paní, 2002.
Waite, Edward Arthur. *The Pictorial Key to the Tarot*. York Beach, Maine: Samuel Weiser Inc, 2000.
Williams, Brian. *The Minchiate Tarot*. Rochester, Vermont: Destiny Books, 1999
Yates, Francis. *Giordano Bruno and the Hermetic Tradition*, London: Routledge Classics, 2002.
Yates, Francis. *The Occult Philosophy in the Elizabethan Age*, London: Routledge Classics, 2001.
Yates, Francis. *The Rosicrucian Enlightenment*, London: Routledge Classics, 2002.
Zipes, Jack. *Fairy Tale as Myth. Myth as Fairytale*. Kentucky: The University Press of Kentucky, 1994.
Zipes, Jack. *Spells of Enchantment*. New York: Penguin Books, 1991.

Terms Used

Alchemy - A medieval discipline based on chemical, spiritual and magical practices, the aim of which was to create the Philosopher's Stone, a red stone that could prolong life indefinitely and also turn base metals into gold.

Arcana - The literal meaning is 'secret', the same root is used in the word 'arcane'.

Baroque - A period in the 17th and early 18th centuries that was known, in terms of visual art, for an extremely ornate style using graphic realism, elaborate surface decoration and much gilt. Musically, Handel, Vivaldi and Bach typify the Baroque.

Bohemia - An area in what is now the Czech Republic that extends for some kilometres around the capitol, Prague. In the past Bohemia also included parts of what is now Germany and Austria.

Chiaroscuro - A monochrome painting that uses areas of dark and light (the term dates from 17th-century Italy).

Cubism - A 20th-century art movement characterised by the use of abstract geometric shapes to represent reality.

Freemasonry - The Freemasons are an old-established fraternal order of influential and powerful figures whose stated aims are a devotion to promoting equality and a commitment to the improvement of society.

Major Arcana - The twenty-two cards that were developed from the "trumps" of early tarot. They include cards such as The Lovers, The Devil, The Hermit, and are considered to be more archetypal and, in some senses, mystical, than the 56 cards of the Minor Arcana.

Marseille - The Tarot de Marseille is the most well-known and widespread of the traditional tarot designs. It has been used as the underlying basis for many modern occult tarot decks (though the influence of Rider Waite Smith may be more apparent). The Marseille tarot probably came from Milan, and was brought to France when the French occupied Milan around 1500.

Minchiate - The Minchiate is a less well-known version of the early tarot. It developed in 16th-century Florence. It's an interesting 97-card deck that includes all four of the Cardinal Virtues (i.e., "Prudence" is included) as well as the four elements and the twelve astrological signs. One or two modern decks have been based on the Minchiate, most notably an elegant recent version by Brian Williams.

Minor Arcana - The 56 cards of the Minor Arcana comprise four suits of ten "pips" and four court cards. The suits are usually Wands, Cups, Swords and Pentacles (which pre-Rider Waite Smith were Coins or Discs)

Querent - The person who asks the question in a reading, i.e., the person for whom the reading is done.

Reading - Using the cards for divination or cartomancy by laying them out in a spread and "reading" (interpreting) the resulting pattern. Some tarot readers believe that the cards can reveal the past, present and future; others see a reading simply as a way of helping to visualise a situation and gain insights into one's attitudes and options.

Renaissance - The period of European history that marked the beginning of the modern period. It is usually considered to have begun in Italy in the 14th century.

RWS (Rider Waite Smith) - The 1909 tarot pack devised by Arthur Waite and illustrated by Pamela Colman Smith, both members of the Golden Dawn esoteric society. It has had a huge influence on the modern tarot.

Rosicrucianism - An esoteric religious doctrine in which the Rose and the Cross are used as symbols of Christ's Resurrection and Redemption. It arose at the beginning of the Enlightenment in Europe.

Sgraffito - Decorations incised into plasterwork, almost always on the facades of buildings. Becasue the pictures are literally cut into the plasterwork it is almost always in two colours (usually black and white) and has a distinct surface texture. It was very popular in the Renaissance.

Spread - A way of laying out the cards for a divination reading.

Seccession style - The Central European name for the style which was known as Art Nouveau in France. Alphons Mucha is perhaps the best known artist of the Czech Seccession school.

Tarocchi - The Italian term for Tarot. The word came into use in the 16th century (before that cards with trumps were often called "trionfi").

Thoth - *The Book of Thoth* was considered to be a book written many thousands of years ago under the instruction of the Egyptian Sage Hermes Trismegistus. It comprised "Enochian" philosphy (from the Biblical Enoch). The knowledge that it contained is supposed to have been communicated by the Enochian angels to Dee and Kelley in Bohemia. *The Book of Thoth* is also the name of the book that accompanies Aleister Crowley's "Thoth" tarot, which is based on his personal interpretation of Thoth philosophy and teachings.

Visconti Sforza - The earliest known tarot is a lavish hand-painted 15th-century Italian deck known as the Visconti Sfroza, after the families for whom it was created.

INDEX

A

Al Sufi   29
Alchemists   17
Šaloun, Lladislav   210
Astronomical Clock   53, 62, 65, 135, 137, 138

B

Battle of the White Mountain   142
Belshazzar   232
Belvedere (Queen Anne's Palace)   141
Black Madonna, The House of the   52
Black Sun,   71, 72
Brahe, Tycho   16
Braun, Matthias   107, 249
Bretfield Palace   245
Brokoff, Ferdinand   182, 218
Brokoff, Jan   262
Bruncvik   224
Burgrave's House   117, 129

C

Cabbala   10, 45
Caduceus   30
Čapek, Karel   131
Carter, Angela   58
Casanova   245
Celetná Street   49, 50
Celtic Cross (tarot spread)   283
Cerberus   212
Černy, David   185
Charles Bridge   33, 90, 155, 190, 200, 202, 204,
     215, 218, 224, 241, 249, 262, 271, 273
Charon   209
Chemical Wedding, The   35, 45
Church of St Peter and St Paul   94, 174, 241
Church of St. Francis Seraphim   202

Clam-Gallas Palace   50, 157
Clementinum   172, 202, 273
Colman Smith, Pamela   10
Crowley, Aleister   220

D

Daliborka Tower   141, 239
Dee, Doctor John   17, 35
Devil's Channel, Kampa   151
Don Giovanni   242, 243, 245
Dukelských hrdinů Street   264

E

Eliot T.S.   8
Elizabeth, Queen of Bohemia   140, 142
Etteilla   9
Estates Theatre   242, 244

F

Faust, Doctor   18
Freemasonry in Prague   151, 259
Furstenberská Garden   239

G

Golden Dawn esoteric society   10
Golden Lane (Street of the Alchemists)   23, 60-61
Golem   18, 45, 162

H

Havel, Vaclav   159
Hecate,   89
Hercules   52, 212
Holy Grail   150
House of the Golden Well   53, 177, 200, 221
House of the Minute   44, 50, 124, 144, 255
Hradčanské náměstí (Castle Square)   174, 182
Hus, Jan   210

I

Široká Street   79, 169

J

Jilská Street   117
Jindrišska Street   200, 215
Josefov   45, 79, 197
Judith Bridge   155

K

Kafka, Franz   61
Kanovnická Street.   207
Karlova Street   53, 132, 154, 157, 177, 200, 202, 221
Karlovo náměstí   144
Karmelitska Street   36
Karoliny Světlé Street   169
Kelley, Edward   15, 17, 18, 20, 61
Kepler, Johannes   69
Knights of Malta   151
Kohout, Petr - see Lasenic, Pierre de
Křižovnícké náměstí,   271
Konviktská Street   59
Kostnice Ossuary, Kutna Hora   77

I

Lasenic, Pierre de   24
Libuše   111, 112, 113, 114
Loew, Rabbi   18, 44, 45, 163, 165
Loki (Norse God)   31
Loreto Chapel   34, 213, 244
Lovecraft, H.P.   21
Lucerna Palace.   159, 268

M

Madame de Thebes (Matylda Prusova)   24, 61
Malostranské Square   53, 127

Martinic Palace 56, 207, 213
Maulbertsch, Franz Anton 97
Melusine 153, 154, 190
"Memento Mori" 77
Midas, King 272
Míčovna (Ball Games Court) 35, 39, 68, 77, 255
Minchiate tarot 47, 51
Monas hieroglyphica 33, 35
Mostecká Street 215
Mozart, Wolfgang Amadeus 76, 243, 245
Mucha, Alfons 55, 204
Municipal House (Obečni dum) 39, 52, 53,, 160, 268

N

Náměstí Republiky 42
Národní Třida 271
Nebuchadnezzar 232
Neruda, Jan 32, 60
Nerudova Street 32, 51, 53, 91, 151, 174, 185, 190, 197, 245
Nový Svět 270

O

Obecní dům - see Municipal House
Old Royal Palace, Prague Castle 265
Old Town Charles Bridge Tower 29, 53, 91, 259
Old Town Square 44, 50, 124, 135, 137, 138, 144, 172, 210, 247
Orff, Carl 63

P

Paganini, Niccola 20
Pařískà Street 169
Petřín 93, 132, 229, 239
Petřín Lookout Tower 207
Philosopher's Stone 150
Pohořelec 247
Powder Tower 42, 52, 53, 232
"Prague Spring" 185

Prokopská Street   197
Průšová, Matylda   - see Madame de Thebes
Puss in Boots   176, 177

R

Rider Waite Smith tarot   9, 93, 243,   276
Rosencranz, Christian   48
"Royal Route"   48, 50, 52, 232
Rudolph II, Emperor 14,   15

S

Saint Wenceslas   137
Saloun, Ladislav   42, 210
Schwarzenberg-Lobkowicz Palace   154,   174,   214
Secessionism (Art Nouveau)   12
Shakespeare, William   90
Smetana Museum   241
Smetanovo nábřeží   98, 135, 210
Spálená Street   91
Spillar, Karel   38
St Catherine of   Alexandria 228
St James' Church, Ungelt   85
St John (of) Nepomuk   172, 262
St Mikulaš Church (St Nicholas Church, Mala Strana)   50,   77,   245
St Peter and St Paul, Church of 95,   241
St Vitus' Cathedral   52,   95, 121, 170,   172, 204, 226,   252
St Francis Seraphim, Church of   202
Stag Moat   226
Storch House, Old Town Square   137
Strahov monastery 35, 45, 51,   72, 97,   228
Strossmayerovo náměsti   264

T

The Marriage of Figaro   245
Thoth, Book of   9. 41
Troja Chateau   187
Týn Church   65,   221,   218

Týn Court   221

U

U Fleků beer hall   82, 177, 207
Ungelt   85, 218
Universalia occult society,   24
Úvoz Street   92, 141, 197

V

Valentinská Street   172, 177
Vampirism   21
Vinohrady   154, 249
Visconti Sforza tarot   28, 51
Vlašská Street   127, 132
Vltava river   91
Vodičkova Street   42, 109, 117, 159, 179, 268
Vrtbovská garden   93, 187
Vyšehrad   114, 218, 232, 259, 262

W

Waite, Arthur   9, 50, 104, 217
Wallenstein, Duke Albrecht von   68, 69, 226
Wallenstein Palace   68, 72, 107, 179, 226
Wenceslas, King   185
Wenceslas Square   185, 179, 259

Y

Yates, Frances   35
Yeats, W.B.   283